Creating eCourses

Creating eCourses

by Amanda Rosenzweig PhD

Creating eCourses For Dummies®

Published by: **John Wiley & Sons, Inc.**, 111 River Street, Hoboken, NJ 07030-5774, www.wiley.com

Copyright © 2024 by John Wiley & Sons, Inc., Hoboken, New Jersey

Published simultaneously in Canada

For general information on our other products and services, please contact our Customer Care Department within the U.S. at 877-762-2974, outside the U.S. at 317-572-3993, or fax 317-572-4002. For technical support, please visit https://hub.wiley.com/community/support/dummies.

Wiley publishes in a variety of print and electronic formats and by print-on-demand. Some material included with standard print versions of this book may not be included in e-books or in print-on-demand. If this book refers to media such as a CD or DVD that is not included in the version you purchased, you may download this material at http://booksupport.wiley.com. For more information about Wiley products, visit www.wiley.com.

Library of Congress Control Number: 2024933671

ISBN 978-1-394-22497-5 (pbk); ISBN 978-1-394-22499-9 (ebk); ISBN 978-1-394-22498-2 (ebk)

SKY10069369_031124

Contents at a Glance

Table of Contents

Introduction

Welcome to *Creating eCourses For Dummies!* This book will become your personal guide and mentor for designing, developing, and delivering your own eCourse, also known as online course. How did I become the author? I am still in awe of the opportunity, but my experiences over 20 years have allowed me to learn the ins and outs of best practices for instructional design, educational technology, pedagogy and andragogy, digital accessibility, and curriculum creation. I somehow became the go-to person for helping others curate curriculum, design courses, use technology appropriately, and just overall give creative solutions to mundane problems, when working in any course modality, including online. I was being asked for help because I had a reputation of giving a resolution. I took pride in that unofficial role, online guru, with no idea that all those years of helping people and building a résumé of experiences, would lead me to an opportunity to write a book and share some of my insight.

About this Book

This book has something for everyone. People who are content or niche experts but have very little training in learning or teaching theory, individuals who are new in their career of teaching and rearing to make a name for themselves, facilitators who focus on professional development at corporations, and seasoned instructors who need some inspiration to rejuvenate their "why." Do not let the title *For Dummies* dissuade you from trusting your abilities; view it as a more efficient approach to learning tips that help create a product you are excited to share with learners. This book trims the fat and focuses on the need-to-know, not the nice-to-know.

Don't feel that reading the book in a systematic manner is necessary. *Creating eCourses For Dummies* can be approached in a variety of ways. The book is written to be a beginning to end journey on constructing a course from scratch. And while there is some overlap in the chapters, each chapter can stand alone. Each chapter focuses on an important concept to create a well-rounded online course. You may have great curriculum developed already but want to spice up your assessments. This book can help you. Maybe you're familiar with course design but aren't sure how to create a course matrix. This book can help you with that task too. It allows you to focus on your needs first and later revisit and refresh concepts that you may have skipped.

Throughout the book are worksheets, examples of tools, and websites to visit. If this information doesn't resonate with you, skip it. Skim the table of contents and focus on what is important for your needs at the time you are reading it. I always say that people look for content when they need it. Knowing where to look saves time.

Foolish Assumptions

I believe any assumption is a foolish assumption. "Teaching is easy" is the most ridiculous assumption to make. Teaching is terrifying, difficult, and exhausting (mentally and physically), but it is also rewarding. I am assuming that those who read the book are doing so to help progress or improve their approach to online design, development, and delivery — newbies and experienced teachers alike. In that assumption, I do use terms that may be technical, but I explain them too. It is important to understand the jargon, or "educationese," because critics, experts, and seasoned consumers look for characteristics that make them think the course they are taking is worthy.

Here are some other foolish assumptions that I or my teaching peers have made in the past:

>> **Students know about and how to use technology.** While there is the thought of "digital natives," many learners did not have the access or resources to use and practice technology. Many learners have not used technology for educational purposes — document headers/footers, slide presentation construction, formula creation, email attachments — and do not have the technology-native expectations we place on them. Our goal is to expose them to digital tools and improve their skill sets, but not at the expense of taking time away from content.

>> **Accessibility is not the teacher's responsibility.** The reality is that the instructor is responsible for creating accessible materials, but many institutions have support departments to help and guide one in the process or potentially complete the process. Having it as a shared responsibility is a luxury. Giving accommodations is reactive. Learners need support; they receive an action based on a request. Creating with accessibility in mind is

proactive because as many barriers as possible are eliminated prior to the learner interacting with the content.

» **Online courses take less work for both instructors and students.** Instructors may think that since there are usually no meeting times, they have more time to spend developing the curriculum (videos, notes, presentations, assessments, practice activities) to ensure the students have a well-rounded experience. Proper development also requires digital accommodations to be addressed (captions, transcripts, alt text, color contrast, heading structure, and so on).

For students, often the time invested is more because it is a heavy text-based environment, which requires committing more time to reading. The responsibility to learn, complete work, and interact with the materials is on the learner. While the online format allows more flexibility and freedom, students must be responsible and accountable for their own learning.

Icons Used in This Book

TIP

The tip icon emphasizes hints and tricks that are helpful in designing, developing, and delivering your online course. These bits of information can save you time, effort, and sanity.

REMEMBER

The remember icon highlights important tidbits that I believe will give you "aha" moments throughout your online course design and delivery experience. You can't remember everything, but these points give you a starting point.

WARNING

The warning icon isn't there to scare you, but rather to give you a heads-up to watch out for difficult situations and common mistakes. Most likely I have already made them, so you don't have to.

TECHNICAL
STUFF

This icon shows up when I want to emphasize important steps or reminders that require a bit more technical skill. Anything having to do with technology is technical, so this icon highlights topics such as digital accessibility and laws.

ACTIVITY

This icon indicates that I want you to try some hands-on work.

Beyond the Book

In addition to the content in this book, there are several downloadable documents you can use as templates to create material for your course. I encourage you to use them as you go, but they are just as useful after you have finished the book. To access these materials, go to www.dummies.com/go/creatingecoursesfd. Consider bookmarking this site so you can easily access it when working on your courses. You want to respect your time and work efficiently.

Like every *For Dummies* book, this book includes a digital cheat sheet that you can access online. Just to go www.dummies.com and type "Creating eCourses For Dummies Cheat Sheet" in the search box.

Where to Go from Here

This book is organized to serve your needs. If you want to learn about accessibility, visit Chapter 4. If you need formative assessment support, Chapter 12 is your starting point. If you want to determine what type of engaging activities you can incorporate, Chapter 10 will guide you. This journey is yours to personalize. The book gives you the opportunity to learn how to design, develop, and deliver a course. It guides you through choosing a topic, creating a schedule, designing the course blueprint, choosing the proper platform for delivery, and pricing to sell. I want you to create a course you are proud of and one that will bring you success with your learners and your bank account.

1

Getting Started with eCourses

Chapter **1**

Examining the Concept of eCourses

I f you are reading this book, then your curiosity has been piqued regarding what an online course is and the effect it can have on your life. The market for online learning is projected to continue reaching hundreds of billions in revenue in future years.

Being a teacher for 22 years and teaching in the online realm for 18+ years, I can say I have seen many things — some good, some exceptional, some bad, and some horrific. I have evolved as a teacher, and when I look back at what I did in 2005 versus what I do now, it's a different realm of reality.

For example, my first course online was just a shell with my notes and slides posted. I can almost guarantee the material was not accessible, as I did not know what that meant in 2005. There were no low-stake assessments, few if any practice materials, and all grades were based on high-stake exams. Immediately after my first semester, I started to make drastic changes to support student success. I knew I could never have learned in that environment, so I had to make an effort to change my outlook, my direction, my vision, my material, my presence, my support — essentially, my everything. Are my courses perfect 18+ years later? No. Are they good courses? Yes. I would state that they are great courses, but they constantly change, shift, evolve, and are under scrutiny by myself, and honestly, I'm sure, by my peers.

It's impossible to know everything, but over time and through certifications, professional development, researching, or continuing education, you can learn. As a student in different programs, I found out about, and now implement, differentiated learning, authentic assessments, learner's choice, scaffolded learning, and more.

Through experience, I now create more compelling course experiences, which, though they may be considered rigorous and difficult, are not dull. Throughout this book you'll find real examples, templates, and ideas to build a course from scratch or to modify and convert material you've already created.

What Is an Online Course?

An online course is taught over the internet, usually via a learning management system (LMS). The LMS is the storage unit for content, assessments, course documents, communication tools, and more.

The topic of online courses is a broad one, as a range of delivery methods and interaction types exist. Understanding your options can help you determine the direction you may want to explore and how to focus your vision.

Types of online courses

Online courses are typically structured as one of the following three types:

>> **Synchronous courses:** Students have the flexibility to take these courses from anywhere, but live meetings are an integral part of the program. Students are required to attend these meetings via phone, web platforms, or in person. Often there are preset meeting times that students will be made aware of prior to enrolling. Some instructors will survey students for the best meeting times, and others will offer a few options for all students to choose from and attend as they can.

>> **Asynchronous courses:** These courses don't entail any planned live interaction with the instructor or peers. They are self-paced and provide material to review and assignments to complete for students to achieve their goals. The course may be chunked into learning units or modules with due dates throughout the length of the course, or there may be just one due date, at the end of the course. Some courses may have no due date at all but rather are purchased for lifetime access.

>> **Hybrid courses:** These courses are a combination of synchronous and asynchronous work. The institution, company, or teacher determines how the course is delivered.

TECHNICAL STUFF

Any type of online course can end with a certificate being awarded by an accredited organization or a professional business.

Why should I consider creating an online course?

There are many reasons to create an online course, but you need to make sure your reasons and approach build on your expertise, trustworthiness and can support the process of designing, developing, and delivering an online course. All of these are addressed in detail throughout the book.

>> **Diversify and increase income by monetizing your expertise.** This income is supplemental at first but can become a sustainable, profitable career path.

>> **Establish yourself as an expert and build your brand to create your mark in the industry.** Focus on information that is most important and relevant to your audience. Avoid boring, unrelated information that may be considered nice to know, but not necessary. Focus on the interesting part, trim the fat, and capture the learner. This can be a branding opportunity (see Chapters 13 and 14 for more on this).

>> **Create a community of practice, a group of fellow teachers or individuals who share common interests.** An online class offers the opportunity to connect with similar scholars and potential collaborators (check out Chapter 6).

>> **Share your knowledge with a global audience.** Even if it is not your career, if you are passionate and have the skill set, teach what you love. With the internet, access to people is at our fingertips. Because your aim is global, language and cultural differences need to be addressed too, but geographical barriers are removed.

>> **Have a direct impact on making education accessible.** *Accessible* means that the course is not only available to learners, but that the material also meets the digital requirements to be usable by individuals with disabilities. You can have an impact on learners' lives and can be a part of their achievements (turn to Chapter 4 for more on accessibility).

REMEMBER

As a creator, you are responsible for digital accessibility to ensure that users with different abilities can enjoy and participate in the online experience.

ENVISION YOUR VISION

ACTIVITY

This activity helps you mold your vision for an online class.

1. Write a one- to two-sentence vision statement of what your ideal online class would look like.

2. Write a few concerns you may have in developing your online class.

Following are some tips for writing a vision statement:

- Review other online teachers' statements to determine how yours can stand out.

- Write down keywords that will be a theme throughout your development process.

- Determine what your biggest goal is and write down steps on how to achieve that goal.

- Have a short statement for branding and a longer one for investors or administrators.

- If you're a visual learner, use a vision board to help inspire your actions.

- Language should be clear and concise. Use present tense. Make it inspiring.

Here are some examples of company vision statements:

- Google: "To provide access to the world's information in one click."

- LinkedIn: "Create economic opportunity for every member of the global workforce."

- TED: "We believe passionately in the power of ideas to change attitudes, lives, and, ultimately, the world."

- Udemy: "Improve lives through learning and to be the go-to platform for anyone looking to learn anything."

- Coursera: "We partner with the best institutions to bring the best learning to every corner of the world. So that anyone, anywhere has the power to transform their lives through learning."

WARNING

A simple search on the internet will provide you with thousands of websites stating it is easy and lucrative to build an online course. I want to be transparent and state that "easy" is a relative term, and financial benefits depend on your dedication, niche, business prowess, and commitment to growth and success. If you are a veteran teacher, then creating content, aligning objectives, using a variety of technology, and understanding pedagogical processes will be simpler. "Easy" is not a term I use because creating a course is a lot of work. However, the work is doable for anyone willing to invest time in learning tools, theories, best practices, and needs of the community.

As a veteran online teacher, I constantly reflect, evolve, and tweak the content to meet the needs of the learner and to keep up with technological advancements.

Focusing on Creating a Great Product

Many online courses are available, so what will make yours different? First, you picked up this book, which means you are eager to discover tips and tools to successfully design, develop, and deliver an online course.

Information is everywhere, and there is so much of it that sifting through it all can be overwhelming. This is why an online course focusing on the necessities is appealing. So don't focus on selling information; focus on selling the learner on the transformation that will occur from taking your course (see Chapter 9).

To begin the transformation, the learner must interact with the material in a sensible manner — think intuitive navigation, clear directions, and engaging activities. This requires you to organize the content in units with defined learning objectives (LOs), a variety of content, interactivity, and a clear starting and ending point per unit. (Chapter 3 helps define your target audience.) The organization is a representation of how you think, which influences the student experience. (See Chapters 5, 8, and 10, which focus on resources and design to increase engagement.)

TIP

I am personally a logical person. My design is usually linear, with step-by-step directions that lead to concrete outcomes.

Remember that you are unique. To quote Dr. Seuss, "Today you are you, that is truer than true. There is no one alive who is youer than you." No one has the exact same personal and professional experience as you, so you want to harness your uniqueness. Students are paying to be influenced, guided, and transformed by you.

In the content you are providing, offer supplemental material that brings your experience to light. Consider providing the learners with case studies, Ted Talks, interviews, blogs, and speaking engagements (live or recorded) that highlight your experience, and others' experience (see Chapter 10 for more on resources).

Offer support materials that help your students achieve their goal. These may be e-books, worksheets, templates, and bonuses (Chapters 10, 11, and 12 focus on course content). Plus, coaching is a great value-add, especially when you sell your first course. In all design efforts, make sure the course is built on the foundation of equity, inclusion, diversity, and accessibility. The material provided should take an individual's social, political, religious, and cultural background into consideration.

TIP

Provide trigger warnings to alert students when information may be considered difficult to encounter. Figure 1-1 provides examples from an accessibility course I teach. The idea and support to do this came from my colleagues at the university. No matter how long you teach, if you are open to learning, everyone can give you great ideas and feedback, and rejuvenate your passion to continue developing and teaching online.

Trigger content warning:

Pp. 191-192 - Discussion of rape and rape prevention education. Feel free to skip.

Trigger warnings: The whole chapter deals with assisted suicide and the right-to-die. Pages 271-273 deal specifically with eugenics in Nazi Germany and in the US. Feel free to skip the entire chapter, or to skim portions to give you the overview.

FIGURE 1-1:
Shadow boxes inserted into directions addressing a reading assignment in an Accessibility Studies course I teach.

A professional goal for you is to gather testimonials and reviews for your courses once they have been taught. Learners are more likely to purchase a course that has reviews because they can place stock in others' experiences. Think about Amazon reviews and how you look at them to determine quality, durability, fit (if clothes), and so on. If the reviews are poor or there are no reviews, you're more likely to purchase a similar item from a different company that has item reviews.

Picking a topic

Two crucial questions come into play when it comes to picking a topic for your prospective course. I need you to dig deep to answer these two questions:

>> Reflect on and be truthful with yourself when you ask, "What skills do I have?"

>> Do research and conduct internet searches to find out, "What do the consumers want?"

What skills do I have?

You may want to look at your resume, a promotion packet, your LinkedIn profile or just wing it, but write down everything you consider yourself to excel at, whether it's career related or personal interests. These are the topics you may be able to design a course about. Hopefully, one of them is a passion item that can become a passion project. A passion project is something you are willing to put time and effort into.

What do the consumers want?

Finding out what learners want can come from many resources. Put on your sleuthing hat and test out your search engine skills. Basically, you are looking to find what topics are most frequently searched. To successfully do this, follow the tips in the sidebar "Tips for searching on the internet" to get what you need from the massive archives that reside there.

TIPS FOR SEARCHING ON THE INTERNET

Use multiple search engines such as DuckDuckGo, Yahoo, Google, Bing, and any others you enjoy.

Some search engines focus on specific subjects or niches. Those may be helpful depending on your field. Google Scholar and Wolfram Alpha are examples that focus on academic writings and data analytics, respectively.

Use your search words carefully and try to avoid prepositions and articles.

Use quotation marks around a word or phrase to help narrow down the search results.

Here are some basic operators you can utilize when searching:

- The asterisk symbol (*) is used in wildcard searches. This provides you with a robust search for many categories related to a word or phrase. Example: Jennifer* actress will give you a list of all the famous actors with the name Jennifer.

- Combination searches use the term AND or OR and will return results with either term. This reduces the number of searches that need to be performed.

- Related website searches can be conducted by placing *related:* in front of a website. Websites that are similar to the original will be returned in the results.

If you are already in the business world, you can meet with clients, peers, and companies to discuss their needs, pain points, and experiences to help guide your decision of topics.

Online course necessities

The goal of this book is to provide you with tools you can use to create usable materials that will help you design, develop, and deliver your course. Each chapter has activities, templates, ideas, tips, and suggestions to build your course. One of the most important aspects is accessibility, which is incorporated throughout the book to ensure the material you create is universally designed for all learners.

WARNING

Be proactive in incorporating it from the start of design. This will decrease the stress, time, and costs inherent in addressing accessibility at the end. It is usually much more difficult to retroactively fix accessibility issues in documents than to create them from scratch.

TECHNICAL STUFF

Research whether there are any legal requirements for accessibility to be taken into consideration. Knowing whether there is an accessibility policy guiding your local, regional, national government is a great way to begin. If there are not clear, defined guideline or policies, use Web Content Accessibility Guidelines 2.2 to help guide your decision making. www.w3.org/TR/WCAG22. WCAG 2.2 provides a shared standard for Web Accessibility internationally.

Structuring your course

Chapters 7 and 8 provide the foundation of course design. These chapters focus on creating a course blueprint (template and structure) and a course matrix (detailed schedule).

The course blueprint is like an architect's blueprint. It provides the design and guidance for the structure of the course. The blueprint is a big picture to ensure there is consistency in the design and delivery of the curriculum. Most blueprints have course information, LOs, curriculum content (static and dynamic; see Chapter 10), activities (no stakes and low stakes; Chapter 10), summative assessments (Chapter 11), and formative assessments (Chapter 12). Course artifacts such as vendor tools and publisher tools (covered in Chapter 5) are mentioned in the design at this phase.

In the course matrix, you focus on the LOs, assessments, and supporting content. The course matrix is usually designed to be in units or modules, but testing blocks, chapters, topics, and other approaches are acceptable. Once this design is determined, trimming the fat (focusing on just what is necessary to learn) and chunking of content (smaller, micro learning pieces) are designed to present to the learners.

Creating your course content

Chapters 5 and 10 focus on content for learning and address a variety of types to choose from. Paid and freeware are discussed in detail, but to give you an idea of types you can create, take a glance at the following abbreviated list. My favorite part of course design is the creative freedom you have in developing materials. Creativity increases engagement, helps retention, and supports your brand.

>> Notes (documents and slides), static and interactive

>> Videos

>> Interactive videos

>> Audio

>> Worksheets

>> Activities

>> Games

>> Assessments

>> Surveys

>> Interviews

>> Questionnaires

>> Publisher content

>> Vendor content

Choosing the right course platform

All of the hard work is done, right? Well sort of, because now your business savvy must emerge. Deciding the right platform to deliver your course and how much you want to sell the course for determine whether you will have long-term success.

Options include websites, standalone platforms, or course platforms. These are covered in depth in Chapters 5 and 13, but you have knowledge of different methods from experience as a teacher or a learner. All have pros and cons, so use what is most efficient and effective for you, as well as cost friendly.

Standalone platforms are a one-stop shop (think Walmart) and everything you need to be successful is packaged in the product. You need to create the course; you got it. You need to host the course; you got it. You need to sell the course; you got that too. Examples are Kajabi (https://kajabi.com/) and Teachable (www.teachable.com). Both have a tiered pricing structure.

A course marketplace is a repository for online courses from many creators. They offer benefits such as predesigned templates and not having to worry about hosting, but there are lost opportunities to refine your brand and gather specific data. Examples are Skillshare (skillshare.com), which is free but with strict guidelines, and Udemy (udemy.com), which has a tiered pricing structure.

Setting a course price

Not all courses are equal, so you need to research factors influencing course pricing. Chapter 14 discusses best practices in course pricing. A quick overview requires you to research the competition, make sure your topic is in demand and the quality of the content is superb and varied to support all learners, and have an exceptional website selling you as a brand (think vision statement).

Reality Check

Moving online is the trend, especially since the COVID-19 pandemic, because it is being demanded by consumers. And while there is great research supporting the success of learners, there are many aspects you want to be aware of. Not all online teaching or learning is unicorns and rainbows. (By the way, I have a love for all things unicorn, glitter, and animals. It is a reminder to breathe and not get caught up in what you cannot control.)

Being the teacher, you will encounter many obstacles — technology not working, costs of software, learning curve to use the technology, the time commitment needed, and creating accessible documents, among other hiccups — but with patience, absolution, tenacity, and commitment, all the requirements can be met.

Students are not as computer and technologically savvy as we believe. Their experience with technology is social media and while it does translate, digital literacy skills such as attaching files, saving to specific folders, or using tools such as plagiarism checkers are not taught.

Students are not required to have a device or internet when they sign up for online courses. We assume and expect they will, but often they don't, or they don't have the means to fix it if it breaks.

As you design the course, it is usually with the thought that the student will be accessing the work from a computer or similar device. In reality, 82 percent of students access work on their phone. You want to design to be device agnostic, but some content is just not a good fit for phones.

You are your number-one advocate. You can manage yourself better than anyone else. You know your brand and your perception of the brand. To do this successfully, be honest about your strengths and weaknesses. Build your brand around the strengths. Find a team or find mentors who can help improve areas of struggle. Use your voice to ask for answers, suggestions, and recommendations from peers, consultants, learners, and future consumers. If you don't have a network, expand it by being present and involved in communities of practice, online forums, conferences, and other networks in your field. Last, never stop growing professionally and personally.

Ready, Get Set, Go

This book was created to help connect fundamental principles for designing, developing, and delivering content for individuals to learn. The book is for all levels of teachers, from beginners to professionals. The material will help navigate old and new tools, with an emphasis on learner-centered activities and multimedia. Throughout the book, important themes are accessibility, universal design for learning, and content alignment with LOs to increase performance, retention, and satisfaction.

Chapter **2**

Identifying the Why for Your eCourse

Why should you develop an online course? Why should you sell an online course? What is your *why*?

The *why* is your purpose that encompasses why you want to do your work. Some call it your conviction, your mission statement, or your motivation source, and it describes what makes you a productive citizen in the community. Many of us fall into teaching, or the job is circumstantial and out of necessity. So, the *why* is not the environment we are in; rather, it comes from within.

The *why* can be established over time, but it takes a practice of self-awareness (think journaling; see Chapter 12) and will be shaped by your values, your motivations, your passions, and your strengths. Being self-aware of your purpose naturally helps you engage in altruistic behavior. Teaching is altruistic, even if compensation is involved.

Finding the *why* is not always easy, but if you get excited about designing, creating, delivering, and teaching, and you can imagine this career in years to come, then your *why* is already there. If you are constantly thinking about ways to improve your curriculum, your students' outcomes, your students' experiences, and how to ensure you and the students are fulfilled, then you probably have your *why.*

TIP

Knowing your *why* provides clarity in your life, which translates into the material you create and deliver. Knowing your *why* harnesses your internal passion, and this helps you focus on your goals.

Your *why* can change because people change over time. Your *why* is not static; it is dynamic. Use the natural progression of your *why* to continue evolving your online courses.

Serving the Online World

The online world of teaching allows endless exploration of philosophies, and approaches while providing flexibility for all participants — teacher and student. In addition, other benefits are seen from the online environment such as an increase in digital literacy and citizenship through discovery, community building, and engagement.

Convenience

There's no doubt that online courses offer the benefit of convenience for both teachers and students.

Convenience from the teacher perspective

As an online teacher, you have control of your time and schedule. You say you want to teach on a beach? You got it. From Italy? No problem. From a train? Yep. You can even teach in your pajamas. You can teach from anywhere as long as there is internet. This can help you achieve the infamous "work-life balance" that's as elusive as a unicorn.

Teaching online has the ability to provide a more flexible schedule than a face-to-face classroom. Depending on the institution employing you, you may have set synchronous hours, or you may be at liberty to create your own schedule, including meeting times. Because you can work from where you want, you are not restricted to a single domicile and can tend to personal and other professional matters. If you are a caregiver, have a family, or are active in philanthropy, online courses provide that litheness with your time.

Because you have more flexibility in how your time is spent, teaching online allows you to be involved with a variety of programs. You can teach K–12, tutor, be a college professor, or facilitate professional development in businesses. The goal of the classes you teach can be to provide tutoring support, enhance professional development, address a personal interest, or get certifications or degrees. The wonderful part is you can be involved in multiple opportunities at once as long as it is permitted by your main employer.

Convenience from the student perspective

You will notice a lot of overlap for the reasons teachers and students enjoy the online experience. For students, it may be more about convenience and flexibility because you can complete the work anytime, anywhere. The same goes for studying. In most cases, there are no physical classrooms, and if there are meeting times, they are virtual. If they are required, many programs offer alternative assignments in lieu of not making the online synchronous session. Online learning allows students to balance work, family, and personal obligations while still pursuing their goals. Since students often need to pay for their own education, online courses allow them to continue working. Many companies support continuing education, and online courses afford students opportunities to earn certifications, degrees, and skill sets while continuing to work their jobs. If they are not working, the courses they take can explain their hiatus in the timeline for work.

Online courses are often more affordable when reviewing all the costs associated with attending classes — commuting (time, gas, energy), potential childcare, and less time working, to name a few.

Educationally, asynchronous learning has benefits too. Students have the ability to reflect on the discussions and construct deeper responses that can further the dialogue among the learners. Formulating answers without the pressure of prompt responses can lead to developing better critical thinking skills. This, along with other soft skills, is important for most companies. Online learning can improve students' time management skills. While online courses provide convenience for when they work, the students are responsible for completing assignments by deadlines. This requires them to manage their time so that they are able to successfully engage in the material and complete coursework.

Self-paced learning

Self-paced learning can be scary, but it also provides a world of control based on the learners' needs. All material is available to the learner at once, but the learner sets their own schedule. There are deadlines, but there are no schedules with due dates until the course is closed. There is a window within which to complete the work (one month, three months, one year, and so forth) when it is convenient for them. This usually differs from an academic classroom that may have weekly due dates and set dates for high-stakes assignments, where the final grade is due to the institution.

WARNING

Even the most experienced online learners can fall behind in self-paced courses. "Out of sight, out of mind" or "my job is so demanding that this course is not my top priority" are often reasons given for not completing a course. In all transparency, I did not complete my most recent self-paced class for a variety of reasons and was fortunate to be placed in another cohort. Remember, no one is perfect, and life happens to all of us.

Self-paced learning often leads to better retention of content because the learner wants to learn or has the time to do so. If you must complete training by 12 p.m. on the same day you have a deadline, your focus on the training won't exist and you won't retain much of what the training presented. But if you could participate in the training after the deadline, you'd more likely be engaged and pay attention. In general, self-paced learning can decrease anxiety and stress, and self-paced learners outperform learners who must sit through scheduled trainings.

Discovery

Think back to your educational journey. Were there classes you were not interested in that you had to take? Of course there were. Not all students want to take a class because not all material interests all people. Many classes are general education requirements, degree requirements, or job-related requirements. Often a student ends up in an online class they are not interested in because of their schedule. Convenience is a double-edged sword. As the instructor, it is your responsibility to help them discover why this material is interesting, important, or impactful to their life. Why care beyond a passing grade?

How do you capture the masses? Make the material relatable by investing in the proper resources (check out Chapter 5). Use examples that students can relate to that are current in society. If you are not active in current trends, have the students pose questions, topics, articles, videos, websites, and other artifacts that help them discover the content. Have them ask weekly questions that are on brand with the news. This puts the responsibility on the student, which helps them become more involved due to accountability.

When the students participate, be present (see Chapter 6). Feedback to the student shows you value their effort, recognize their time investment, and acknowledge their contribution.

TIP

When the course is fun for the student (discovery), students feel valued. When the teacher uses different strategies for discovery, retention increases.

Retention

Retention addresses learning and how long information can be recalled and implemented over time. Retention also addresses return rates of students. While these definitions are surface value, they give you an understanding of the term in different contexts without discussing nuances of how different variables and data can alter the whole story.

Institution retention

Retention is necessary for learners to be successful in a job and the world, and retention is required for institutions to be successful. An institution's retention does not always paint the proper picture of student success, but it is a predictor of graduation rate. An increase in student retainment should lead to an increase in graduation rate. More graduates lead to more individuals prepared to enter the workforce. Institutions benefit from increased graduation rates and tuition earned; the economy benefits from the skilled workforce.

We know it is not this straightforward, but it makes sense when considering how online courses can help reach these goals.

Knowledge retention

WARNING

If learners do not retain knowledge, then the effectiveness of your course or program is questionable, and it is at risk of failure.

Can you remember back to being a student and being lost or uninterested? Did you ever think the teacher just didn't understand you, or they didn't understand how to teach? I know I did, and whether my thoughts were warranted, they were still legitimate.

As a teacher the best quality you can offer is empathy and humility. Put yourself in a position to feel or recognize where your students are. If you can do that, then you can adjust your approach to teaching from that perspective. If you begin to see a drop in attendance, work completion, or students dropping from the course, reach out and ask for feedback. Sometimes it may be due to circumstances out of their control such as health, finances, family, or work. But sometimes it's a disconnect that can be addressed to bridge the gap of separation.

Look at steps that can be taken to improve the learning experience — ease of use, intuitiveness, navigation, clarity of directions (covered in Chapters 7 and 8), and document accessibility (Chapter 4). Use feedback and analytics to help determine where you can improve (see Chapter 12). While some content can't be altered quickly, other changes can be implemented swiftly. It can be a simple fix to help students retain knowledge and their enrollment.

TIP

Putting yourself into the student's shoes, you can adjust content and navigation quickly as needed. Always go through your course in student mode to experience the student perspective prior to publishing the course. This will allow you to experience the course; verify dates and visibility settings are correct; experience the gradebook; and find mistakes, obstacles, or unclear directions.

Table 2-1 offers advice for knowledge and institution retention.

TABLE 2-1 **Strategies to Help Address Knowledge Retention and Course/Institute Retention**

Strategy	Explanation
Faculty presence	Helping faculty understand, develop, and practice online presence. Encouraging faculty to interact with students through collaborative activities.
	Helping faculty recognize motivations and emotional struggles, and providing support and training to help students manage expectations and responsibilities.
Feedback	Helping faculty create tools to gather input from learners and their needs in the online sector.
Support tools	Providing appropriate information that is accessible to students who need financial support or incentives; emotional or mental health support; and wraparound services such as food, housing, and transportation security.
Course design and development	Providing training and support to create courses that employ a variety of learning modalities and alternative assessments that will engage multiple cultural backgrounds and provide social interactions for community involvement.

Engagement

Student's paying attention, participating, and putting in effort is engagement. The depth of engagement is a predictor of the learner's willingness and ability to retain and apply the information. Barriers to engagement exist, and trying to alleviate these prior to or early on in the course experience can improve retention and experience.

Distractions are a barrier. Distractions are varied and range from text messages, emails, and work to pets, family, and friends. Past learning experiences have shaped the view of a participant's perception. Lack of teacher support, boring presentations, or poor performance can affect commitment. As discussed previously, lack of relativeness to the learner's direct needs may decrease their engagement.

Relevancy is a powerful tool to help entice learners to be more active, present, and work toward completion of assessments. Optimizing student engagement requires connection, community, and compassion.

Connection

In online courses, instructors can be considered invisible. Students are not consistently seeing the instructor so there are no facial or body queues, or inflections of their voice to relay important information. So, an online instructor must be present in the classroom — literally present. This entails a welcome message, a welcome page, and a voice (literally and figuratively) that gives feedback to assignments. While a lot of feedback will be generic and sent to the class, opportunities to give individualized feedback help students form a sense of belonging. They feel that you notice them and are invested in their success, which can increase their motivation and confidence.

When asking questions or posting responses in the course discussion forum, engage the students in the discussion and prompt higher level thinking. Redirect comments and pose questions that explore a student's answer.

Here are a few tips to help you connect with your students:

>> Addressing students by their first name helps increase a sense of belonging and can increase course satisfaction and engagement. Using a name shows respect and recognition.

>> Recognizing completion of activities helps students feel celebrated. In contrast, reaching out to individuals withdrawing or considered high risk can show they matter. Creating a safe environment for communication can guide them to success, if not in the current course, hopefully, in their future courses.

>> In many learning management systems (LMS) you can set up automated messages or send mass messaging that appears to be individualized to students. This effort is critical in building a community with the students and helping them recognize that they have a support system in place.

Community

Community is often the highlight of going to a brick-and-mortar institution. However, the presence on campus decreases the flexibility of an education. So how can these two factors, both important, be intertwined? It takes work, but it also increases engagement, retention, and satisfaction with student experiences in the online course. Students sacrifice other social aspects of their life to take online courses, so ensuring there is some effort to invest in a community is the responsibility of the facilitator.

Community can be created through asynchronous and synchronous activities such as discussion boards, video messaging, meetings, break-out rooms, gamification, social media, and more. (Find more ideas in Chapters 8 and 10.)

Flip (info.flip.com) is a great free platform that allows individuals to interact with their peers through video, audio, and text asynchronously.

TECHNICAL STUFF

Compassion

Rigor and compassion can be equals in an online course; one does not need to overshadow the other. Often online students are taking this modality for convenience and flexibility so they can continue to work, raise their family, focus on health, or for other personal reasons. Because of their lifestyle, empathy and support is important. They may need an extension on an assignment, but more than that, they may need guidance on how to manage their time, meet their upcoming due dates, and prioritize their responsibilities.

Ways to create a safe environment that is based on compassion are to provide tools and opportunities to access platforms and resources (usually provided by the institution or business), be present via communication channels (email, chat, phone, virtual meetings), and be open to listening.

Seeing How You Benefit

As long as you have a good reputation and are respectful to and respected by colleagues, students, and administrators, there are many advantages to teaching online. Most align with convenience, but there are other perks too:

>> You can set your own hours and create your own schedule, helping you achieve a healthy, worthwhile work-life balance.

>> You can work from anywhere.

Furthermore, you are no longer commuting to the workplace. Not commuting saves money and can improve other aspects of your work-life balance:

>> Not commuting saves on gas and car maintenance, and you may be able to lower insurance costs permanently.

>> Not commuting saves on clothes from purchasing work attire to dry cleaning.

- ➤ Not commuting saves on eating out. Think about how many times you forget your lunch, want to join your colleagues, or are too tired to prepare meals for the week due to the lost time commuting.

- ➤ Not commuting may allow you to earn tax breaks — deductions for a home office, phone bills, internet services, depreciation of equipment, and more.

- ➤ Not commuting potentially gives your employer more effective work hours and gives you hundreds of hours back from work-related activities.

- ➤ Not commuting may afford the opportunity to save money on childcare, dog walking, or dog daycare.

Flexibility

Yes, flexibility is being mentioned again. It is one of the most splendid benefits of teaching online. One can explore the world without asking permission to be away from the office, while still fulfilling their responsibilities.

WARNING

Time zones can be challenging — both with due dates and meetings. If you teach a class that serves the world, make sure you're prepared for early mornings or late nights to serve all students' needs.

Increased salary

Online teaching, online course design, and online curriculum development offer opportunities to earn beyond a fixed income. Working online makes it possible for teachers to earn more through many avenues connected to the online teaching community.

There are opportunities beyond teaching an online class. One can sell lesson plans, tutor online, teach preparatory courses for standardized testing (ACT, SAT, LSAT, GRE, MCAT, and so on), mentor or coach other schools or businesses, and facilitate professional development courses. Working online can also provide opportunities to earn money doing other activities, from pet-walking to selling crafts to being a photographer. There is no limit to what you are capable of achieving.

Better work-life balance

If you are currently a teacher in the traditional sense, then you are probably overworked. How can that change with online courses? Online courses allow more flexibility when creating a schedule. The schedule can change from week to week or course to course. If your schedule changes frequently, that inconsistency may affect student engagement and retention, so be transparent with the students from the beginning.

In my opinion, the best part about teaching online is that it can be done from home or wherever I may be at the moment, and it can be done in loungewear. Your job is to create a space so that your content can be understood and your students feel supported, seen, and served.

Invest in yourself via professional development. Explore opportunities through your institution or company, read journal articles, join societies, and attend webinars and conferences. These activities allow you to expand your knowledge and network with people who have similar interests. In the long run, it may pay off as building a community of practice and eventually individuals who can help you expand your brand. (Check out Chapters 13 and 14 for more on these topics.)

Since you are working from home, you are responsible for having boundaries at home, both physical and mental. Schedule times that are for you and your family — uninterrupted times or a day that you are offline and disconnected. Practice reflective journaling (see Chapter 12) to maintain focus on your goals, your course evolution, and to release stress and anxiety.

REMEMBER

Give yourself a break, give yourself grace, explore life outside the classroom, and invest in your personal health, physically, emotionally, and mentally. Celebrate small and large milestones, as each accomplishment is a step on your path.

2
Planning for the Best Outcomes

Chapter 3

Identifying Your User and Their Needs

As you are reading this book, you're probably thinking about what the best way for you to experience an online course is and how you can provide your user with the best support and experience. Obviously, you want it to be awesome, amazecraze, eye-catching, and fun, but is it that easy?

Designing a course for all learners is important, and thinking about all aspects of user needs before design and development occur is imperative. As you begin the process, there are many questions to consider. Is the course usable for the widest set of users? Is there limited need for adaptation of material? Does the course design account for accessibility and inclusiveness? Is it flexible in use, simple and intuitive to use, and require low physical effort?

In this chapter you uncover the basic knowledge and skills to use universal design for learning to create the best user experience. You also find out more about the importance of usability and accessibility in design. I introduce basic design ideas, personas, and time spans, as well as give you some exercises on how to create that initial architectural build or idea of your course.

Introducing Universal Design for Learning (UDL) and User Experience (UX)

Universal Design for Learning (UDL) is a set of principles and an educational framework that increases learning opportunities for all learners. It's based on three principles, each of which has guidelines to provide evidence-based approaches that help improve learning through the use of available tools and resources. Each principle aims at helping educators improve the presentation of information, engagement of students, and creation of inclusive assessments. These principles are applicable to course design and instructional materials and strategies, which makes them versatile and advantageous to implement because you are integrating one pedagogical or andragogical approach instead of many.

The design affects User Experience (UX). UX addresses how students interact with your course. UX design directs the whole experience a student has with the course to ensure they are engaged and compelled to participate to completion.

Using Universal Design for Learning to meet every user's needs

UDL is an instructional framework that supports differentiated learning by encouraging flexibility of presentation and assessments in the classroom. UDL follows guidelines that promote multiple means of representation, action and expression, and engagement. The essence of UDL is to present information in a variety of ways to reach and support the most learners.

REMEMBER

UDL focuses on changing how you design the environment instead of changing the learner. Intentionality of design reduces barriers so all learners can have a great user experience and experience meaningful learning.

From the beginning of lesson development, you anticipate and plan for all learners. The goal is to ensure the greatest range of students have access and can engage in learning. There are no specific tools and technologies. The students use the tools and resources you provide but in different ways, not prescribed.

Some content is dense, and reading a text can be exhausting as well as ineffective and an inefficient use of time. Adding alternative visual, auditory, or hands-on content creates interactive and adjustable lessons. Visual and aural elements can bring the material to life and allow users to interact with it at their own pace.

There is nothing inferior about text, but we have an over-reliance on it, therefore underutilizing pictures. It's time to embrace the alternatives. Think of more billboards, less text-driven messages; Figure 3-1 illustrates this concept.

FIGURE 3-1:
Visual messaging can be more effective than conveying the same point through text.

Obviously, learning is enhanced when the content is relevant and interesting, but lessons are often not presented with these outcomes in mind. Think about those textbooks, some weighing 5 pounds, without pictures or color. And the icing on the cake? These are the texts you had to read in classes you struggled to remain interested in. Zzzzzzzz, whoops, did I snooze off? I'm sorry. Is that what you want your legacy to be?

TIP

Think about learning patterns and big ideas. As the educator, you can show learners why content is important and therefore increase engagement via interest. This can reduce loss of learning and increase retention — an active mind is a happy mind.

TIP

Table 3-1 offers a rubric you can use to ensure your eCourse is meeting UDL guidelines.

UDL leads to UX

UDL helps with user experience (UX) because it focuses on supporting the processes of teaching and learning and can be used by anyone — educators, instructional designers, curriculum specialists, and entrepreneurs. UX focuses on how relevant and meaningful your users find your eCourse as they interact with it.

TABLE 3-1 **UDL Rubric**

Provide Multiple Means of Engagement	Examples
How can I engage all students in my class? Do I give students choice and autonomy? How do I make the learning relevant to students' needs/wants? Is my classroom supportive of all students?	On the first day of the semester, administer a survey with questions: Ask students their preferences and interests. What do they believe their strengths are? Use this information to tweak lessons. Create a choice menu for activities. Many LMS allow differentiated learning and choose-my-path learning.
Provide Multiple Means of Representation	*Examples*
Are there alternatives for printed texts, pictures, graphics, and so forth displayed? What alternative options are provided to students who need support in active learning with static material (text versus video, text versus activity)?	Make sure the digital material is adjustable in font type, size, color, and other reading features. Immersive readers are great tools to support reading. Do your tools have alternative formats? Can they be converted by you or through a program to text to speech, html, epub, mp4, and so on?
Provide Multiple Means of Action and Expression	*Examples*
What leeway is there for flexible time and pacing for assignments? What are the alternatives to offer all students instead of paper/pencil (infographics, vlogs, blogs, comic strips, songs)? Do I have the proper assistive technology? (While by law the institution should provide this, often it is not available, and knowing options will help you support the students.)	Provide checklists, calendar guides, interactive task lists to help keep on track of goals. Allow knowledge representation to be shown through multiple formats (art, writing, graphics, presentation, video, audio). Provide alternative formats for students to interact (text to speech, mp4, epub).

Think of UDL as the house designers/architects. They are thinking about the tools and layout that allow for ease of movement and usability of the living space. UX considers the size of the refrigerator, the number of chairs around the table, the quality of the carpet, that sort of thing. It can even go so far as to determine who gets to live in the house.

In terms of your eCourse, you consider the interface being used, the design deployed, and the quality of material developed. Even further it can be linked to the community created within the course. UX encompasses course structure, sequence, delivery, and evaluation. UX is the individual's ease of living in the house. Everything is accessible and meets their needs for full involvement and enjoyment.

ACTIVITY

ALLOWING USERS TO CHOOSE THEIR TOOLS

Students need to explain how to make a peanut butter and jelly sandwich. Details can vary, but it is so much fun to see where students start and what assumptions they have for background knowledge of someone making a sandwich.

Some students have made peanut butter and jelly sandwiches and are excited because they believe this will be easy. Other students may have never made one and are nervous. And honestly, some students dislike writing and dread this exercise.

Because all classrooms have a wide range of backgrounds and skills among the students, when you create this assignment, plan it with a range in mind of how the students can approach the lesson.

Background:

- Learners know the goal, and expectations are clearly stated for grading.
- Flexible options are available for students.
- All resources are available for students from the beginning of the lesson.
- Students will build their own learning (individually or in groups).

Options:

- Write an essay on how to make a peanut butter and jelly sandwich.
- Create a video explaining how to make a peanut butter and jelly sandwich.
  - TikTok
  - Reels
  - I video
- Draw a storyboard of the process to create a peanut butter and jelly sandwich.
- Tweet the steps of making a peanut butter and jelly sandwich.
- Compose a song explaining the steps of creating a peanut butter and jelly sandwich.

Creating more effective instruction with UX

When designing for UX, you're employing empathy for the user; that is, having the ability to understand someone else's needs, experiences, and desires. When you approach your eCourse outside your role of instructor, you are understanding it from the user's perspective. That's a start, but it's not enough.

TIP

Don't just imagine the users' experiences; instead, go and talk to them. Listen to their needs and listen well. Watch and observe, talk, and find out how they use the "tools." Use all senses to learn, because many individuals do not solely rely on sight, sound, or touch. We do not want the designer to sympathize with someone because they cannot provide proper experiences. If that is the case, *do not use* the tool or the process.

ACTIVITY

USER EXPERIENCE EXERCISE

Audio Description (Descriptive Audio or Video Description) relays the relevant visual content in a video so individuals with low vision or blindness can understand the meaning. While this action is part of the law, ADA, Titles II and III, and the Rehabilitation Act, section 504 and 508, help ensure equity is provided for individuals with disabilities. While this sounds simple, consider the process.

Watch any 30-second video, whether from YouTube, a clip from your favorite movie/tv show, or a Broadway classic, and describe in a meaningful way the audio description of what is occurring surrounding the speaking, if speaking even occurs.

Can you do 30 seconds of the audio description for a clip of *The Lion King?*

Try it: *The Lion King* clip without the audio description: https://youtu.be/0d164QwwtW4?si=swbdQoLwXXE1kj1E&t=105 (starts at 1:45 to mimic the audio description example below).

Now listen to this audio description of *The Lion King:* https://youtu.be/7-XOHN2BWG4?si=0EAr5QkTEGeQBsIw.

Who can this help? Is it just for low vision and blind users? If you said no, you are correct.

Multi-taskers, those on the autism spectrum, people experiencing temporary blindness, those who struggle with language development and others can also benefit.

Part of designing well is talking to the users. Asking for input is important, as seeking feedback directly improves your courses. Don't be afraid to ask what they didn't like instead of what they did. Focus on finding issues for improvement instead of seeking approval.

Defining Your Target Audience

Who do you want to teach or capture the attention of to mold minds or instigate exciting quests? Your target audience will vary based on the purpose of your course, your personal goals, and your profession. Your approach may also affect the audience you draw: Are you a TED Talk storyteller, an activity aficionado, or a melting pot of let's try it?

Think about who can take online courses. *Anyone!* I mean anyone. Online courses can be taken by students, educators, professionals, lifelong learners, and clients, and the courses can offer flexibility and convenience for the participant.

If you design using UDL and keep the user in mind, accessible courses will become second nature and access to courses will become your secret sauce.

So where do you start with determining who you're teaching to or for? Design what you believe to be your ideal learner and figure out your audience. It may not be as simple as paint by numbers, but it shouldn't be rocket science, either!

Personas: Conjuring up your ideal learner

Who are your learners? What are their goals? You must look past demographics and see the whole picture. Learners are the sum of all their past experiences — personal, professional, and educational. What are their preferences in learning? Do they know them? What is their familiarity with and access to technology? Is cultural, racial, and ethnic upbringing going to influence how words, analogies, and images are perceived?

Learners are diverse, complex, and ever evolving. Getting to know your learners and identifying them early will help you create a safe environment in which they can learn and grow. The way to do this is to be real!

Look at past data of student performance and feedback; observe their actions and what assessments they excel at or find meaningful. Survey the students to garner feedback that will help you grow as a facilitator of knowledge. Most importantly, speak with them. Discover the good, the bad, the ugly, the fun, and the fails.

K-12

If you teach K–12, you may be asked to reach children virtually and online with little training or technical and professional support.

When tackling teaching online K–12, so many factors need to be considered:

>> Are you teaching tadpoles (elementary children) or the big fish (high schoolers)? The grade will ultimately change the feel, experience, and design of the course.

>> Do the students have access to technology? Computers, internet? Support? If not, what tools can you provide the students?

>> Are you supported by the parents, or do you need to create a guide to help parents both technically and educationally? Are the lessons parent dependent?

>> How can increased autonomy be developed for younger students?

Guess what? You are not alone. There is a road map that will help you be successful. There will be turns, loops, merges and verges, potholes, and obstacles along the way, but it is always how you react, not what is occurring, that matters.

AN EXPERT BEYOND YOUR FIELD

When you're designing an eCourse, you become a self-proclaimed expert from the instructional view and the student's view. You are tech support, and this knowledge will allow you to seamlessly move through the day without having to rely on others as often.

Make notes of what questions are commonly asked by students and parents and use them as a FAQ or reference guide for both students and parents. Create a guide to meet your needs. Be selfish and allow this guide to be you 24/7.

Plan time in the day for tech lessons with students and parents. If you build in time for this, you won't feel that you are constantly racing the clock.

Last, know that the different grade levels will have different learner needs. As you are developing lessons, do so in a variety of ways, allowing for alternative assessments and delivery. Small steps make a big difference to you, the child, and the parent.

Higher ed

Is everyone online student material? No, but everyone is not a baker, a pilot, or an underwater welder. It takes a certain individual to naturally excel at online learning. The most recent research has profiled online learners in higher education, and here are some of the most common characteristics.

Undergraduate online college students are usually single, white women from 19 to 23 and 27 to 30 years of age who are not of Hispanic, Latino, or Spanish origin and have no children living at home. Around 50 percent are employed full time, with an average of six years' work experience and an income around $50,000. Most are not first-generation college students and enroll within a school in their state. The graduate school population of students has similar demographics but they're between 30 and 35 and make around $10,000 more on average. A commonality among all online students is convenience and flexibility. They can study and complete the work anywhere at any time. Also, career advancement is usually a motivating factor supporting the online enrollment.

REMEMBER

As an instructor, you must be able to motivate the students to work hard, be flexible, apply self-discipline, and finish assignments in a timely manner. Your fancy videos and interactives, while awesome and impressive, are not going to meet the students' needs if you are not addressing student pain points, guiding them on how to apply what they are learning, being present and answering questions, and being able to predict their needs before they realize them.

TIP

What higher education students really want:

>> Access to courses that are mobile friendly

>> Actionable content that is relevant to the real world

>> A great user experience from navigation to aesthetics

>> Clear expectations and outcomes

>> Opportunities for connection, community, and collaboration

Incarcerated person

Understanding all students is important, and being able to adapt to alternative students opens up the breadth of the audience you can tap into. Being able to teach incarcerated individuals, including those having environmental, cultural, and economic disadvantages, allows you to expand your reach and have a greater impact on the learning space. Special skills are needed to facilitate the learning of disadvantaged groups. Knowledge of and the ability to implement innovative or instructional techniques are essential. The facilitator must understand principles, theories, techniques of education (pedagogy/andragogy), and content of the subject matter. Using the following steps in developing and deploying the curriculum is helpful in creating a successful foundation for any course, but especially for students with specific needs.

1. **Diagnosis of the need**
2. **Task analysis and planning of the curriculum**
3. **Implementation of curriculum**
4. **Tracking of progress (assessment)**
5. **Evaluation**
6. **Modification of curriculum**

Being an educator in the correctional environment requires one to adapt and adjust to situations presented. The limitations on technology options and integrations to engage students in meaningful learning scenarios are often limited. A community of practice is one way that educators can support each other through the culture shock, by sharing teaching strategies and skills specific to a restrictive environment and discussing pragmatic options for deployment of content. Because both the student population and the classroom conditions in correctional education differ from traditional education, it is important to have development opportunities specifically designed for the correctional educator. These opportunities are offered through correctional education associations and department-organized training opportunities.

Businesses

When training employees at businesses, creating a learning culture is important. You are bringing knowledge into everyday activities, and the employees represent your company. Delivering and assessing the skills development is important to build an exceptional team.

Online courses allow the training to maintain relevance, be innovative, and be continuous with limited delay in knowledge. Your training can ensure you are competitive in the market, reduce technical issues (IT nightmares such as malware, phishing, and scam emails), and improve the employees' effectiveness on technology. A goal is to enhance the efficiency of employees' productivity, which leads to profitability.

REMEMBER

In businesses, there is often a skills gap between what the employee wants and who may be applying. But a creative, cost effective, and scalable solution is micro credentialing. Micro credentials are bite-size qualifications that demonstrate a skill, knowledge, or experience in a field.

If you go this path, identify the skills and competencies you need to upskill or reskill the employees, and you can partner with higher education institutes or businesses to offer the micro credentials. These mighty badges can create a culture of continuous learning.

TIP

When choosing to use online delivery for business training, you must keep this in mind:

>> Facilitation of personal development should be provided with the training.

>> The programs should be customizable for your company's needs.

>> The program needs to support scalability.

>> Robust analytics need to be generated.

Personal growth

Individuals who take online courses for personal growth want to enjoy the time they invest in the course. Your job, as the facilitator and/or creator, is to make it fun!

You want to attract your learners' attention in the environment. When creating the course for learners, ask yourself this:

>> Would this activity or design captivate me?

>> Am I having fun or is there a more dynamic, alternate way to deploy this knowledge?

>> Is the course engaging?

The secret to success is keeping the course exciting, flexible, engaging, and interactive. With these thoughts in mind, your product may be unrivaled.

TIP

Regardless of the learner, creating micro learning helps you capture the attention span of your audience.

Chunking material into smaller pieces allows your learner to consume it more easily. Focusing on one objective instead of a chapter makes it seem that they are moving through content and meeting end goals more quickly. It also helps to improve retention.

Knowing How Much Time You Have: Course Length

Course length is often predetermined by parameters out of your control. Truth is that the course should be long enough to deliver your learning outcomes and nothing else. How much time and willingness do learners have to devote to a course? Understanding who the learner is and the constraints they have may help you design a course with reasonable workloads. You don't want to be the course that everyone takes for the "easy A," but you don't want to have the reputation of the evil sage on the stage.

Regardless of who the learner may be, think about two things:

>> As a subject matter expert (SME), your knowledge is more in-depth, and you don't want to make the course too complex.

>> What the learner needs versus what they want should be taken into consideration. The goal is for your customers (the learners) to walk away with skills and knowledge that are applicable to their job or real-world anecdotes.

REMEMBER

Regardless of course length, you can determine your schedule by reviewing your objectives and chapters and aligning them with a single day, a week, or a preset block of time to fit your course length. A well-designed matrix (schedule aligned with activities, objectives, and timelines) will allow your learners to be aware of expectations and you to guide them to success.

Quarter system

When creating courses that use a quarter system, understanding student experience is essential. Students have smaller course loads as they take fewer credit hours during a shorter period of time. In addition, having four quarters allows for greater course flexibility as they can take more classes over the school year. The classes are fast paced, but if you do not like a class, it is shorter lived.

Quarter systems on average are nine to ten weeks. As the instructor, you have to be vigilant about creating an environment that is need-to-know material versus nice-to-know material. Less time with the material means less time learning and creating those critical thinking abilities.

Semester system

Semester systems are generally 15 weeks long. The length allows individuals more time to learn and more time to form relationships with their professors. But schools are businesses, and there are alternative terms that can be offered within a semester. Two-week intensive courses allow students to earn a better grade or take a course when time is of the essence. Imagine finishing an entire course like Human Anatomy and Physiology in two weeks! What, no thank you. But there are students who do this, and they are successful. Their success is based on the teacher's design. The teacher trims the fat of the course and focuses on work that will engage the student while supporting their learning of the content. Similar to quarter systems, there are shorter terms within a semester that allow students to have flexibility in start dates.

Open-ended

There are a lot of reasons individuals sign up for free or affordable learning nuggets offered through Massive Open Online Courses (MOOCs) and other providers. You can dabble in a lot of subjects and determine where your interests are sparked by exploring trendy or timeless topics. You can stay up to date in your field because it is convenient and fits into most individuals' busy lives. You can earn free or affordable certificates. You can meet your peers from around the world and form communities based on topics of interest.

Last, flexibility is key, as open-ended courses are self-paced. You do not have to abide by the parameters of time constraints. As a teacher designing the course, you can determine what the ideal weekly workload should look like and assign work to fit that mold.

Weekly schedule

If learning is a hobby, there are many short courses that technically can be completed in a day or so, but students are often given seven days, a week, to complete. Many of these are micro credentialing or certificate courses used for CEUs or professional development. However, they provide a niche in the education and business world. These courses are efficient, effective, low-cost to run, and informative, but can be very lucrative. If your audience is a short-course audience, dividing your objectives into short activities that are demonstrated daily will help you create a well-designed, beneficial course where the learner earns experience daily.

Chapter **4**

Focusing on Accessibility

Worldwide, it is reported that over one billion people have a disability. That's one in six individuals. In the United States, a quarter of the population lives with a disability, and an even higher number experiences situational disabilities, which are temporary or situational circumstances that interfere with tasks.

Digital accessibility represents a set of practices that is meant to remove barriers for people with disabilities, thereby improving the experience for disabled users. Digital accessibility promotes inclusion and diversity, and it helps to ensure that everyone can access important services and information, such as education and training.

Why Accessibility Is Important

For all individuals to participate and contribute to a digital world (for education, business, and social purposes), all information needs to be accessible, which means perceivable, understandable, operable, and robust. The material must be navigable and intuitive. All people, regardless of visual, auditory, physical, speech, cognitive, and neurological needs, should be considered when designing, creating, and implementing digital tools and platforms. Accessibility expedites delivery of information and allows a larger consumer base to obtain information.

Accessible design: What it means to create an accessible online course

Creating an accessible course is a marathon, not a sprint. Instead of thinking "accessibility is for disability-related issues," consider shifting your mindset to be more constructive. Accessible design improves ease of access for your users. There are many terms that you'll want to become familiar with as you strive to enhance accessibility. Don't get overwhelmed with the alphabet soup of acronyms; embrace it.

The following sections describe the defining characteristics of an accessible course.

LAWS AND POLICIES

Different countries have different laws and policies in place to govern accessibility and disability rights. In the United States, it's the Americans with Disabilities Act. In Canada, it's the Accessible Canada Regulations (ACR). In Europe, it's the European Accessibility Act (EAA). There are many guidelines and laws followed in Asian countries, such as China's Information Technology Requirements and Testing Methods for Accessibility of Web Content (GB/T 37668-2019). India enacted the Rights of Persons with Disabilities Act (RPWD act), and Ireland and the United Kingdom have several acts that govern digital accessibility, such as the Disability Act of 2005 and the Equality Act of 2010, respectively. The goal of this information is not to be overwhelming, but for you to know that tools to help guide you and make decisions are available no matter what country you reside in.

- **Americans with Disabilities Act (ADA)** was signed into law in 1990 and prohibits discrimination and ensures equal opportunity for people with disabilities (PWD) in employment, state and local government services, public accommodations, and transportation. There are different Titles in ADA that address specific aspects of life.

- **Section 508 of the Rehabilitation Act of 1973** requires vendors who want to work with the U.S. federal government to provide accessible websites and software tools.

- **Web Content Accessibility Guidelines (WCAG)** is the most recognized, comprehensive standard for accessibility around the world.

- **World Wide Web Consortium (W3C)** is the industry-recognized body for setting web accessibility standards.

- **Web Accessibility Initiative (WAI)** develops standards and support materials to help others understand and implement accessibility.

Intuitive

In the 1990s, Jeff Raskin was teaching PageMaker to employees. At the time he asked them to use the computer mouse to click on the OK button on the screen. An employee picked up the mouse and clicked it against the screen. Today, using a mouse is second nature to most individuals, but at one time, the mouse's design and purpose were not intuitive.

Intuitive design is creating an experience with the digital materials that is easy for the user. Is the design inviting or disinviting? Is the structure repetitive and similar throughout to help create an ease of navigation? Is the location of reading materials, assignments, tasks, collaborative opportunities, in the same format and place for each section? Can the user use the material immediately, without having to think about how to use it? If so, then it is considered intuitive. But intuitiveness is based on who the user is, too. Determining what experience your users may come into the course with will influence your design ideas.

Navigable

Have you ever gotten lost? Your sympathetic nervous system kicks in, and you feel nervous and anxious. You are overwhelmed and don't know where to go. Well, that's what it can be like if your course is poorly designed. Great navigation is a nonnegotiable component of an online course. Course navigation facilitates a positive course experience and ease of use. Navigation should be consistent, logical, and entail minimal scrolling, clicking, and searching. You want the user to spend time interacting with the content, not searching for it. Many steps can be taken to ensure navigation is intuitive and well designed. Many are discussed later in detail, but a sneak peek follows:

>> Have a "Start Here" video to help students learn how to navigate.

>> Clarify where users should be going (via next buttons, page links, and so forth).

>> Consistency is key — across weeks, chapters, content pieces, and the course as a whole.

>> Include hyperlink shortcuts.

>> Ask friends or colleagues for feedback.

>> Embed material within the course.

Perceivable

Can things be invisible to the senses? Can you smell through the TV? Information must be created so it can be presented to users in ways by which they can perceive it. The users need to understand the information being presented. Individuals who are blind or sight-impaired need alternative text that describes pictures to them. Those who are deaf or hard of hearing can read a transcript or use closed captions. Second-language learners can use transcripts or closed captions to help them understand the content.

Operable

Making a course operable often requires some knowledge of how to operate assistive technology. *Operable* means a user can use controls, buttons, navigation, and interactive elements. This can require different assistive technologies such as keyboard strokes, screen readers, voice recognition, screen magnification, alternative keyboards, and eye tracking tools. Operable also includes time to read and use content.

Understandable

While this may seem obvious, content is not always delivered in a manner that improves comprehension, learning, and remembering. This often can be associated with navigation. Creating pages that have similar flow, so relearning actions is minimal, helps make the experience predictable and readable. Also make sure that you don't use a lot of abbreviations, jargon, and acronyms without defining them early on. Alphabet soup is difficult to learn.

Robust

Robust is a fun guideline because it focuses on creating content that can be interpreted by a wider variety of users and the technology they choose to use when interacting with the documents, websites, and media. You don't want to use websites or tools that are only supported in specific browsers or aren't supported by a particular operating system. While you may not be creating the material to be delivered, you are responsible for ensuring that the tools you choose are compatible with current and future operating systems and assistive technologies.

Assessing Platform Accessibility

When creating online courses, the company or institution will often determine what Learning Management System (LMS), or platform, you will be using to deliver the content to your audience. If this is the case, you will need to learn the LMS interface. Even when an LMS is accessible, the course you create, the content you create, or the material you choose to deploy can create an inaccessible course. Another aspect to consider is that most LMSs support plug-ins that work across products by the Learning Tool Interoperability (LTI). LTI integrate many learning tools and content in a standard way. In a click or two, the data exchange between the LMS and learning systems can be automated. However, the plug-ins can introduce accessibility problems.

Regardless of the LMS, whether you choose your own or are required to use a specific one, the potential to introduce accessibility issues is great. Instructors and course developers need a foundational knowledge of technology accessibility. Many great tools are available on the web to help guide instructors, and many LMSs provide built-in accessibility checkers that provide feedback on how to improve documents, fix issues, and create more-accessible documents. Often these tools are add-ons, and many provide alternative formats to the user such as text files, PDF, immersive reader, EPUB, audio, braille when supported, and more.

Utilizing resources to support your accessibility journey

You need to be aware of the laws and guidelines surrounding accessibility, but they are there to serve a purpose.

To provide users with a sense of support, many industry standards and regulations exist for making technology accessible. When technology was in its infancy, the Web Accessibility Initiative (WAI) through the World Wide Web Consortium (W3C) published the Web Content Accessibility Guidelines (WCAG). WCAG is a set of independent formal guidelines recognized globally. These are considered the strictest and most inclusive.

Many laws, such as Section 508 of the U.S. Federal Rehabilitation Act and the Americans with Disabilities Act (ADA), share common goals of accommodating individuals with sensory, cognitive, and mobility impairments. Section 508 has incorporated WCAG as the federal standard for website and app accessibility. In 2018, Section 508 was revisited, and the requirements for information and communication technology (ICT) were enhanced by the adoption of WCAG 2.0 AA as the standard for website, electronic document, and software accessibility. With this addition, federal agencies and organizations receiving federal funding must follow the guidelines because they're part of the law.

TIP

Should you memorize the guidelines? No. Should you be aware of them? Yes. Don't get overwhelmed; instead, do internet searches on an as-needed basis. All the WCAG guidelines are posted on the internet, and there are ample resources to help walk you through how to accomplish compliance.

Checking accessibility

Many of the tools you will use to build content have an accessibility checker built in, which is great. But I must emphasize that no accessibility checker will be able to evaluate a document completely without human touch. The tools cannot emulate human attributes such as context and common sense.

Following is a list of some free tools that are available to check different aspects of accessibility:

>> **Web Accessibility Versatile Evaluator (WAVE)** is one of my favorites (see Figure 4-1). It's an evaluation tool that identifies many accessibility WCAG errors and helps humans evaluate the website. WAVE can be used as a plug-in, or a website URL can be directly placed in the website's search bar. Consider using the WAVE tool on a website you use daily and look at the accessibility reports.

FIGURE 4-1:
Web Accessibility
Versatile
Evaluator
(WAVE).

>> **Accessibility Checker** (see Figure 4-2) is an audit tool that checks websites for major errors based on legislation around the world. The scans provide detailed reports on each error, whom it affects, and how to resolve the issues.

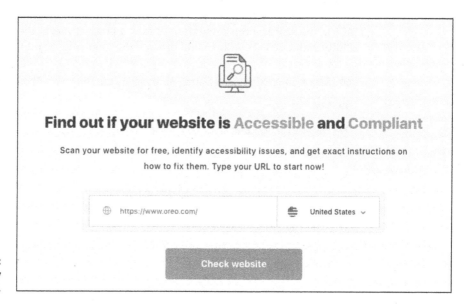

FIGURE 4-2:
Accessibility
Checker.

>> **PAVE** is a PDF web tool that helps fix existing PDF documents with tagging documents for use with assistive technology.

>> **Universal Design Online Inspection Tool (UDOIT)** allows faculty to identify web accessibility issues in the Canvas Learning Management System. UDOIT is free by downloading the source code at UDOIT's GitHub page.

>> **Accessibility Color Wheel** helps you choose color pairs (text and background). It simulates three types of color blindness and uses contrast checkers.

>> **Microsoft Accessibility Checker** uses a set of rules to identify many issues that may affect people with disabilities use of a file. The accessibility checker can provide information on the issues and potential ways to fix them.

>> **Adobe Accessibility Checker** is present in Acrobat Pro, and it helps review common WCAG standards. The tool allows you to check accessibility and can guide you on how to fix issues such as reading order and structure.

VPAT and ACR

Companies are responsible for supplying you with accessible documents/tools, and they are increasing accessibility to their content. Companies should provide a Voluntary Product Accessibility Template (VPAT) on their website or by request. A VPAT that has been filled out is known as an Accessibility Conformance Report (ACR). The ACR is a representation of how a product meets the applicable accessibility standards. An ACR should provide the following, at minimum:

>> Report title: "[Company Name] Accessibility Conformance Report"

>> VPAT version

>> Name of Product (and version, if applicable)

>> Product description

>> Date of publication

>> Contact information

>> Evaluation methods used

>> Applicable standards: WCAG 2.0, WCAG 2.1, WCAG 2.2, Revised Section 508, EN 301 549

Best practices are to have third-party experts in digital accessibility complete the ACR instead of the company doing it in-house. If the product is not a website, the company can provide conformance statements that directly address WCAG 2.0, 2.1, or 2.2 AA.

To see what a VPAT looks like, download the current template from the Information Technology Industry Council (ITI) website at www.itic.org.

Getting Accessibility Tips

Planning, understanding, and using digital accessibility may be overwhelming. I always say it is a marathon, not a sprint. To be effective and most efficient, digital accessibility should be done proactively, and while you do not need to be an expert, educating yourself and knowing where to find support is essential and useful. While there are many accessibility tips to promote usability, this section covers a few that can be implemented swiftly the next time you edit or create a digital document.

Images (alt text, in line)

Images support content and often make it easier to understand content. When properly described in context of the content, images help orient individuals with the content. Images need Alternative Text also known as Alt Text. Alt Text is meant to convey why land how the images relate to the content. Making images accessible allows users with screen readers and speech software to understand the non-text content. In addition, Alt Text can be read if images do not load. Sometimes a website is slow to upload because images consume bandwidth. Images are often tagged and indexed to increase search engine optimization and find content relevant to the search. It is possible to turn off images in the browser you use, such as Chrome. Creating text-only versions only creates more barriers to users as they are less accessible and functional. All users should have an equivalent user experience.

TIP

Images can be categorized into different groups and the alt text provided based on the images' purpose, as follows:

>> **Informative images:** Alt Text should be a description conveying the meaning of how the images relate to the text or purpose.

>> **Decorative images:** These are solely for aesthetics and don't convey information pertinent to the content.

>> **Functional images:** These describe functionality based on well-known symbols or icons. Can you think of images that are recognized around the world and convey the same context? Think about *Danger, Wet Floor, Stop,* and *Exit.*

>> **Complex images:** Think about graphs, figures, and diagrams. These can become very complex. Information is provided surrounding the image in the text portion of the content.

In addition, in Word documents, screen readers will only recognize an image if it is inline. If it is floating, the screen reader won't alert the user to its existence.

ACTIVITY

PICTURE PERFECT

Open a Word document (the steps are very similar in PowerPoint and Adobe) and insert an image from your computer or the documents picture repository, or copy and paste an image from the web.

Do one of the following: Select Insert > Pictures > This Device for a picture on your PC. Select Insert > Pictures > Stock Images for high-quality images or backgrounds. Select Insert > Pictures > Online Pictures for a picture on the web.

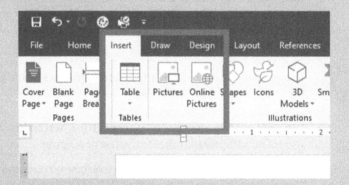

There are numerous ways to add Alt Text to images, pictures, shapes, and more.

To add alt text to a picture, shape, chart, or SmartArt graphic, follow these steps:

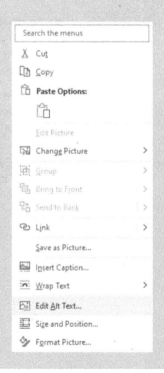

1. **Right-click the object and select Edit Alt Text. . . .**

2. **Select the object. Select Format -> Alt Text.**

   The Alt Text pane opens.

3. **Type a detailed description of the image for someone who can't see the image.**

   Describe the meaning of the picture in the context of the text.

Making a picture inline through picture formatting is necessary for assistive technology to recognize the picture. There are different ways to accomplish this but usually selecting the picture, and selecting layout options is the easiest.

You can change a figure's behavior by using the Wrap Text menu in the Arrange section on the Format tab, which appears when you select the figure.

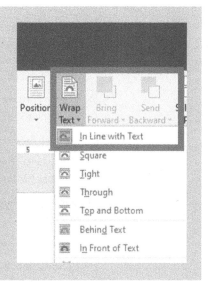

Meaningful links (hyperlinks)

Hyperlinks connect a hypertext file to another location or file, and the linked information is usually a website, video, or document file. Hyperlinks often are a different color than their surrounding text, which is helpful for sighted users, but color is not sufficient for accessibility. In addition to color, underlining links is a good indicator as long as it is always present and not dependent on hovering over the link. The contrast between the hyperlinked text and the background should be 4.5:1.

In general one wants to avoid link text such as "click here," "read more," or "view video/document here" as the link should make sense without depending on the surrounding content. Here are some tips:

>> **Embed hyperlinks:** This provides a concise string of text. If a full URL is used, a screen reader will read every character of the URL.

Accessible: Amazon purchase site for *Creating eCourses For Dummies*.
(The link is embedded in the "purchase site" text.)

Not accessible: https://www.amazon.com/Creating-eCourses-Dummies-Career-Education/dp/1394224974/ref=sr_1_1?crid=29C8YS4KQ8J7L&keywords=creating+resources+for+dummies&qid=1706816844&sprefix=creating+ecourses+for+dummie%2Caps%2C169&sr=8-1

>> **Create concise hyperlinks** to allow users to scan and determine if they want to click it and access the content.

Concise: Accessing *Creating eCourses For Dummies* cheat sheet.

Not Concise: Click on this link to access the page that provides the *Creating eCourses For Dummies* cheat sheet.

>> **Descriptive hyperlinks** explain what the user will link to and improves their experience.

Descriptive: Cheat Sheet for Creating eCourses

Nondescriptive: Cheat Sheet

Captions, transcripts, and audio descriptions

Have you ever forgotten your headphones and been in a noisy area, such as an airport or train, when you want to watch a TV show online? How would you do this? You would turn on the closed captioning feature. If the video didn't have closed captioning, you would be disappointed. If closed captioning were your only method of consuming the content, you would have run into an absolute barrier. There are laws that require captioning for all TV programs shown on the internet, and when designing your courses, videos will play a large role in conveying meaningful content.

Do a web search on "YouTube Caption Fails" and watch a few of the results without volume. Did you laugh? Were you confused?

So what is the difference between captions, transcripts, subtitles, and audio descriptions? Do you need all of this?

Vocabulary lesson

Captions are texts placed on the screen of the video in the language of the video. They can be closed, meaning they can be clicked on or off, or open, in which case they stay as an overlay of the screen. Subtitles are captions, but they are in a different language than the original video. Audio descriptions are audio that describes the environment and actions happening on the screen. Last, there are transcripts, whose purpose is to provide information for individuals who may not be able to attain it from audio and/or video.

To time stamp or not? To add speaker names or not?

Both time stamps and speaker names can clutter the written page, but both offer important information based on use cases. If there are a lot of individuals in the conversation, providing speaker names is helpful to follow the flow of the conversation. Time stamps are useful in situations such as searching content, reviewing the time investment of a speaker, and creating chapters.

You can minimize stress by creating proper tools for your users.

TIP

Plan ahead. Create a script of what you will say. Scripts are useful for a multitude of reasons. They keep your content concise and on point. You can control the length of recordings more easily. The script can also be converted to a transcript with many of the digital programs available for use, many of which are free.

If you choose to free-form your video content, no worries. Many video platforms can create captions based on your speech (speech-to-text AI) or files provided. Verified YouTube users can upload different file types such as SubRip Subtitle file (SRT), or Video Text Tracks (VTT) files to the video *or* you can allow AI to create the captions. VTT files can be customized and styles such as fonts and colors can be adjusted. These are often seen in social media. SRT files are plain text files that are smaller file sizes and better for professional videos. Editing is involved to ensure it is accurate, but it does help create a solid foundation for creating alternative information outlets.

Color contrast and use of color

Have you ever tried to read something and found that the colors chosen in the message or graphic made it difficult? Color choice is very important because if there isn't enough contrast between text and its background, it can be difficult to read. Because computers can affect luminance, hue, and saturation, color contrast is determined in a way that people who have color vision deficiencies will be able to differentiate between the text and background. Light color fonts with a light background or dark color fonts with a dark background may be okay for those who have perfect vision. But many individuals who have color vision deficiencies find it difficult to distinguish between such colors.

What does this mean? The minimum color contrast ratio between text and the background color must be 4.5:1 except for large scale text (18-point or larger in font size or 14-point bold in style), incidental text, and logos.

How do you figure out the 4.5:1 ratio? You let the computer do it for you. There are plenty of free color contrast checkers, as well as color contrast checkers built into accessibility checking programs.

The colors are usually defined as HEX (hexadecimal), or RGB (red, green blue). These are friendly, universal ways to communicate color to computers. Color contrast checkers as well as software programs often allow you to enter either HEX or RGB. A web search may allow you to pick your exact colors, or your institution or business may have predetermined marketing colors.

There is no reason to memorize HEX or RGB codes. I only know two by heart: black (HEX #000000) and white (HEX #FFFFFF).

TIP

Here is a great website to check color contrast: WebAIM Contrast Checker (https://webaim.org/resources/contrastchecker). Figure 4-3 shows examples of maximum contrast and partially failed contrast using the WebAIM Contrast Checker.

Good examples versus bad examples of color contrast can easily be found on the web with a simple search. You will be surprised at how many color combinations are used that are not considered compliant, such as red on green.

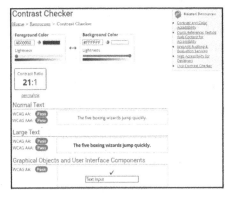 

FIGURE 4-3:
The WebAIM Contrast Checker shows maximum contrast (left) and partially failed contrast (right).

Microsoft products and accessibility

Microsoft provides a robust repository of accessibility training materials such as walk-throughs, step-by-step instructions, and video directions. They strive to use inclusive design to support the spectrum of disabilities, including hearing, vision, learning, mobility, neurodivergent, and mental health. The versions of Windows differ, but the most recent versions are the most accessible and most innovative by providing live captions, voice access and typing, narrator, focus mode, color control, advanced display and vision settings, color features, eye control, and immersive reader.

In addition, Microsoft products have a built-in accessibility checker that verifies files against rules that identify potential issues for people with disabilities. The accessibility checker defines the check of the document as an error, warning, or tip. It is available in numerous of their apps and platforms.

PDFs and accessibility

Portable Document Format (PDF) is a destination file format. PDFs are usually created in another application, and the original document should be designed for accessible use. Adobe (Acrobat Pro) supports you when creating accessible documents. And when created properly, accessible PDFs can support searchable text, fonts with characters that can be extracted to text, hyperlinks and navigational aids, title information and document language, security that does not affect assistive technology, proper reading order, alternative text descriptions, audio controls, no flashing elements, and more. Acrobat allows a quick predefined automated accessibility check. It also has a full check for accessibility and provides an accessibility report. As with Microsoft, there are support guides online that can help you properly develop a file.

If you have Adobe Pro, open any PDF file and run the accessibility checker. You can also have it read out loud to you. Experiencing assistive technology gives you a real appreciation for how well documents are designed.

Making Accommodations in Online Courses

Online education and opportunities allow many students access to education, and it is an alternative for students with learning disabilities. The online world affords students enhanced opportunities for academic success.

While typical accommodations are given for online students, one must consider how to move past typical and think about student needs and characteristics. No one accommodation will work for the masses, and no decisions should be made about them without them.

Typical online accommodations include

» Extended time on assessments

» Reader

» Scribe (an individual that types or writes responses verbatim for the user)

» Braille display

» Adaptive or assistive technology

» Distraction reduced environment

» Alternative format

» Note taking

» Memory aids

» Alternative formats including audio, braille, etext, and tactile graphics

» Communication Access Realtime Translation (CART) (also known as real-time captioning)

» Interpreting

» Religious accommodation

Chapter 5

Choosing the Right Resources for Your eCourse

C hoosing the right materials for your online course is key for the user's success and experience. Figuring out which platform to use helps determine instruction too. Depending on the course and the platform, it may make sense to select materials before you decide on assignments or vice versa.

Comparing and contrasting different formats of resources will provide advantages and disadvantages for users' different preferences, time needs, and engagement desires. Whether the material offered is in the form of reading, video, audio, activities, or documents, you can offer an assortment of options. Evaluating the quality and relevance will help you provide resources that support users' needs, interests, and context.

When I first started creating online courses, my resources were scarce, but once I understood users' needs, my needs, and types of materials available or I could create, I was able to create credible, quality, and relevant material.

Locating the Resources You Need

Choosing the proper material for your courses can be confusing. We hold the students or users in online classes to the same expectations as students in a face-to-face class. In traditional classes, you give feedback to students frequently, read body and facial cues, and answer questions as they occur. In an online classroom, those opportunities can be missed, so we often give more assignments to gauge understanding and give frequent feedback. So where do you go to get information to create assignments?

Peer support

No one understands your needs better than your fellow instructors or facilitators, also known as your peers. Your peers can provide you with premade assignments, guidance, content, and tools. More importantly, they are a source of discussion for teaching and learning, which focuses on best practices, teaching strategies, and types of assignments. In reality, peer support is even more. It allows collaboration, networking, socialization, an opportunity to vent (it's necessary), and mental and emotional support.

In all honesty, I have wanted to walk off the cliff many times. But what stops me? I have peers who are going through experiences similar to mine. I can turn to them and express my stress, overwhelming feeling of ineffectiveness, and lack of time to complete everything.

Teacher peer support is the humanistic way of coping with the stress. I ask my peers to share work. We create a repository of activities, assignments, videos, and assessments. These effective learning opportunities are impactful because we share the work, and the onus is not on one individual.

Last, if there is not an effortless way to find peer support within your company or institution, there are many professional learning communities (PLCs). Educators work together collaboratively, regionally, nationally, and internationally, on topics and subjects. PLCs allow people to find great resources, emotional support, and networking with individuals they may never see in person. An internet search can help locate different PLC that you may be interested in joining. Many PLC are free, some are invitation only, and others may require fees.

Open Education Resources

Open Education Resources (OER) are free teaching and learning materials that anyone can access, use, and often modify. OER include textbooks, lessons, videos, quizzes, notes, worksheets, and more resources that support learning. This approach is popular due to the cost–effectiveness, access, and inclusivity to education.

Implementing OER can be tedious as you must go through all the material for quality control and understand Creative Common attributes as well as less support from the resources. Creative Common attributes allow users to distribute, remix, adapt, and build upon the material as long as they give attribution to the creator(s).

OER have gained popularity because of many factors, yet while there are many advantages, there are also some potential disadvantages.

Following are the main advantages:

>> **Cost savings:** Because the cost of textbooks is high, students often do not obtain their texts immediately or ever, causing them to fall behind as soon as the course begins. OER are an alternative, allowing students access immediately without the burden of prohibitive costs.

>> **Collaboration:** OER promote collaboration among educators. This leads to innovation, creativity, and sharing best practices.

>> **Access:** Due to affordability, OER may offer a solution to the barriers of some countries that don't have access to education materials.

>> **Relevance:** Because OER are under Creative Commons, the material can be updated frequently, keeping it relevant, up-to-date, and engaging for the users.

Here are some disadvantages:

>> **Quality control:** Because it is open resource, anyone can work on products, and they can create material that they perceive themselves to be experts on, whether or not this is true.

>> **Copyright issues:** OER rely on open licensing. It is important to understand copyright and attribution. Creative commons licenses have key features in common. Will there be commercial use? Are derivative works allowed? Will there be ShareAlike terms?

Types of licenses

Creative Commons is an international nonprofit organization that provides infra-structure through tools and licenses, which allow individuals and companies to share and use their work by granting copyright permissions. The licenses allow content to be copied, distributed, remixed, built upon, and edited within copyright laws. The usage of the work depends on the type of license. There are six different creative common licenses.

The elements shown in Figure 5-1 are included in creative common licenses.

BY — Credit must be given to the creator

NC — Only noncommercial uses of the work are permitted

ND — No derivatives or adaptations of the work are permitted

SA — Adaptations must be shared under the same terms

CC0 (see Figure 5-2) is Creative Commons Public Domain and is a public dedication domain that allows creators to give up all copyright, such that their works are in the worldwide public domain. People can distribute, remix, adapt, and build upon the material in any way without conditions. CC0 is not a license.

PUBLIC DOMAIN

Following are the six types of licenses and their characteristics:

>> **CC-BY refers to attribution** (see Figure 5-3) and is the most lenient and accommodating license. This license allows maximum dissemination, and one must attribute the author. All Creative Common licenses require this condition. BY is a part of all CC licenses.

CC **BY**

- **Share:** The material can be copied and redistributed in any format.

- **Adapt:** Users can remix, transform, and build on the material for any purpose, even commercially.

- **Attribution:** Appropriate credit, a link to the license, and information about any changes that were made to the material must be noted.

>> **CC-BY-SA is ShareAlike** (see Figure 5-4). Creative Commons ShareAlike ensures that if you adapt a work, it must be licensed under the same or a comparable license. Fun fact: Wikipedia uses this license.

FIGURE 5-4:
Creative
Commons
Attribution
ShareAlike
license.

- **Share:** The material can be copied and redistributed in any format.

- **Adapt:** Users may remix, transform, and build on the material for any purpose, even commercially.

- **Attribution:** Appropriate credit, a link to the license, and information about any changes that were made to the material must be noted.

- **ShareAlike:** Any changes must be noted and distributed under the same license as the original work.

>> **CC-BY-ND is NoDerivatives** (see Figure 5-5). Creative Commons NoDerivatives states that no adaptations to the original work can be made, but you can share the work as is. Changing the color of, blurring, or removing part of an image is considered an adaptation. However, if there are spelling or grammatical errors, when changing from a digital to a physical copy or combining many NoDerivatives into a collection, correcting these errors is not considered an adaptation.

FIGURE 5-5:
Creative
Commons
Attribution
NoDerivatives
license.

- **Share:** The material can be copied and redistributed in any format.

- **Attribution:** Appropriate credit, a link to the license, and information about any changes that were made to the material must be noted.

- **NoDerivatives:** Material that has been remixed, transformed, or built upon may not be distributed.

>> **CC-BY-NC is NonCommercial** (see Figure 5-6). This license allows others to remix, transform, or build on your work noncommercially. The new work must acknowledge the original work, but derivative works don't have to be licensed on the same terms as the original work.

- **Share:** The material can be copied and redistributed in any format.

- **Adapt:** Users may remix, transform, and build on the material.

- **Attribution:** Appropriate credit, a link to the license, and information about any changes that were made to the material must be noted.

- **NonCommercial:** The material cannot be used for commercial purposes.

>> **CC-BY-NC-SA is NonCommercial-ShareAlike** (see Figure 5-7). This license allows you to change, reuse, and distribute the work, but no commercial use or monetary compensation is allowed. Noncommercial in these licenses can by vague, and some case uses may be in the gray area such as placing a picture in a tuition-based education course.

- **Share:** The material can be copied and redistributed in any format.

- **Adapt:** Users may remix, transform, and build on the material.

- **Attribution:** Appropriate credit, a link to the license, and information about any changes that were made to the material must be noted.

- **NonCommercial:** The material cannot be used for commercial purposes.

- **ShareAlike:** Any changes must be noted and distributed under the same license as the original work.

» **CC-BY-NC-ND is NonCommercial-NoDeriveratives** (see Figure 5-8). This is the most restrictive license. It allows people to download the work and use the work. No changes can be made, credit is given to the original source, and it cannot be used commercially.

FIGURE 5-8:
Creative
Commons
Attribution
NonCommercial
NoDerivatives
licenses.

- **Share:** The material can be copied and redistributed in any format.

- **Attribution:** Appropriate credit, a link to the license, and information about any changes that were made to the material must be noted.

- **NonCommercial:** The material cannot be used for commercial purposes.

- **NoDerivatives:** The material, whether remixed, transformed, or built upon, may not be distributed.

OER repositories

In addition to creating your own resources or collaborating with a network of peers, many OER repositories are available for use that can be browsed by subject area. Many state library systems have robust repositories of OER classes ready to be imported into an LMS. The following are a few of the most robust ones:

» **OER Commons** is a public digital library that allows you to explore, create, and collaborate with educators around the world.

» **Merlot II** is a collection of 45,000 peer-reviewed resources, including open textbooks.

» **OpenStax College** provides textbooks (digital or hard copy) as well as instructor content.

» **Digital Public Library of America** is a collection of tens of millions of images, texts, videos, and audio from the United States.

>> **Khan Academy** provides education to anyone anywhere.

>> **Community College Consortium for Open Educational Resources** is a community of practice for open education, providing resources, support, and opportunities for collaboration for learning, planning, and implementing successful open educational programs at community and technical colleges.

>> **MIT Open Courseware** offers educators and students full courses designed by MIT professors. The entire course packet with interviews, syllabi, outlines, readings, assignments, and projects is available.

ACTIVITY

ACTIVITY 1: CREATIVE COMMONS LICENSES

Select the best CC license for the scenario given. Use the six types explained earlier in this chapter.

1. Ms. Shriver takes a picture of a microscopic image and loads it to her website she curates for students. She does not mind if others use it, but they cannot alter it and must attribute her. Which CC license will best suit Ms. Shiver's needs?

   a. CC-BY

   b. CC-BY-SA

   c. CC-BY-ND

   d. CC-BY-NC

   e. CC-BY-NC-SA

   f. CC-BY-NC-ND

2. The music teacher recorded a new song with the intention for others to use it and remix it but for noncommercial purposes only. Which CC license will best suit the music teacher's needs?

   a. CC-BY

   b. CC-BY-SA

   c. CC-BY-ND

   d. CC-BY-NC

   e. CC-BY-NC-SA

   f. CC-BY-NC-ND

3. A writer created a short story and posted it on a blog. The writer does not mind others using it if they give proper attributions, make no changes, and do not attempt to use it commercially. Which CC license will best suit the writer's needs?

   a. CC-BY

   b. CC-BY-SA

   c. CC-BY-ND

   d. CC-BY-NC

   e. CC-BY-NC-SA

   f. CC-BY-NC-ND

Answers: 1. c, 2. d, 3. f

ACTIVITY

ACTIVITY 2: EVALUATING OER

Find an OER resource, evaluate it, and determine whether you can use it for creating a lesson. Here are some checkpoints to use when evaluating the content.

- The OER information is accurate.

- The OER reflects controversies (as needed), theoretical perspectives (as needed), and explores the content accurately in terms of the subject.

- The OER contains no grammatical or spelling errors.

- The content is written at an appropriate level so that it is clear and understandable.

- The content and design are easy to navigate and intuitive to use.

- If media is included with the OER material, the quality is high.

- Closed captioning and transcripts are provided for video and audio resources. Hyperlinks, alt tags, and styling format are ADA compliant.

- The OER content is accessible on multiple devices and is dynamic.

- The OER content promotes active learning, collaboration, and engagement, and provides multiple materials (videos, audios, graphics, interactions, checkpoints) and multiple instructional approaches to help students learn.

- What type of licenses does the resource permit?

Publisher resources

Publishers are powerhouses for a reason. They have the resources, talent, finances, and expertise to create tools and content to help guide instructors to disseminate material and assessments in multiple modalities.

The best instructional materials align with the elements of the course, such as learning objectives, assessments, and activities. In addition, most publisher materials align to specific textbooks. You must be careful that there is not a disconnect between the publisher's textbook learning objectives and your content presentation flow and course learning objectives. Instructional materials can be engaging or demotivating to students, so it is important to thoroughly vet the content the users will access, explore, study, and reference as they move through the course. Carefully selecting, organizing, refining, and planning how to use the content for maximum effect on the user's experience should be a priority. Of course this is true for OER too.

The publisher's tools can be a lifesaver to new faculty or when the institution or company adopts a new textbook or platform. Often the material is already in a digital format to be imported seamlessly into the platform — slide decks, test banks, interactive activities, the textbook, videos, and more.

TIP

It gives newbies and veterans a "course in a box." It is based on chapters and the textbook learning objectives, but you can evolve and tweak as you go. While this is not ideal, most teachers have done it. I have been assigned a course two hours before it began, and you can bet I had no idea what I was doing. I posted a note that the course would begin soon and to review the syllabus.

With all these tools, it is important for the facilitator or instructor to consider how the user in the course will use the material most effectively and efficiently. The users see you as the subject matter expert. They do not want to read the textbook and teach themselves. They want you to be present and guide them with your opinions and explanations of events and content. You put a personal touch on the subject matter and make the content meaningful, tangible, and applicable to the real world. Use the publisher material as a foundation and then personally develop the material to reflect who you are as a guide.

Before you integrate material into your course from a publisher, be sure to address the accessibility of the material. Often, some materials may not meet the WCAG guidelines and are not useable to people with or without disabilities, especially when they rely on assistive technologies. Requesting an ACR (covered in Chapter 4) from the publisher is helpful but doesn't tell the entire story. If your institution or company has an accessibility department, it's smart for them to vet the content and run it through a series of usability tests.

PUBLISHER TOOLS: CHOOSING YOUR OWN ADVENTURE

When selecting what type of material you want to deploy in the platform to guide users' learning and experience, consider these questions:

- Does the publisher resource provide the appropriate coverage of content without having to over-supplement with outside materials?

- Is it organized in a useful way for readers to follow?

- Is it the correct reading level for the audience?

- Are the pages designed well and do they tell a story with the content?

- Can the users read, watch, hear, and interact with the content? Is a variety of materials provided?

- Can the users create content or activities that support their learning path?

- Do the materials and text properly align with the course's learning objectives?

- Is it visually appealing and does it provide figures, drawings, and graphs that help explain concepts?

- Is the digital material able to integrate into the platform?

- Does the digital material allow Single Sign On to the platform?

- Are the assignments and assessments assignable for a grade and synchronized to the platform's gradebook?

- Is the material and textbook accessible with WCAG?

- Is the material dynamic and usable on multiple interfaces — mobile, tablet, PC, Mac, and so on?

- Is there a support center for technical issues for both instructors and students?

- Is the price affordable?

In general, publisher materials are advantageous. They give new teachers and veteran teachers a starting point as well as innovative ideas for presentation flow. However, there can be disadvantages, and it is always important to consider both sides. Publisher material is usually associated with chapters. If or when you move to OER material, the chapters probably won't align and can cause confusion to students. You would be responsible for removing any chapter references from all material. Next, and more importantly, most instructor resources are only accessible if you have adopted their resources as a required text. If not, this can cause copyright issues and subject you and the company or institution to legal questioning. Often OER resources are not robust in helping start a course.

To use a publisher or textbook or not

No matter if you choose to use publisher or OER resources, it is important to recognize that students may need guidance on how to use a textbook effectively and efficiently. Many methods are available to help guide them in learning proper textbook use such as the SQR5, Survey, Question, Read, Respond, Record, Recite, Review; and the Study Cycle, Preview, Attend Class, Review, Study, Check and then repeat. Both methods help students become active readers and gain more from the content. Search online for these methods if you are not familiar with them. Both methods can be a game changer by helping students to effectively use and organize their materials, and effectively manage their time.

Determining the Best Vehicle (Platform) for Delivery of Content

With an array of platforms on the market, narrowing it down can be hard. Budget and learning goals have a considerable influence on which platform is chosen for use. Many factors need to be considered to home in on the right platform.

Making it work: Platforms mandated by your job or career

The Learning Management System (LMS), sometimes called a Course Management System (CMS) or Platform, is a critical part of user success. If your institution or company has chosen your LMS, you want to ensure you and your users are prepared for whatever comes up, and you want to make the most of the LMS.

First, you want to learn how to build and personalize your course with accessibility in mind. Once you know the basics of how to load content and organize your material, you can start to ensure optimization of learning with your materials. Focus on microlearning and creating content that focuses on a single learning objective. You can then begin to focus on assessments and monitoring user progress or performance.

>> Seek out trainings offered by your company's or institution's training department.

>> Provide training resources to students. A platform is not useful to students if they don't know how to use it effectively. Embed directions in assignments and activities on how to do an assignment submission or an activity.

>> Use the LMS community of learners. Most LMS have community guides and resources that are robust and helpful. Sign up for all online trainings — even if you can't make them, they'll often send you the recording.

>> A simple internet search for your LMS training guides will pull up many schools' training repositories too. Don't re-create the wheel. Spend time focusing on what is present already and use that to grow and learn.

>> Use the plug-in for third-party tools as the vendors supplying the plug-ins usually offer extensive customer support.

Deciding where to start

Here are some factors to consider when you choose your own platform:

>> If you are choosing your own platform, you need to determine the number of accounts, students, and faculty. Oftentimes, platforms charge per user.

>> Do you have abilities to host your own site, or will you need to be under someone else's domain?

>> Is your course going to be public or private? Do you want to make it available for anyone or just to certain students?

>> What type of data and reports do you want to have access to? Do you want individual student reports, aggregate data at the course level, outcome data measurements, engagement reports, interaction reports, and so forth?

>> What are you teaching? The discipline you are teaching will help you decide the needs. Basic platforms allow embedding of content such as videos and freeware. Advanced platforms allow use of multiple platforms, multiple assessments, group collaboration, plug-ins from vendors, peer reviews, and more.

>> Is it accessible for all? Is it compatible with assistive technology?

If you are starting small and want feedback prior to investing in content, activities, and a platform, you can use basic website tools such as WordPress, Google, Squarespace, Weebly, and Wix, to name a few. Basic HTML will allow you to create more robust, interactive features, and how-to videos can be found online for free. Many platforms offer upgrades if you decide you need more advanced functionality.

Some online platforms are specific for online courses. These sites can support student accounts, provide analytics, and sometimes offer instructional features that are specific to their platform. Moodle, Coursera, Litmos, and Udemy are all examples of these platforms.

There are Learning Management Systems (LMS) that provide user interfaces geared toward education. Many LMS offer free access to a basic version of their LMS that you don't need a licensed instance for your company or business. LMS examples are EdApp, Blackboard, Schoology, Canvas, CourseSites, and Desire 2 Learn.

EXPERIENCE HELPS EXPERTISE

Create a user experience account and play around in the platform. Dabbling in different ones will help you understand what best meets your needs. Here are a few that you may enjoy:

- I suggest creating one in Canvas by going to canvas.instructure.com. They allow free site creation and have a wonderful support community with all the how-to directions.

- Consider using Moodle by creating a free account with no licensing fee at moodle.org.

- A mobile-based free LMS is EdApp, and it provides an editable course library, creator tools, admin portal, and the learning portal. Create your own account at edapp.com.

- Try Google Classroom at edu.google.com/workspace-for-education/classroom/. It's free to anyone who has a Google account. While there are a few limitations for personal accounts, it allows you to experience an alternative to a paid-for LMS.

Adaptive learning platforms adapt to and personalize the user experience. Some of these adaptive experiences are built into vendor offerings, but there are also stand-alone ones. Adaptive platforms allow you to assess student's proficiency and provide differentiated learning. Examples of adaptive platforms are D2L Brightspace, Knewton, and Smart Sparrow.

WARNING

Be careful when seeing "free," though, as any support services or customization may come with hidden fees. Understanding company structure can be insightful regarding the type of attention, troubleshooting, and turn-around time you can expect for issues. With the evolution of online learning and technology enhancements and changes, it is important to have a platform that has a team receptive to input and growth.

Try to keep your content agnostic of platform mention as this allows you to migrate content easily between platforms without having to rework the documents and videos.

Chapter **6**

Your Presence Is a Present

When you are in a face-to-face classroom, your presence is apparent as there is physicality for the students. However, in an online course, being present takes planning and dedication. Online courses require more attention to the three different relationships that occur in the course:

» The teacher-student relationship

» The student-student relationship

» The student-content relationship

In an online classroom, students often complete their work by themselves and don't recognize the presence of their teacher or their peers. Student satisfaction, perception of their experience, and the memorability of the course and the content are affected.

A few statements may help teachers understand student needs and perspectives. Students want/need their instructor to

» Care about them as people.

» Listen to their concerns. Often, they just need to vent. You can ask whether they just want you to listen or provide options for solutions.

>> Believe in them.

>> Teach with stories that apply to the real world or their world.

>> Support them.

This chapter can help you meet those needs.

Time Is Ticking

As the adage goes, you only get one chance at a first impression. This holds true in an online environment. The atmosphere you intend to create, the community you build and present to, and the interactions you generate through communication prior to or at the beginning of the course are sufficient information for the users to make all kinds of judgments; for example, whether their facilitator (that's you) is trustworthy, competent, boring, exciting, and so on. This is the first time they determine what your intentions are for their experience in the course. Online courses can cause one to feel disconnected, so if you are present, via video, text, and/or images, you can engage your students from the first second they "meet" you.

TIP

A quality introduction gives your users the chance to hear and see your passion for the content firsthand. This is your chance to humanize yourself and establish a teaching presence. Remember to add alternative text, captions, a transcript, and if necessary, an audio description file.

Considering customer service

This may be controversial, but teaching is becoming customer service–oriented due to parental involvement, eager-to-please administration, and students who are part of the instant gratification culture. Since COVID-19, the line between education and home has become hazy and demands on teachers have become exhausting. But customer service doesn't have to have a negative connotation. Reframing your thoughts of customer service in terms of your experience at a restaurant or retail store may help you become proactive and anticipate types of problems that may occur. You can then help users avoid frustration, inconvenience, and disappointment.

REMEMBER

In education and training, most people tend to think only about the teacher and the content, but in reality, teaching is like an iceberg. Students may only see a small piece of it, but the bulk of what goes into producing an online course is hidden from the masses.

Consider the parts of the iceberg that are underwater:

» **Content production:** Creating and curating content is where most of a facilitator or teacher's time is spent. This time-consuming process is required to be there for users. They look at it and consume it, but often they don't recognize the investment of time and effort it takes to produce such learning tools.

» **Privacy:** Using tools that make it easy to redact or hide information facilitate privacy compliance.

» **Supporting a varied base of users:** Employing empathy allows you to better support your users. Users come in with different levels of knowledge, experience, and technical capabilities. Providing the material and directions upfront (proactively) will help all users be successful. If they don't need detailed instructions or how-tos, they'll skip them. Make sure you masquerade as a student so you can experience their workflow and ensure you have everything set up properly.

» **Prioritizing requests:** You want to respond in a timely manner, but that can become overwhelming if you are receiving masses of emails, phone calls, and requests from colleagues/administration. Each day, set aside a time that is dedicated to triaging this information and determining what needs to be done immediately, within a few days, and what can be tabled for some time.

» **Creating feedback opportunities:** Providing opportunities the moment the learner finishes the work or activity not only helps students recognize areas they need to improve on, but also provides the instructor information to close the gap between what is wanted versus what they are doing. Feedback helps the instructor pinpoint learning barriers and allows for adjustment of the presentation, teaching, and assessment to better support the user.

Personal availability

While teaching begins in the classroom, there are numerous ways to connect to users beyond the classroom. To increase a sense of belonging, which is important for increasing retention and reducing attrition, being accessible is important. Office hours are a way to accomplish this but consider being creative with the name. Office hours are often intimidating to users so consider calling them "student hours," "connection hours," or "Q and A." These slight changes in wording may help increase attendance and use of the reserved times.

You must be accessible for students at times that are convenient for them, not just you. This doesn't mean you need to be available 24/7, but it does mean you should schedule meeting times based off of student feedback that you can gather in a short survey. For users who are local, consider holding your office hours in the campus food court or a coffee shop that is near the institution. You may be considered more approachable outside of your office.

TIP

Following are some ways to connect outside of the classroom:

>> Encourage users to make appointments through calendar links.

>> Set aside time to be available through live chat or video conferencing.

>> Create a social media page for the class (but set ground rules).

>> If you have live classes (virtually), arrive early and stay a few minutes after.

>> Create a Google number for texting and calling.

>> Schedule consultations with your students to check in on their progress.

WARNING

Be careful to set boundaries to ensure that personal and classroom spaces do not become blurred. Avoid the creepy treehouse effect that occurs when teachers interact in spaces seen as personal by students. If social media is something you want to do, use media platforms that don't have real-name policies. The students can create a disposable account for the course's purpose.

ACTIVITY

SCHEDULE YOUR APPOINTMENTS ONLINE

Create an online appointment scheduler using free software and deploy it in your classes. Software that you can use for scheduling includes:

- Meeting scheduling for Google Calendar (free)
- Calendly (free version)
- Doodle (free version)
- Outlook Scheduling Assistant (free if you use Microsoft 365 or Exchange)

Once the platform is chosen, it's time to add specificity for your scheduling. A few best practices are to show availability, not your whole schedule, and designate the scheduling times into sections of 15- to 30-minute blocks. If necessary, you can add small increments to buffer between meetings.

Adding the meeting link directly in to the calendar makes it easier to be connected and organized. Whether it's Zoom, Google Meets, or WebEx, you can link the process together, eliminated extra steps for you and the user.

Student Community and Course Atmosphere

Isolation can occur in online learning among students. To avoid these alienating experiences, cultivating an atmosphere of engagement and trust is valuable. This task is going to be mediated by technology but is dependent on the instructor's role.

The instructor can promote community by employing different strategies that can be accomplished asynchronously and synchronously. Options are covered in more detail in upcoming sections, but here are some basic tips:

>> Plan communication.

>> Establish presence and immediacy.

>> Provide expertise sharing.

>> Implement collaborative and engaging learning techniques.

>> Meet synchronously.

>> Offer alternative assignments.

TIP

Keep a notepad or computer document on which you write notes about each class and students for reference. This will help you remember conversations or correspondences with students. While you may forget due to the volume of communication occurring, the student will not. Being able to quickly reference these past interactions gives the student a sense of a continuous conversation, where they feel seen.

Immediacy shortens the emotional distance created by technology or geography between teachers and students, students and students, and students and content. The goal is for students to form a connection, which usually improves their performance.

TIP

Online communities help users meet common goals, improve learning, develop networking opportunities, prevent isolation, and improve the learning experience.

Asynchronous and synchronous options

How and when will you communicate? Will your communication be in the form of an email, text messaging, comments, or announcements, or maybe a combination?

Do you provide feedback frequently? Is it in bulk to the group or individually? Are you touching base before and after high-stake assignments? Frequent and effective communication helps encourage immediacy between the students, students and teacher, and the student and content.

>> Asynchronous classes allow students to access content during times and locations convenient to them. There is not a real-time component.

>> Synchronous classes run in real time with instructors and students attending together at the same time, but it can be from different locations.

Planning communication (asynchronous)

Intentionality in communication helps improve "customer service." In the course policies (syllabus, addendum, course expectations), provide students with an expected time return on grades and feedback. Providing students with immediate, automated responses is still powerful, but if you are hand-grading material, state a time estimate for returning grades and feedback. Built-in feedback fulfills that immediate gratification that the younger generation has become accustomed to. In more personal replies, always use a salutation or the student's name. Do not make the responses extraordinarily long or too curt. Try to incorporate words like "we" and "our" to exemplify that you are going through the journey with the user.

In addition, you can create forums for questions regarding course content, course feedback, and an "In the News" related to the content. These can be anonymous as long as ground rules are established for using the forums. State whether you participate in these or monitor the forums.

Planning communication (synchronous)

Provide students the opportunity to meet virtually or face-to-face in real time. This may not be possible for all, but live interactions can improve the community atmosphere. In these settings, students start to recognize faces and names, and share information. Having synchronous sessions a couple days a week at varying times, and making them optional, can help increase participation and improve engagement in the community.

In virtual meetings, try to use chat and voice to form connections. I know it sounds like I'm asking you to juggle firesticks while balancing on a ball, but just like any skill, the more you try and practice, the better you become over time.

Last, consider humanizing yourself to the users by showing pictures and telling relevant stories. Students forget that their teachers, mentors, and facilitators were all in their shoes at one time.

ACTIVITY

GRAB AND GO FEEDBACK

MCreate a document that you can reference and copy from for feedback. Consider using ChatGPT and CopyAI to help you get a foundation of comments in the document.

Caveat: In reality I have written my document myself as it started prior to ChatGPT and AI being readily available or acceptable. However, having variations of information as a foundation is helpful. It's definitely encouraged to tweak the output to showcase your writing style and personality.

Example of a prompt you can put into a free chat generator:

URL: https://chat.openai.com/

Prompt: Write five variations of feedback to student's based on a good performance on a high-stakes exam. Include good time management, organization, study methods.

Results:

- "Your exceptional performance on the exam speaks volumes about your effective time management, organization, and study methods. Keep up the fantastic work!"

- "Congratulations on your outstanding results! Your ability to manage your time wisely, stay organized, and employ effective study methods truly set you apart in the exam."

- Your success is a testament to your excellent time management skills, organizational abilities, and strategic study methods."

- "Your stellar performance on the exam reflects your adeptness at time management, organization, and study techniques. Your dedication to these aspects of learning is truly admirable."

- "Well done on your achievement in the exam! Your success underscores the importance of good time management, organization, and effective study methods. Keep up the great work!"

I have created a document over the past ten years that has feedback in numerous categories such as low-earning grades, medium-earning grades, high-earning grades, did not complete the assignment, end of semester performance, and study strategies such as time management, note taking, organizational skills, short answer tips, test taking tips, and study cycle. Some of these are written for face-to-face or online-only students, but many are modality agnostic.

Warning: As you get to know your users, be careful not to use the same feedback on siblings and friends. Make sure you address the student by their name prior to copying and pasting the feedback from your document.

Establishing presence and immediacy (asynchronous and synchronous)

Creating your presence begins with the course instructions and course design. You are the tour guide in your course. This is done through clear directions and expectations for participation, assignments, and due dates, intuitive navigation, and creating activities and videos to build your presence.

There are different types of presence: cognitive and social. Both can be asynchronous or synchronous. Cognitive presence helps students identify a problem, explore the problem (individually and/or in a community), construct meaning from their exploration through integration, and come to a resolution where learners reflect, self-evaluate, and apply their new knowledge.

Social presence is how the user is socially and emotionally connected in the environment and to their peers. Social presence can motivate participants to be more accountable for their learning and participation. Users that feel there is a community will usually have less stress, better learning outcomes, and more connectedness. This belonging should occur throughout a course experience but often is the first event to occur in an activity prior to adding academic content.

Providing expertise

As the teacher, you provide much of the content, but your organization and repository of resources help draw users to the community. Bring in relevant resources such as news articles, journals, guest speakers, and more. Depending on the media, the users may interact with it in real time (synchronously) or on their own time (asynchronously).

Create online groups. This provides students with peer support for the course while helping them learn how to navigate connections, manage time, and collaborate on content. The groups can be managed via discussion boards (asynchronous), video conferencing links (synchronous), text messaging or chat (asynchronous or synchronous), or social media (asynchronous or synchronous).

Implementing collaborative and engaging learning techniques

Adopting collaborative, engaging, active learning is difficult because students are often comfortable being disconnected, disengaged, and lonely. They have become accustomed to feeling isolated. By fostering a space for collaboration, the users are taking ownership and accountability for learning. In addition, it helps provide team building opportunities, experiences with group dynamics, and often improved achievement.

As the instructor, you can emulate responsible collaborative work by partnering with different groups in meetings. Transparency is helpful and increases trust when you are clear with the students about the purpose of an activity. What should they gain by participating? Should they take notes? What is their role in the activity?

There are so many collaborative learning strategies, but here are two of my favorites:

>> **Jigsaw technique:** No, this is not a tool in the shed, but it does help build on processing and retaining information. This can be an asynchronous or a synchronous activity. You place students in small groups and assign each student a small piece of content to learn. They are then responsible for teaching it to the group. The group will then work together (collaborate) and synthesize a cohesive story. To take it one step further, they can create an activity to share with the class either via video, an infographic, or live.

>> **Scaffolding technique:** Yes, this is analogous to building structures with construction scaffolding. Instructors can't expect students to magically work in groups successfully unless they 1) model how to accomplish this and 2) provide support as they learn to work together and then slowly let go of their hands. To scaffold successfully, set expectations early and provide examples and guidelines on how to accomplish the expectations. In addition, before the students can work in groups, there may be prework that helps them learn about the topic so that their group contributions are more meaningful. Scaffolding can be accomplished via either asynchronous or synchronous class discussions.

Meeting synchronously

You're teaching an online class, so why should you meet your students live? Well, there are always advantages and disadvantages to every method, but first focus on the advantages of what synchronous meetings can add to your class:

>> Students can ask questions as the content is relevant to their learning.

>> Instructors can vary their approach and content coverage based on how they gauge students' understanding of material.

>> Students can create a schedule that allows them to attend so they have task-oriented goals to stay on track.

>> Instructors can create live group work experiences.

>> Students form a relationship with the instructor as they are "really there."

TIP

Perception of experience is usually more enjoyable and positive when the student believes the instructor cares and is present. Creating immediacy between instructors and students helps students perceive that they had a great experience even if they don't earn the grade they want.

And now for the disadvantages:

>> Student schedules may not permit them to attend. Even if it is recorded, they are not experiencing it live, creating more "catch-up" work. Procrastination is real, and they can always "do it later."

>> Most students can't digest content and reflect as deeply when they are confined to a timed, live session.

>> Accessibility standards may be difficult to provide such as a live interpreter, accurate captions, and audio/video descriptions.

Offering alternative assignments

Alternative assignments can determine what students can and cannot do instead of what they do or do not know. They promote application, synthesizing, and creation of material in a manner that promotes creativity through multimedia and technology.

Alternative assignments make it easier to determine students' knowledge and skills concerning the learning objectives. Students are assessed on their abilities and transferable skills, not what they can memorize.

There are many alternative assignments. Here are some that I have implemented in all modalities of the classroom (online, face-to-face, hybrid, virtual, and HyFLex, which is covered in Chapter 12).

>> Open book exams

>> Group testing

>> Choose your own adventure (differentiated learning)

>> Write, draw, tweet, or video your answers

>> Create a play or skit

- » Create infographics
- » Create a learning tool such as a trivia game in Jeopardy or Family Feud format
- » Oral testing
- » Retake options that focus on correcting answers and reviewing content

TECHNICAL STUFF

Alternative assignments are also known as *authentic assessments*.

Online Doesn't Have to Be Lonely

It's completely natural to be nervous about teaching online or taking online classes. Learning online poses a challenge that is not necessarily technological but human.

REMEMBER

We must remember as instructors that technology doesn't teach; teachers teach.

The good news is that there are many tools and ways to connect with others so that you aren't doing it alone.

Starting with empathy and transparency

Presume that someone may be having a tough day and consider what you can do to avoid adding to those feelings. You are not a therapist, but the longer you teach, the more you will think you earned a minor in psychology/therapy.

Listening is key if a student contacts you, but try not to judge "tones" in emails. While there is no cadence in an email, we all read into emails. If we feel it affects our judgment, our character, or our decisions, we may jump to conclusions. If there seems to be a question about the tone of an email, student language, or the motivation behind the email, contact the student directly to discuss the concerns.

TIP

Tell students at the beginning of every content piece what they will take away from the lesson, what they will be doing during the lesson, and how the learning of the material will help support their long-term course goals. These frequent check-ins are overt efforts to open lines of communication.

Asking students for an introduction

This assignment can be optional but consider asking students to post a brief introduction and share a photo of themselves. If there is a synchronous online portion to the class, ask students to turn on video cameras. Address students by their name to give them a sense of belonging and let them know they are not a number but a person.

Helping students getting to know their peers

If you want students to study with others in an online class, it may be feasible for them to meet up, but most likely it won't be. If it isn't, your institution may provide platforms for collaboration in virtual meet-ups such as Zoom, Teams, WebEx, or Hangout. If not, you can use such platforms as Free Zoom, Facebook, Skype, WhatsApp, Snapchat, and more. The social side can be vital to success in online learning by keeping students motivated.

Advertising study support

Many institutions provide tutoring services, success coaches, and peer-assisted support. If these are not an option or time does not permit using them, there are tutoring services available online — some free, and some not. Again, this goes back to having support via peers through online collaboration.

ACTIVITY

HOW GOOD ARE YOUR COMMUNICATION SKILLS?

Reflect on what you do or do not do in the classroom. If you are a brand-new teacher, write about what you believe you would like to accomplish. This filled-out table is for referencing and reflecting and is not an artifact in the course.

Using the following table as a guide, you will review your syllabus and/or addendum, your schedule, your course introduction, and yourself (actions). Some material is not expected to be in the written documents but is an action you take to improve user inclusivity in the course.

If you don't have all these criteria, that's fine. The book is meant to help develop pieces to allow you and users the ultimate online experience. You will be reviewing and explaining the following:

- Your current communication strategies for online courses
- How you will communicate and what type of communication you have with your students before the semester begins
- Your current expectations for your course
- How you envision your students' first experience in the course

There are no right or wrong answers. This written reflection allows you to determine areas you can improve or areas in which you are excelling. If criteria being reviewed is not present, or you believe it can be evolved and developed further, please make notes of the information you want to focus on creating/editing/evolving.

Criteria	Review Your Syllabus and/or Addendum for These Specific Topics
Response Time/ Communication	Do you explain to the students how to access their LMS email or institution or preferred email?
	How will you communicate with your students during the semester (videos, emails, texts, phone calls)?
	How quickly are you expected to respond to student emails? (Does your institution have a policy on email return? A common rule of thumb is 24 hours to return an email on weekdays and next business day on weekends and holidays.)
	Do you give feedback on graded assignments? What type(s) of feedback should students expect on graded assignments? What is the time frame for posting grades? Is there a difference between multiple-choice, fill-in-the-blank, and short answer/essay tests or papers?
	If discussion boards are used, how often (if any) do you post in discussion boards?
	How often do you post announcements?
	Are your office hours and contact information available (in the syllabus and in the LMS)?

(continued)

(continued)

Criteria	Review Your Syllabus and/or Addendum for These Specific Topics
Presence/Immediacy	How do you communicate with your users before the online class starts?
	How do you communicate with your class the first day that the course is available?
	What do you provide that welcomes the users to the course?
	How do you create immediacy (connection) with your users?
	Is there immediacy among users (introduction assignment or forum)?
Expectations	Are there directions to teach users about LMS notifications?
	Are your expectations for class goals, assessments, due dates, and responsibilities clearly defined for users?
	Do you state what the user can expect from you, the instructor?
Navigation	Is it clear what the users should do when the class starts?
	Do you create assignments to be prerequisites to access other assignments?
	Is navigation intuitive and does the navigation have limited distractions and clear direction?

3
Putting All the Pieces Together

Chapter **7**

Deciding What to Put in Your Course

Think about your best experiences in the classroom and the not so wonderful ones. What made the moments memorable? What made learning doable? What activities kept your attention? Also consider the moments when you were uncomfortable, disengaged, or just bored. You can use those experiences to help curate materials, supplements, and activities to ensure your students have an experience that is memorable, engaging, and motivating to continue their academic journey. These are the pedagogical reasons and drive for becoming an online teacher, but you must have technology skill sets too.

Honestly, you need to have a hard conversation with yourself before you start and make sure you are ready with basic technology skills. Ask yourself these questions. Can you create folders on a hard drive? Do you know the basic skills for using document tools such as cut, copy, paste, collapse, expand, and save? Can you attach files and communicate via email? Do you know how to access different internet browsers and have basic skills such as locating the URL, or clearing the cache and cookies? Last, do you have the knowledge to manage the course and courseware via your learning management system? If you are comfortable, then you're ready.

This chapter helps you identify the whats and whys behind your course-building journey.

What Should the Audience Know?

Determining the purpose of your course helps you create the material the audience, also known as the consumers or the students, want to know. Identifying your audience is your task, as this helps you create an action plan with deliverables. Often instructors believe that the audience is interested in the subject or has some pre-knowledge and experience, but that's not always true. It's important to know your audience because you want them to feel comfortable when they are learning from you.

If your course is for college credit or a certification, you'll need to align standards and learning objectives with assessments and be able to demonstrate student mastery through data analytics. Often these objectives are set by industry, boards, or societies that manage a subject, discipline, or standard.

If your course is for personal enjoyment, conduct a survey to determine customer needs. Use search engine optimization to help understand what people are looking for on the internet. If you search "how to" and the first thing that appears is "how to add captions to a video," then there is a market looking for training in this area.

When developing for-profit courses, consider these steps.

>> Determine the audience (age, gender, education level, geographic location, education level).

>> Understand what the audience wants from the course.

>> Know what the audience needs to value the course.

TIP

If you want to create a course to prepare students for the Kaplan Nursing Entrance Exam, which is required to get accepted into some registered nursing programs, create personas for who you are going to develop the course for. For example, Roberto is a 27-year-old licensed practical nurse with a small child. He is in a transition program to become a registered nurse. This information tells you that you want to target students in their last year of prerequisites for the nursing program and students that identify as pre-nursing majors. In addition, you can identify the following traits of the persona — challenges, goals, values, desires, and everyday activities.

REMEMBER

Every niche will have an audience with different expectations and perceptions. If you are teaching photo editing, the audience will expect to have video recordings of the software tools and how-to explanation videos to properly use the software.

Making the content applicable

Your course is the avenue to a relationship with the students. The content and your presence are the mediators. Content relevance is about your users' perception of your material's pertinence to issues, topics, and/or interests. The usefulness of content helps users progress toward their goals. How well your content helps them accomplish that goal is important to how effective your content is overall.

When deciding what your content will be, follow these steps:

1. **Identify the desired results.**
2. **Determine what you consider acceptable evidence for the outcomes.**
3. **Plan your instruction and your experiences.**

Identifying desired results

What are the learning goals of the lesson?

The learning goals can be written to represent your learning objectives (LOs). Whether you state the learning goals explicitly, goals must be set so students understand where they are starting and where they should go. What are the students going to be able to do at the end of the course? Design your course with the end result in mind. Aligning assessments with course LOs is much easier when your objectives are measurable.

How do you write learning outcomes?

Writing an effective learning outcome

LOs help students know what they are expected to know or be able to do upon completion of a course. Ensuring that the LOs you provide the users are helpful in achieving their goals and providing measurable data for you is important.

Use an action verb to articulate the actions the students will be able to do. These actions can be observed and compared with the desired results. And the results focus on the what the students can and can't do.

TIP

Choosing the action verb helps describe the desired result the student will obtain. Often people reference Bloom's Taxonomy or Fink's Taxonomy.

Bloom's Taxonomy is a framework that consists of six categories: remembering, understanding, applying, analyzing, evaluating, and creating. These categories describe the cognitive processes in which users will work with the content and their knowledge.

Fink's Taxonomy is unique because it does not rely on scaffolding categories. Instead the levels of Fink's Taxonomy are interactive among each other and focus on human emotions such as thoughtfulness and recognizing feelings. Finks Taxonomy includes foundational knowledge, application, integration, human dimensions, caring, and learning to learn. A goal is for the instructor to incorporate all in a unit or lesson so that the learning has an impact on the student.

Examples of action verbs that are measurable are "analyze," "define," "describe," "compare," "arrange," "translate," "compose," "measure," and "diagram."

Writing learning outcomes (LOs) is a talent and an art form. LOs need to be specific, measurable, and student-centered:

WARNING

>> **Specific:** When developing the LOs, how will you know as a teacher that a student has mastered the material? What will the student need to do, say, or demonstrate to show their mastery? These answers help you write specific LOs.

LOs should be specific, and the goal should be clear. Avoid using verbs such as "understand" or "know" because they're too vague. How do you interpret what someone understands or knows? Comparing what a graduate student knows to an undergraduate is wildly different.

>> **Measurable:** The learning goal can be measured quantitatively or qualitatively. Measurable LOs inform students of your expectations. The LOs help clarify what the students are expected to learn and/or perform.

What should participants hear, read, explore, and practice? What skills should the participants show mastery in? What should the participants retain?

>> **Student-centered:** If you were limited in terms of what the students could learn from your course, what would those skills, knowledge, and abilities (SKAs) be? Answering this question helps you identify and write student-centered learning outcomes. Student-centered outcomes focus on what the students can actually do at the end of a lesson or a course, not what you aim for them to do.

PRACTICE WRITING A LEARNING OUTCOME

ACTIVITY

Writing effective LOs is an iterative process. Feedback, data analysis, and your experiences will help refine and revise the LO. As you do this, check to ensure the LOs remain aligned with your course assessments and needs.

1. **Identify the thing you want the students to learn.**

   Example: The three states of mind.

2. **Identify the level of Bloom's Taxonomy.**

   Choosing the appropriate level of learning influences what assessment measures the student's learning.

   Example: Defining the three states of mind is the remembering level of Bloom's Taxonomy.

3. **Select the action verb that you want to observe and describe the level of learning.**

   Example: To define the three states of mind, you might use "state," "name," and "list" as the action verbs.

4. **Add additional information to give students context for their LOs.**

   Example: Define the three states of mind when writing a paper.

   Review the examples to help visualize how the process can be completed.

   Original version: Understand how to write a learning outcome.

   Revised version: Identify the elements needed when writing a learning outcome.

   Original version: Describe a learning outcome.

   Revised version: Create a learning outcome.

Skill sets for succeeding in an online environment

Online courses offer freedom and flexibility, but with the freedom and flexibility comes more responsibility for the online student and teacher. As an online facilitator, you need to create an environment that encourages written communication and open communication, self-motivation and self-discipline, time commitment, time management, and decision-making. As a teacher you need to foster a culture that encourages the students to embrace online learning and develop and highlight their skills.

To help your students shine, you must be visible. This means being accessible to students; present and available; and ready to accommodate their concerns, needs, and requisitions. Response time is important.

Welcome students to the online course in ways that support them and let them know that you are committed to their continued success. Emulate the behaviors you want to see in your students — communicate.

Following are some important tips to help students succeed in online classes:

>> Provide students with weekly or daily time management suggestions and give them a time management schedule. (You can review an example schedule online at www.dummies.com/go/creatingcoursesfd.)

>> Remind students that they need to take responsibility for what they do and don't do, and they need to recognize the consequences of their decisions.

>> Emphasize that it's up to the student, to read, watch, and complete the assigned material.

TIP

Send an email to students a couple of weeks before the start of the course to introduce yourself and share information they will need to be successful, such as whether there will be scheduled synchronous class meetings, the syllabus and schedule for the class, when the course will become available, and how they will access the course. Reach out a few times before the course starts to include students who may have enrolled more recently.

Mapping the course with a matrix and blueprint

What's the difference between a poorly developed course and a course that allows students ease of navigation and a clear pathway for learning? In a word, planning. Before you start building anything, you need to spend some time thinking about your goals and developing a plan.

Although you build a single course, the reality is that it's delivered to an audience that's not homogenous. The learners come from different backgrounds and levels of motivation, skill, and experience. This makes crafting a great learning experience a bit of a challenge. The more prepared you are, the easier it is to create an experience that can meet many individuals' needs. Mapping the course helps you create a blueprint of your vision of what the students will learn. This blueprint is guided by a detailed schedule that termed the *course matrix*. Online course matrixes must be detailed and clear. The blueprint and course matrix are addressed in detail in Chapter 8.

>> **The matrix** is a detailed schedule that provides users with material such as, but not limited to, an alignment of their LOs, assignments, learning activities, and due dates or suggested time management schedule.

>> **The blueprint** includes the matrix but is really a large outline to help you organize the material into chunks or smaller, digestible pieces. The blueprint helps you build the course into navigable and organized sections to be completed in units or time frames.

The course matrix can be designed in a variety of ways, but you can outline what should be present. Here are some example headings in a course matrix (not all have to be used):

>> Week/Dates/Due Dates

>> Learning Outcomes

>> How users can practice and show mastery

>> Learning Activities/Assessments

>> How feedback is provided

>> Supporting Content, or What you need to complete the work

Back to the blueprint, let's discuss what a blueprint can do for you.

My goal is for you to have a detailed outline of your course. The outline is intended to serve as a guide to construct a course. The content doesn't need to be made at this point, but the outline should include ideas and titles that explain what will ultimately be present. As you proceed, you should bear in mind the time divisions into which you've organized your course. Many faculty and facilitators organize courses into "weeks," but others use larger groupings such as testing blocks. I refer to these groupings as "modules," but you may refer to them however you like (for example, units, lessons, chapters, and so on). Each module has associated learning activities, readings, graded assignments, and assessments — all of which culminate in the final grade for the course.

Your outline should be detailed enough for a colleague to take your directions and make your course shell with modules, pages, quiz holders, activities, notes, videos, and other supplemental material.

Create a bulleted outline

TIP

Once you have put thought into the overall course schedule, create a timeline in which each activity, assignment, and assessment in your course is present. These activities, assignments, and assessments can be divided into weeks, modules, or units.

What features should you consider in your course outline? Here are some ideas:

>> **Start-here area:** This ideally contains the syllabus, addendum, schedule, important information about the Learning Management System, a welcome video and letter, and study tips.

>> **Presence plan:** This is a communication and feedback plan, a posting of information for success. This is not necessarily its own area but often part of the course documents (see Chapter 6). It explains what the instructor expects from students and what students can expect from the instructor.

>> **Modules (also known as folders):** These may include pages for each chapter, a testing block, or a weekly setup, depending on the course design; see the example in the next bulleted list.

>> **Content types:** Content may be in the form of videos, notes, presentations, interactions, or learning artifacts.

>> **Summative assessment placeholders:** Summative assessments may be in the form of an exam, a project, or a presentation. They evaluate students learning at the end of a chapter or learning unit.

>> **Formative assessment placeholders:** Formative assessments provide feedback that help the instructor improve student experience and course design. They can be in the form of a survey, discussion board, or a concept map.

>> **Placeholders for no-stake assignments:** These are practice assignments.

>> **School information:** This info includes technology resources and support, learning management system guides and directions, and policies and procedures.

>> **Census assignment, if needed:** Many institutions may have a day that enrollment is locked for financial aid purposes. These institutions may require some type of verification of identity or regular and substantive interaction between the user and the instructor.

>> **Proctoring information, if needed:** Many institutions require a form of proctoring to ensure the test taker verifies their identity and to maintain the integrity of the assignment. To ensure users are aware of the requirements, directions need to be provided.

Here's an example of a bulleted outline course:

- Module 0: Start Here and Course Welcome
- Overview of objectives
- Syllabus, Schedule
- School information
- Orientation/Overview of the course (interactive videos are usually the best way to convey this information)
  - Navigation demonstration
  - Assessment introduction with grading structure if necessary
  - Explanation of technical requirements
- Census assignment, course agreement, or start-here assignment
- Proctoring information, explained with a practice assignment, if needed
- Introduction to the class (Video Post, Discussion Board, or Treasure Hunt)
- Module 1: Testing Block, Weekly Unit, or Chapter
- Overview of objectives and learning outcomes
- Learning content (notes, textbook/readings, videos, supplemental tools)
- Practice material (worksheets, interactions, concept maps, supplemental no-stakes content)
- Community building exercise (video blog, discussion board, or some type of freeware engagement tool)
- Interactions to consider:
  - Student to student interaction
  - Student to content interaction
  - Student to teacher interaction
- Summative feedback (low and high stakes depending on the module setup)
- Formative feedback

FILL OUT A MODULE LESSON PLAN

This activity helps you plan and develop the material needed to design and implement a single lesson plan. This plan can be based on an entire chapter with multiple learning objectives or a portion of the chapter with a single learning objective.

Learning Goal(s)/Objective(s)	
Chapter or Tools to support or guide the LOs	
What the student will know after completing the learning goals	
How the student will demonstrate knowledge	

Pre-Work (what the student needs to know prior to completing an assignment)

Content Description	
Resources Needed	
Media/Technology Needed	
Special Requirements	

Learning Activity

Learning Objective	
Resources Needed	
Media/Technology Needed	
Technology Support (List any support links and numbers, common issues to be aware)	
Activity Description	
Interactivity	

Homework

Resources Needed	
Media/Technology Needed	
Technology Support	
Activity Description	
Questions/Issues	

Determining the Development Time Span

When you develop an online course, the time span for delivering the information is important to consider. Does the course follow a 2-week, 4-week, 8-week, 9-week, 10-week, 12-week, 15-week, 16-week, self-paced, or other timeline? The timeline changes how you approach your content and how you assign work.

In a two- or four-week course, you may only have a handful of high-stakes graded assignments with deadlines but numerous practice and preparation assignments. In longer courses, you have the ability to assign more low-stakes remediation and exposure work to help prepare for the high-stakes exams.

In an online course, students engage with the same course material, discussions, and activities within a week (or module); however, they complete assignments, activities, and contribute to the discussions at times that are most convenient for them.

If you use a weekly time frame, make all assignments due at the same time weekly. As an online instructor, you need to create your week based on arbitrary deadlines. Try to avoid a Monday to Sunday schedule so you don't create a situation where you need to work over the weekend answering student questions and posting material for the following week. Consider a Tuesday to Monday schedule. This helps accommodate students who work during the week by giving them the week-end and supports students who are weekend workers as well.

Use pre-planned weekly check-in points, so students are not left on their own for too long. Most learning management systems allow you to post material and then deliver it at a predetermined date. This allows you to preplan communication for an entire course.

Consider the pacing of the course and plan appropriately. Reading through many discussion postings and lessons can be time consuming for the online student as well as grading for you.

REMEMBER

It is important to avoid assigning daily due dates because many online students will not be able to participate daily. Also, consider your work and personal schedule for when due dates will be assigned. You are expected to return feedback in a timely manner.

Figuring out how much time you'll need to develop the course

The time to develop a course is tricky because the minute you complete a section, you'll have ten more ideas you want to implement. Take one step at a time.

Try one new activity or pedagogical approach each time you teach the course and use student feedback to guide your evolution of material.

Initially when developing an online course, you may depend heavily on your peers, publisher material, and material scavenged from the internet. Developing an online course often requires more time than a face-to-face course. You must transition what you would demonstrate or explain verbally into clear, step-by-step instructions for all activities, usually both verbal (video) and written methods. There are numerous variables in estimating the time it takes to create an online course, such as course length, learning different technologies like the learning management system and publisher or vendor tools, transitioning face-to-face activities into online activities, creating digital formats that are accessible, and loading and organizing the content in a navigable and intuitive manner.

Developing material for the first time takes more time than converting existing content, but sometimes the modifications needed can require more rework than starting over. Consider how much reworking it will take to make the document accessible based on what is present versus the time it will take to create an accessible document from scratch.

There is no magic answer, but there are definite ways to be efficient and effective with your time — the blueprint and the matrix. Both are your guides to what is being built, where it is being placed, and how much time the user must spend with the content to show proficiency.

Building as you go

In a perfect world, we would have the course fully built prior to opening it to the users. But who is perfect? Not me! I was a couple of weeks ahead of my students in a brand-new course assigned to me a week prior to classes beginning. But it was okay because I had a detailed schedule with learning objectives aligned to assessments. I knew what the vision was for the course, and I built it in a repetitive manner to ensure the students' navigation was simple and using the learning material was intuitive.

Your job is to facilitate learning, not constantly teach how to navigate your course design.

Arranging material logically from beginning to end

Creating the order is truly a design practice. There are many great design frameworks, and all offer pros and cons. Instead of focusing on one specific framework, focus on ideas and actions. No matter which area or module a user is experiencing, they need to be guided with a beginning, a middle, and an end. The beginning is the introduction of the objectives, actions, and the alignments. The middle is the learning, engagement, and exploration. The end is when the experiences and actions come together with measuring skills, knowledge, and abilities.

Understanding the importance of alignment

Alignment was mentioned earlier in this chapter because it is important for students to recognize the parallels in your module that show the relationship between the activities, assignments, technology, and material to the objectives.

Teachers are proud of the material they create, but they cannot, I repeat, they cannot include all of their work in a course. Users will not be able to sift through it to find what is important or essential to their success. Your goal is to guide them and help them focus to achieve measurable outcomes. I like to call this trimming the fat. Only providing what is truly necessary or providing extensive guidance regarding what is "need to know" versus "nice to know." Explicitly labeling content and guiding users to that content is important for intuitive navigation and a positive user experience.

Achieving alignment

By using the learning objectives, you allow yourself to self-select what is most important for the user to learn and demonstrate with their skills, knowledge, and abilities (SKAs). Filtering which objectives make the cut is the first step in achieving alignment. *Alignment* is when the activities, assignments, technology, and/or material support the user in demonstrating their SKAs relative to the learning objective.

Get started by building your outline for each module. What is the learning objective(s) for the module, and what must be present for the student to achieve the LO goal? If the LO and the material presented don't support the goal, then they are not properly aligned. At that point either the objective needs to be reworked or the material provided needs to be evolved to guide the students into producing actions. If you have material that you truly value but is not aligned, consider it no-stakes, practice supplemental content.

TIP

Make sure that your outline is detailed. This outline can be the module introduction for the users as an overview of what is to come. What material and activity will help them learn and achieve their goals? In addition, the matrix serves as a guideline to the time frame for completing the module.

Envisioning the User Experience

Regardless of the design, it needs to be accessible and inclusive to the majority of learners. Universal Design is a set of best practices that help instructors and facilitators meet the needs of all learners. The process and practice consider that when designing, the material you create, for example, can be read by mobile devices and screen readers. Universal Design focuses on the wide diversity of learner needs, not just abilities.

When developing your vision, the outline, remember to focus on the facilitation of delivering content for learning. Your learning management system is not just a storage hub but a vessel for exploration, experience, and engagement.

Ensuring intuitive navigation

Intuitive navigation sounds obvious, but the importance of analyzing the movement and experience of users ensures a positive experience in the course. Intuitive navigation helps users find what they want quickly and easily, and their movement seems logical and seamless. Navigation that is intuitive reduces frustration, improves user experience, and keeps them from abandoning their goals. When navigation is clear, users are retained, and this increases matriculation or returning customers.

Avoiding poor navigation begins when you create your blueprint outline by prioritizing navigation in the design process. What are the needs and goals of the user, and how can the organization of your content lead them to these goals in an easy and understandable manner?

TIP

The following are best practices for creating intuitive navigation:

>> **Use consistent labels and descriptive language.** The terms need to communicate the contents' meaning or function concisely.

>> **Organize material effectively.** Place related items together and use headings to help with navigation and accessibility.

>> **Take advantage of icons.** Icons are such fun tokens and visual designs that help you recognize content or function immediately.

>> **Ask for feedback from your users.** Don't be afraid to tweak as you go to ensure that your course design is intuitive and easy to use.

Making the experience repetitive

The process of navigation in your course needs to be consistent. This statement holds true for icons, imagery, and buttons. To avoid confusion, make sure that moving through your course modules doesn't change from page to page or activity to activity. Yes, different assessments may require a different approach, but the goal should be content driven. Use different tools to help guide users, such as line breaks, banners, bullets, and boxes.

We respond to cues in our physical environment, and in the online world, those cues are often visual. We use those visual cues to help make decisions on where to go. The onscreen elements, when used repetitively, help users navigate your course.

REMEMBER

Your goal is for the users to learn skills, gain knowledge, and showcase abilities — not constantly be learning how to navigate and use new technology.

Time Management Schedule

Study Hours Needed for _____

You will need to invest a minimum of _____hours *(Choose the appropriate time.)*

These are estimated hours based on feedback from previous semesters. Some weeks and chapters may be more demanding than others.

The number of study hours that I need weekly for study in _____

Time	M	T	W	Th	F	Sat	Sun
12–1 a.m.							
1–2 a.m.							
2–3 a.m.							
3–4 a.m.							
4–5 a.m.							
5–6 a.m.							
6– 7 a.m.							
7–8 a.m.							
8–9 a.m.							

Time	M	T	W	Th	F	Sat	Sun
9–10 a.m.							
10–11 a.m.							
11–12 p.m.							
12–1 p.m.							
1–2 p.m.							
2–3 p.m.							
3–4 p.m.							
4–5 p.m.							
5–6 p.m.							
6–7 p.m.							
7–8 p.m.							
8–9 p.m.							
9–10 p.m.							
10–11 p.m.							
11p.m.–12 a.m.							

Place the class abbreviation in the hours that you plan to commit to daily preparation for this class. Allot specific times that you will be available to review lectures, notes, and assignments.

Place the following letters for all the hours that are occupied by these activities. You will be surprised at how busy you actually are!

W: Work

SA: Social activities

C: Commuting

S: Sleeping

E: Eating

O: Other class

R: Responsibilities (family, appointments, and so forth)

OS: Studying for other class

Number the remaining empty boxes 1, 2, 3, and so on. This is the number of hours you have available for participating in this course.

What is your total number of hours available for studying this course? _____ Is this a realistic schedule based on your other commitments?

Does this number match or exceed the number of hours needed to complete this course as you have indicated at the top of this chart?

Yes No (*Circle One*)

If **Yes**, you have the time available to participate in this course.

If **No**, consider how you can prioritize your time to ensure you are successful in the course.

Chapter 8

Designing an Interesting, Informative Course

The early chapters of the book focus on giving you the greatest likelihood of achieving the desired goals through proper planning. I discuss why it is important to take specific actions in courses such as designing for a broad audience (Chapters 3 and 4), being present (Chapter 6), having a plan (Chapter 5), creating measurable learning objectives, and having a blueprint (both in Chapter 7). Each of these actions is important, and each represents something the user needs to be successful. In this chapter, you involve the learner by creating a clear and consistent structure that is inviting and intuitive. As you plan, design, create, and build, you will begin to reflect and revise. When users begin to interact, you will truly begin to evaluate your framework, and you'll be able to evolve your course through feedback that analyzes the design and the delivery, which in turn will help you tweak and develop iterations to come. This process is a marathon, not a sprint.

TIP

Through your reflection and student feedback, keep a journal of issues, questions, and design hiccups that occur through the course. Use these notes, questions, and ideas to help improve experiences over time. (Refer to Chapter 12 for more information on journaling.)

Creating a Presence by Welcoming the User

Chapter 6 focuses on your presence in the classroom. A whole chapter devoted to this? Yes, because this sets the tone for the entire semester and creates an environment in which users want to participate, learn, and be present themselves. While an online course may be a great monetary opportunity, users must feel their investment is worthwhile, and your presence affects their perception of the course's and experience's worth. You may not be everyone's cup of tea, but you can always say you were there for their success.

Students need to feel welcome from the moment they enroll in the course. Whether it is via an email prior to the Learning Management System (LMS) being available or their first time logging into the course, you are their guide, facilitator, and knowledge purveyor, and by greeting them, you increase their comfort level and form a proper relationship from ground zero.

There is no shortage of ways to welcome students to your class, so be creative. I cover the most common ones plus a couple of out-of-the-box ideas. Welcome videos, welcome letters, and online meet and greets are great ways to begin the course, but if you want to be a little spicy, consider an escape room, treasure hunt, or interactive video.

Saying hello through a welcome letter, welcome video, or a meet and greet

I encourage teachers to do all of these because individuals prefer learning in different manners. Thus, a video may reach an audience that a letter may miss.

Welcome video

A welcome video is a terrific way to create a dialogue between you and your users. A welcome video allows you to familiarize your students with you and the course. Realizing a human is behind the course structure and design eases some anxiety. Allow students to see you as approachable and present while setting the tone for positive interactions for the remainder of the course. If the students view you as easy to communicate with, then it is easier to build a relationship with them. They want to feel welcome after investing their time, and often money, into a course.

A welcome video can be composed of many parts, but they can be siloed into two main categories: 1) instructor information and 2) course information.

Instructor introduction should welcome the student with an introduction to yourself such as your title, field, and interests within the field or research. Offer any succinct advice about succeeding in your online course. If comfortable, you can provide personal information about your hobbies, interests, animals, or family. Of course, this is optional.

A course walk-through is essential to help students understand your navigation vision of the course. Remember that you built it and probably think it is intuitive. But a walk-through ensures that students have a personal tour guide to get started. The course walk-through should share important information about how the course is designed and best practices to navigate it for the course documents, important school information, textbooks/readings, learning content, and assessments. If there are requirements to be completed to access information or if there are unique assessment paths, those should be covered in the navigation video. In addition, state how the design of the course is going to help the students achieve their goals and what student expectations are for the course.

TIP

When recording the welcome video and navigating through the course, make sure to describe what you are doing, too. This ensures inclusivity for individuals who may be visually impaired.

How can you create the most awesome welcome video? Follow these steps:

1. **Create a script to help keep yourself on track, concise, and conscious of time.**

   (This also helps with the development of captions for accessibility.)

2. **Review the script and practice it a few times.**

   Determine whether you want to ad lib some. You want to be comfortable and sound natural.

3. **Ensure your camera, microphone, lighting, and recording environment are properly set up.**

   - Lights should be in front of you to illuminate your face.

   - Your environment should be quiet and distraction free to ensure the video quality is not affected.

   - Use a plain background that is usually on the lighter side in color. Make sure your clothing contrasts and does not blend into the background.

4. **When recording the video, project your voice and ensure your cadence is good.**

   Also relax your body and try not to shift or swivel too much in a chair.

5. **Save the video and ensure that the captions are accurate.**

    If you use YouTube or other captioning services, a transcript is often created automatically with timestamps.

Welcome letter

No matter how much work you put into a welcome video, not everyone will watch it unless it is a course requirement to access other content. I encourage writing a welcome letter in addition to making a welcome video.

The welcome letter should not be a transcript of the video but a personal letter that includes a greeting and introduction. You can include background information on yourself that is both professional and personal. You choose your comfort level. If you want to include the first steps to access the course, make sure they are concise. You can provide some information about course success, personal pictures, and hobbies. An example of my welcome letter is at the end of the chapter.

Meet and greet online through live video platforms

Office hours often hold a negative connotation to students, so framing the online meeting opportunity as a meet and greet or social hour can alleviate student fears. No matter how convenient online education can be, having the opportunity for face-to-face communication is attractive. By hosting this in the beginning or throughout the course, the students will feel more comfortable approaching you and trusting you. This method shows you take your presence for students as an important factor in their success.

All material you create needs to be accessible. This requires pictures to have alt text and be inline on documents. Videos need an accurate transcript and accurate captions, and live meetings need closed captions turned on.

Beginning a course with out-of-the-box approaches

Out-of-the-box approaches offer a fun opportunity for both the students and faculty to have a memorable moment at the beginning of a course. A couple of examples that I have dabbled with are treasure hunts and escape rooms.

Treasure hunts

Treasure hunts, also known as scavenger hunts, are a great way for students to learn how to navigate the course. You can do this by having students complete activities, watch videos, and read documents such as the syllabus that require them to find the answers and document them by typing/writing the answers or taking screenshots and turning them in via a quiz, survey, freeware tool, discussion board, or an upload assignment. Have a document in which the clues or answers are in white, so the document appears blank. The students need to change the font color to read the clues or answers.

Here are some examples of questions:

>> What time are assignments due?

>> What is the makeup policy in your own words?

>> When are office hours?

>> What are the testing requirements?

>> Where in the course do you find your learning material?

Escape rooms

Escape rooms take gaming into account and can bring an opportunity for students to figure out answers that reinforce lesson content and increase engagement. Students answer questions, decipher puzzles, or solve problems to enter the next level. To begin the process of creating an escape room, you must write down the goals of the assignment/exercise. In this case, you are focusing on a welcome to the course exercise. Figure out the theme of the escape room so it has consistent images and text. Is it medieval, 1960s, a cartoon, a movie, or a television show? You want to determine the amount of time spent in an escape room. Since they are supposed to be fun, I suggest keeping it to 15–20 minutes. You want to figure out your last lock clue and the prize, which may be access to learning content, and then work backwards to clue one. Escape rooms can be built directly into the LMS, Google, Jamboards, or Microsoft Office. They may depend on the tools available to you or what is accessible and not blocked for the users.

You can hide clues in videos, hyperlink text, hidden text, QR codes, pictures, interactive slides, and more. You can highlight letters in an anagram for the code word, make the clue the correct answer letter in a multiple-choice question, have the response correspond to a clue in the syllabus, or provide clues in videos to make sure students watch them.

REMEMBER

Educational games increase motivation, and the interactive techniques required in activities such as escape rooms allow students to apply knowledge, receive feedback quickly, and improve their confidence. The online escape room simplifies logistics and costs that come with physical escape rooms.

TIP

Try to complete your activities such as an escape room using assistive technology, such as screen readers and keystrokes, to ensure the activities are accessible to all users. If they are not accessible, the design will need to be modified to be inclusive of all users.

Community building and environment decorating

When creating an online course, you want to create an environment that encourages community building, which is introduced in Chapter 6. In this chapter I discuss components of social online learning and describe specific examples.

Say my name

Names are part of our identity. When one's name is called or stated, it allows that person to be seen. Mispronouncing names can create feelings of disrespect, sadness, exclusion, and isolation. Encourage students to give phonetic pronunciation if they believe it may be difficult to pronounce their name from just seeing it. Ask them to offer tips or guidance such as "It rhymes with _____" or a nickname they prefer. Last, ask them to record a short audio and post it. Many LMS have audio recorders included in the Rich Content Editors, such as discussion boards, so this can be done without extra steps. Many vendors focus on creating a community with different products to mimic social media and include pronunciation tools, and these tools may be integrated into the LMS.

Welcome with an online discussion forum

Online discussions can be a great way for you and the students to interact. How you frame the discussion is important, and you want to make sure you start the forum by introducing yourself too. Most students and faculty roll their eyes when they hear the term "discussion board," but you can be creative and use it in an atypical manner.

You can use discussion boards for icebreakers and getting acquainted exercises. These bring some reprieve to the typical use of a discussion board focused on content. Icebreakers and getting acquainted exercises provide the opportunity to send and receive messages about people, observe others in your own time, and establish initial relationships with individuals in the class.

What is an icebreaker? An icebreaker is a type of activity or game that helps individuals converse on a surface level. They are designed to get people talking about topics and establish a social relationship.

What is getting acquainted exercise? Many people say this is another name for an icebreaker. I see getting acquainted exercises as an opportunity to go deeper in conversation and discuss attributes of the individuals in a more in–depth manner.

Here are some icebreaker examples:

>> **Two truths and a fib:** This example is a classic where each user writes three statements. Two are true and one is a lie. Their peers vote on which statement is a lie. On a set date, the original author shares the truths and lie with the class.

>> **Piece of advice:** Ask students to share a piece of advice that has influenced or resonated with them in their life.

>> **Where in the world:** Ask students to place the coordinates to anywhere in the world or a picture unique to an area that they would like to visit.

>> **ABC alphabet game:** The students have to post a term describing a subject with the letters of the alphabet. The first student to post uses the letter A. The second student to post uses the letter B. The third student to post uses the letter C, and so on until each student has posted. If there are more than 26 students, then the 27th student starts the alphabet over. This works best with nonthreaded replies in discussion board settings. The subject can be the course content, the student who is posting personality, food or drinks, movie names, actors, animals, and so forth.

And here are a few getting acquainted examples:

>> **Backpack:** Choose five items that you would carry in a backpack to represent who you are and state why they are important to you. You can use visual representations from the internet or your personal pictures, videos from YouTube (make sure they are appropriate for class), or words and phrases. The students should respond to at least one other student with a statement, an emoji, or a GIF to engage in discussion. Students will learn about their peers' passions, families, values, similarities, differences, and likes. Students can feel more connected when they are allowed to express themselves in a variety of ways.

>> **Make a music playlist:** Have students compile a playlist of six songs that represent their past, present and hopes for the future, choosing two for each phase. They can share links to the actual songs via YouTube, iHeart, or digital jukebox tools. Then students can respond in a question-and-answer session

to determine how a song represents a phase of their life. Through questions and answers, they determine shared interests, differences, and music genres.

TECHNICAL STUFF

When students post hyperlinks, have a quick video or short directions on how to post hyperlinks as descriptive text. This ensures that all users know where the hyperlink leads, and screen readers are provided with appropriate information.

Verifying your students are your students

Online courses through public universities must include at least one assessment that meets Federal Regulation §602.17 and HLC Policy Number FDCR.A.10.050. These regulations state an institution must establish that a registered student in a course offered through distance education is the student who engages in the course. Processes must be in place to protect student privacy and notify students of any charges associated with student identity when they register.

Verification assignments allow faculty to ensure the student taking the assignment is the student who is enrolled in the course. There are many ways to complete verification assignments, and how you choose to complete them is dependent on your needs, class size, and class type. A for-profit or free Massive Open Online Course (MOOC) does not have the same regulations as a for-credit college course.

Proctoring tools allow verification to occur through multiple steps that can include a photo of the individual and a photo of the individual's identification, which, while up to the faculty member, can be a state identification, driver's license, passport, military identification, school identification, or another approved identification. Another alternative is an assignment where the students submit a picture of themselves holding their identification next to their face. Last, one-on-one meetings to verify the individual can occur, but this is time consuming, so it depends on class size and the faculty's schedule.

Deciding Between Need-to-Know and Nice-to-Know

What is the difference between need-to-know and nice-to-know? Teachers with specialties, or subject matter experts (SME), can become wrapped up in the minutia and believe everything is necessary for a student to know to be successful. But you must be realistic with time in and out of the classroom. Need-to-know is the foundational material to understand the bigger picture. Nice-to-know is specific and detailed. The more content that's presented, the greater the amount of time needed to be successful. Being mindful of time investment is important for both teacher and student achievement.

Trimming the fat

Trimming the fat is a colloquialism that, when used with curriculum, means you focus on the essential *learning objectives* (LOs) or the need-to-know versus the nice-to-know. This doesn't mean you can't provide the nice-to-know, but it should be signified in the material as supplemental or lagniappe (something extra) and not something the student will be assessed on.

Determining the essential learning objectives for a course helps you develop learning activities and assessments that map to those objectives. These LOs allow you to observe and measure a student's knowledge, skills, and attitudes. How do you determine what is essential? Essential LOs allow the student to successfully continue in the program or the course sequence, prepare for professional exams and certification, and have confidence that they can complete activities in a professional and timely manner. These LOs are the make-or-break or the course foundation. Asking yourself some questions may help to determine the essential LOs and trim the fat of the nice-to-know LOs:

>> What should students be able complete, do, or perform after the course that they cannot do prior to the course?

>> How well do the students need to demonstrate mastery of the LO?

>> How will I evaluate the achievement of the LO?

>> Which LOs will be the most influential for the student's success professionally and academically?

>> Which LOs, if not taught, would be seen as the course being incomplete and students not achieving their goals?

>> What is the most important takeaway from this course?

Determining the type of learning you want to impart to the student can help guide the development and choice of LOs. Cognitive, psychomotor, affective, and interpersonal are some of the main domains of learning. *Cognitive* relates to the students' knowledge and mental skills. *Psychomotor* refers to the physical skill sets, *affective* focuses on feelings and attitudes, and *interpersonal* represents interactions and social skills. If you start with the most complex and challenging LOs, you can break them into smaller parts. What does the student need to do before showing mastery of the complex outcomes? Last, determine what basic skills students will need to achieve success. When writing the LOs, use the acronym SMART: Specific, Measurable, Achievable, Relevant, Timely.

SMEs tend to think everything is important. Ask yourself these questions to help reduce the amount of content:

>> What is an example of when knowing this would come up in a job?

>> Is there a time or situation where students will need to rely on this content?

>> What would happen if they did not learn this content?

If students can't apply the information from the course in their jobs, is it really need-to-know?

Time is always of the essence

There never seems to be enough time to do everything, and in reality, that's true. But as a faculty member you must balance teaching, parents, partners, a social life, and other obligations. And students often must balance the same load as you as well as multiple classes. Because time is limited, you must recognize that and manage it so you can allocate the most time to what you believe is most important.

Parkinson's Law states that the work we must do will expand to fill the time we devote to completing it. For teachers, tasks such as grading and prepping content expand to take up as much time as we give them. If you have an hour, a task will fill the hour; if you have a full day, it will fill the whole day. When preparing or when grading, set a timer. These suggestions are true for students too. Students retain more knowledge when they use spaced retrieval practice as part of their studying. Spaced retrieval practice is when you have a set amount of time to devote to learning and you then spread the time out over multiple sessions, so the sessions are spaced out over time.

As a teacher, you can help set up your students for success by giving them a suggested time management schedule for each chapter, unit, or content piece. This can be done in a variety of ways. I like to give my students an interactive check list that states what they can do for each content piece, an estimated amount of time for each activity, and the due dates. Any other information you may find pertinent can be added.

Another helpful suggestion to guide your students is to provide them with a check-in guide on how you would approach the material. This can be sent via announcements on your LMS, a Group Me or Remind Me app, an email, or a Slack channel, to name a few.

Here's an example of a weekly suggested time management schedule. This example is taken from *Human Anatomy and Physiology* "Chapter 4: Tissue (Histology)":

>> August 22–23: Open and download Chapter 4 (Tissues (Histology) notes. On these days you should concentrate on Chapter 4 only. Read through the notes two or three times so you are familiar with the terms. You can also rewrite the notes in your own format using colors to associate with headings. (This creates an active learning style, rather than a passive one.) If you choose to do this, write the notes in your own words (like a story), and write 2–3 times your normal size. As you write, say what you're writing out loud so that you create an aural, visual, and active connection.

>> August 24–26: Listen to online lectures and take your own notes for Chapter 4. Use the charts provided to help organize the tissues presented in Chapter 4. Drawing the tissues improves association. Creating silly analogies also helps. Example: Adipose tissue looks like marshmallows.

>> August 26: Open the homework and begin working on the assessments. These assignments are not meant to be completed in one sitting.

>> August 26–28: Create a chart of each tissue type and fill in its location and functions. Practice the worksheets provided in the notes section.

>> Provide the students with a list of questions or activities to answer or complete. These directives can help them focus on the LOs and be a knowledge check.

If you can discuss these prompts, describe the events, and apply the knowledge, then you are prepared for the assessment.

- Create a chart or draw the cell junctions. Include the different functions and the locations of the cell junctions. Think of analogies for each junction (Ziplock bags are analogous to tight junctions, tunnels are analogous to gap junctions, bolts holding a desk to the ground are analogous to hemidesmosomes, and so on).

- Create a flow chart of the germ tissues and the adult tissues that differentiate from the germ tissues.

- Draw and describe the connective tissue makeup (different cell types, fibers, and ground substance).

- Create a diagram for just connective tissues. Draw each tissue to help you learn the structures, locations, and functions. Label the important parts identified in your materials.

- Create a diagram and chart for just epithelial tissues. Draw each tissue to help you learn the structures, locations, and functions. Label the important parts identified in your materials.

- Create a diagram and chart for just muscular tissues. Draw each tissue to help you learn the structures, locations, and functions. Label the important parts identified in your materials.

- Create a diagram and chart for nervous tissue. Draw each tissue to help you learn the structures, locations, and functions. Label the important parts identified in your materials.

- Name and describe the four membrane types in the body. Where are they located, and what tissues represent the membrane?

REMEMBER

This exercise places the responsibility on the student to create their own study guide. They are allowed to be creative using colors, drawings, notes, tables, charts, and diagrams. They appreciate the guidance provided but they have to do the work to become familiar with the content.

Student-centered learning

Learning occurs differently for every individual. Some individuals prefer linear learning and others nonlinear learning. Some people learn well when information flows in an organized step-by-step manner, and others may excel when they follow a dynamic, interactive path. Is one more effective than the other? Many factors determine the best approach, such as student level (freshman, sophomore, upperclassman, independent learner) and the purpose of the course (certification, degree based, personal growth).

Linear learning occurs when the course design is divided into steps. It can be chapters, modules, or weeks, and the material are in a fixed order. The linear route allows guidance to the learner and delivers the knowledge at the same point in time to each user. Linear learning provides clear direction, structure, and organization; measuring the impact of the student's learning is straightforward through exams and assessments. Linear learning is used frequently in lower-level courses as students need more guidance.

Nonlinear (dynamic) learning has no fixed path, so students follow different approaches based on their preferences and skill levels. This method focuses on individuals being stimulated to learn new things, and their efforts determine their abilities. In this approach, students seek information that is relevant to them and based on their prior knowledge level and comfort level with the information being presented. Nonlinear learning allows flexibility and allows one to focus on areas of interest. It helps with being adaptable, but it can appear chaotic or unstructured since there is a lack of direction for where to start. Nonlinear learning is seen in higher level courses, graduate level courses, and courses taken for self-improvement learning.

Both methods can support student-centered learning, but nonlinear lends itself to students planning their learning path and their assessments more easily. Teachers can give the same choice in assessments in linear and nonlinear learning design. This gives students the ownership to make decisions on their learning — the why, the what, and the how.

>> **Why** is the relevance of the subject and skills since the students are investing the time and effort to learn. Students need to see how this will help them in their future careers.

>> **What** the student learns involves their choosing the content and exploring what is interesting to their personal goals and growth.

>> **How** the student demonstrates they learned can be done in a variety of ways. Teachers can offer choices as to how the students demonstrate their skills, knowledge, and aptitude.

As a teacher, you can provide two or three options. The third is open-ended, where students propose their own assessment or product based on some parameters provided. This is like differentiated learning where the lesson assessment is tailored to meet an individual student's interests, needs, and strengths. When creating material for the masses, differentiated learning is difficult to accomplish, but by offering choice, you create an environment that supports a wider array of students' learning needs.

When developing curriculum, content, process, and product are addressed. The content is what students learn, the process is how the students comprehend the information, and the product is how students exhibit their learning. No matter the approach, if the teacher keeps the content, the process, and the product at the forefront, they then encourage students to meet the learning objectives and continue to advance in their academic path.

Following are examples of choice for students when participating in a discussion board and answering a prompt:

>> Answer each question in 100 words or less. You are writing the answer in your own words to practice explaining the overall content.

>> Tweet style. You can answer the discussion board questions in a tweet for each question. Tweets are 280 characters (not words) or less. Because these are limited in length, it takes a lot of creativity and the ability to synthesize the material. It requires you to understand, create concise information, and really express your understanding in limited space.

>> A video blog where you discuss the answer. You can include drawings in your discussion or discuss them as a monologue. You can be as creative as you want, but you can't use other videos. Please keep video blogs under two minutes.

>> Be creative in your approach but make sure you are meeting the expectations in the rubric.

Here are examples of choice for students when participating in a project such as a Public Service Announcement:

>> Creating an infographic

>> Shooting a TikTok video or short YouTube video

>> Writing a letter to an editor

>> Creating a presentation

REMEMBER

With learner's choice, the chances are greater that these experiences will be an appropriate fit for most learners.

Design Thinking: Conception to Completion

When creating a course, using design thinking is a fancy way of saying you are focusing on the user the course is being built for. Design thinking produces better processes, content, and assessment if the user is considered from the beginning.

What you are teaching your students must be clear to you when designing the course. These objectives allow students to know whether they understand the information. You want your learners to know: 1) What skills they will acquire, 2) What knowledge they will acquire, and 3) How long it should take them to acquire these skills and knowledge. To do this, think about what captures one's attention. Engaging course content captures the user's attention and encourages the learning process. An intentionally designed course outline (modified blueprint) provides a beginning, a middle, and an end for each major objective, unit, or module for both the learners and instructors, ensuring everyone understands where they are. The users can track their progress and focus on the learning outcomes.

Creating an immersive experience helps the user stay motivated, connected, and engaged. To do this, a variety of visuals, multimedia, and applicable world examples help with retention and comprehension.

Building the blueprint

Blueprints, introduced in Chapter 7, are a way for an instructor to plot out the teaching and learning that goes into a given course, providing a chance to express a detailed outline and picture of the course.

In the early stages of planning your course, having the blueprint prepared with the topics, assessments, resources (or ideas of resources), practice content, and other information pertinent to success in learning is beneficial. Having the layout to your vision helps yourself and others to have a clear idea of the course.

Many aspects are involved in planning a course, so having your ideas articulated in a central location is a valuable way to see progress, flow, and process. Seeing everything allows one to make sure there are no gaps in the coverage of content.

To begin, knowing how many modules (lessons) helps organize your blueprint. The weeks in a term can guide this, but a good rule of thumb is to have 12 modules. This number works well in 7-, 8-, 9-, 10-, 12-, 15-, and 16-week terms. Usually, 12 modules allow courses to be taught in a variety of weeks so redesigning and reworking the content is not needed, and it still allows for testing and projects to be assigned or worked throughout the terms. Each module is broken into more palatable or digestible subtopics or units to cover content. This approach is less intimidating for the designer and the student. Two main approaches to modular design are chunking and scaffolding.

Chunking

Chunking reduces cognitive load because the course is broken into smaller units that are more meaningful. This breakdown can be daily or weekly units, and if there are texts for the course, the units may align with the textbook's chapters.

These units can be presented in a variety of ways to the users based on the LMS being used. Some LMS are organized via modules or folders and others are presented using pages. Depending on the LMS, modules can be placed within modules and pages can be placed within modules. Here are some ideas on how to chunk:

>> **Modules (Folders):** Each module can represent a distinct content piece, and then units within the module are presented. Each module may represent a unit corresponding to a topic, day, or week.

>> **Pages:** Each page may contain content related to one topic, or the pages may be broken into multiple topics by days or weeks.

- External links via URLs

- Course tools to publisher material
- Files

Pages and Modules are very common tools to use to chunk information. If using this approach, the use of formatting is helpful. Examples include

- » Headings and subheadings
- » Paragraph spacing
- » Styles such as bold (strong) and italics (emphasis)
- » Bullets (use alphanumeric lists only when there is an intentional order of events or tasks)
- » Images (remember alt text)

Scaffolding

Scaffolding is a pedagogical strategy to help students reach their goals. Lev Vygotsky was known for his theory of learning and development. A key construct of this theory was the *Zone of Proximal Development* (ZPD). ZPD is the area between what a student has learned and can perform on their own and what they can do with guidance from a more knowledgeable individual. Scaffolding is how students are supported in the ZPD.

Scaffolding challenges students to learn past their current knowledge; they learn content with support from others that may be too difficult to learn on their own. This method increases the chances of students meeting the learning objectives because explicit instruction (guidance from the more knowledgeable individual) can be provided on how to complete the action.

TIP

When making assignments, the approach and the information provided as support documentation are important. Also, consider students' array of background experience and education exposure. Having the supplemental resources for discovery (nonlinear learning) may provide insight for beginning learners and enhance the experience for advanced learners. Here are a couple examples:

- » Discussion boards are more successful when there are specific rules for interactions. Providing examples of good versus poor discussion posts can be helpful, but modeling good interactions can help students learn from your actions.

>> Projects often are put off until the weeks before they are due. If the project is broken into smaller pieces with due dates throughout the term, it allows students to receive feedback as they are creating the material and make adjustments as needed. This encourages pacing and scaffolds their learning based on previous actions and guidance.

REMEMBER

Implementing scaffolding technique works best in a student-centered classroom. Using a variety of instructional approaches helps them form connections to the material they are learning and relate it to information they already know. When students can create or choose how they demonstrate their knowledge, it increases their motivation to succeed.

With chunking and scaffolding in mind when building the blueprint, the next important concept is pacing. Usually, there is a predefined amount of content that must be covered for a myriad of reasons such as transferability, course sequencing, certifications, and so on, so understanding the course pace is important. You don't want it to be too slow and bore students, leading to decreased motivation, nor do you want it to be too fast such that students become lost and overwhelmed. In online courses, you can't read facial cues or body language to know how students are reacting to the material. As the expert you must determine, being sensible of course, what can be accomplished in the time frame allotted. Your students are learning the content, and often the technology, so realistic expectations are important.

TIP

Having a calendar is helpful to visualize the course pace for you to properly pace the content and for students to handle the course load. Create tentative work times and due dates for the content, assignments, and assessments. Is there a lot of overlap? Do students have time to review and comprehend the material over a day or two? Do you have time to give timely feedback? The schedule that you provide students with gives them an overview of their next few weeks or months and allows them to adequately plan and manage their time.

ACTIVITY

CREATING INTERACTIVE ELEMENTS

Creating an interactive checklist helps students understand the activity and tentative time that needs to be allotted to the activity.

Use the checklist document found at www.dummies.com/go/creatingecoursesfd as a guide for you to develop your own interactive schedule. You can tweak and develop this file into a usable student time management guide.

Using an outline to create your blueprint

In Chapter 7 you start to build a rudimentary blueprint. Now you can create a more in-depth one using the outline that follows.

As you proceed, you should bear in mind the time divisions into which you've organized your course. Many faculty organize courses into "weeks," but others use larger groupings. I refer to these groupings as "modules," but you may refer to them however you like (for example, units, lessons, chapters, and so forth). Each module has associated learning activities, readings, graded assignments, multimedia, and assessments — all of which culminate in a final grade (letter or Pass/Fail) for the course.

The blueprint ensures that these elements are present for students:

>> **Course description:** Most likely the institution's course catalog or the company provides a broad description of the course. This can be a good place to start. Copy, paste, and modify your course description into the field within the template located at the end of this chapter.

>> **General course goals:** What are the overarching goals of your course?

>> **Student learning objectives:** Each module has objectives that you want your students to achieve. These should be measurable (refer back to Chapter 7).

>> **Artifacts:** The materials and tools students use to support their engagement and learning of content.

>> **Performance:** These are the assignments that students need to complete to demonstrate mastery/proficiency in learning the material.

Depending on the platform you are using to deliver the course, some information in the blueprint may change, but in general the blueprint is not affected by platform type.

Including About Blueprint Content (ABC)

When students land on an LMS home page, there should be navigation links to guide them on where to go next. The teacher should make a list of all the navigation links necessary for success in the course. Justifying the need for the link is important, as less is more in course design.

Every course should have these modules:

>> **A how-to module:** This may be either a course or school how-to that references Frequently Asked Questions, school- or business-specific

information, LMS guides, technology help desk options, study tips, tutoring options, and other important information.

>> **A welcome module:** Welcome modules may be termed "Getting Started," "Visit Me First," or "First Stop to Success." Use a name that you believe will help guide students. The welcome module should include the welcome letter, welcome video, syllabus, schedule, and specific course information such as a census assignment and proctoring information. Often this module must be completed by meeting different criteria set by the teacher. These criteria can vary but may range from the student viewing material, marking material as done, submitting information, and/or scoring a grade. Controlling a student's movement through certain material can benefit them as they are more likely to interact with content if it is the required path to access the course learning material. The schedule, syllabus, and course guidelines are important for student success and are often overlooked or skipped by the learner.

>> **Learning modules:** These should be repetitive. They can be set up by content, weeks, chapters, testing blocks, or any other way you find supportive of student learning. However, each module and page should be set up consistently with the same structure, layout, and organization of material.

TIP

You can find a course blueprint template in table form at www.dummies.com/go/creatingecoursesfd.

Below is a brief overview of what you will want to make notes of, label, and evaluate in your course. This exercise will allow you to think about the big picture and the navigable experience.

Course name:

Course description:

Course goals:

Landing page (area students enter the course): On the landing page is a banner introducing the course with the dates and course length. Beneath the banner is a brief introduction to the students on first steps and the instructor's name.

Below this information there can be interactive elements to bring students to specific modules within the course. For example, Start Here, School How-Tos, Learning Modules, Testing Module, Office Hours.

Navigation links available to students: Home, Announcements, Modules, Grades, Office Hours. Minimum links to avoid confusion and make navigation more intuitive.

Course body: Modules or pages are set up to present information on each chapter, unit, or LO in a repetitive format for each assessment or project.

TIP

Consistency is key, and sticking to these ideas will help with course flow, navigation, and student experience.

>> **Consistent naming conventions:** Clearly labeling modules and activities with titles and ensuring users know how to interact with the material.

>> **Consistent layout and order:** Keeping modules or units organized systematically, and clearly defining the beginning, middle, and end of a lesson as well as providing due dates.

>> **Consistent schedule:** Ensuring the class due dates support a learning routine.

>> **Consistent design:** Making style elements consistent in text fonts, sizes, colors, and formats. You can find public domains and creative commons licensed images (Library of Congress, Unsplach.com, Flickr, Pixabay.com) as well as cool design programs that offer a free experience (Canva and Piktochart).

>> **Using icons:** Icons provide users with visual information without using text. Example: most of the population is familiar with the text message icon of a comment bubble with three dots. This type of iconography can be used for student to become familiar with course content and actions.

The following should help you with your blueprint:

Title of Module	Content Located in Units (pages, external URLs, assessments, assignments, learning artifacts)
Icons, Font, and Color Choices	All Discussion Boards have a comment bubble icon in the title.
	All readings have a book icon in the title.
	All videos have a video camera icon in the title.
	All assignments have a paper and pen icon in the title.
	Font color is usually black but will call out important information in 14-point red, bold font and place it in a shadow box.
	Each page has a banner title in the organization's colors.
	Horizontal break lines are used to separate parts, steps, or pages to help clearly delineate and chunk content.

Title of Module	Content Located in Units (pages, external URLs, assessments, assignments, learning artifacts)
School How-To	LMS Help (page)
	Student Information System (page)
	Bookstore Information (page and URL)
	Student Help Page (URL)
	Resources for Students (page and URL)
	Technology Resources (page and URL)
	Tutoring Options (page and URL)
Office Hours	Question and Answer Discussion Board
	Office Hours Link and How-To Document
Start Here	Tips for Success (checklist for success and study skills/organization/time management tools)
	Start Here Page (syllabus, schedule, orientation, addendum, welcome letter)
	Syllabus Walk-Through (interactive video)
	Proctoring Tool Information (page)
	Practice Quiz with proctoring tool also serves as verification of identity
	Optional Midterm Bonus
	Course Community Discussion Board — Icebreaker (rubric associated with grading)
	Study Cycle/Metacognition — Interactive Video
Tests	Test (summative evaluations)
	Tests are multiple choice, short answer, fill in the blank, matching, T and F
	50–100 questions
	65–120 minutes
	Proctored
	Formative evaluations (anonymous surveys)

Title of Module	Content Located in Units (pages, external URLs, assessments, assignments, learning artifacts)
Test 1 Learning Content (Chapters. . .)	Introduction to Test 1 Module (page of objectives for each chapter)
	Test 1 Study Material (page of links to interactive notes, links to video playlists, links to transcript files, and links to practice worksheet files)
	Read, Watch, and Do Section (Practice Supplemental Material — all are pages with links embedded in them)
	Reading textbook chapters
	Listening to illustrations
	Animations and worksheets
	Concept maps
	Interactive assessments
	Practice material (not graded)
	Test 1 Review Information (page with files and links)
	Flashcards for the test
	Practice quizzes (not for a grade)
Test 1 Graded Material (Homework and Bonuses)	Test 1 Resource Assignment (discussion board activity when the students discuss what supplemental tool they used, a screenshot, and pros/cons of the tool) (rubric associated with grading)
	Discussion Board (discussion board to answer short answer questions as an alternative assignment. Students have choice on how they answer the prompt.) (rubric associated with grading)
	Differentiated learning via MasteryPaths for each chapter (a series of assignments that are released based on performance on a baseline quiz; embedded in the module)
	Bonus options (vary for each testing block)
	Games such as Kahoot!, Jeopardy (embedded in a page or as an URL)
	Alternative assessments using freeware (posted in a discussion board or submitted as an assignment) (Types that may be used are Thinglinks, Flips, Padlets, Concept maps, Analogy presentations.)
	Crossword Puzzles (submitted as a file assignment)

Title of Module	Content Located in Units (pages, external URLs, assessments, assignments, learning artifacts)
Test 2 Learning Content (Chapters. . .)	Exact same setup as test 1 but with content that aligns with test 2 material.
Test 2 Graded Material (Homework and Bonuses)	Exact same setup as test 1 but with content that aligns with test 2 material.
Midterm Exam Material (Review)	Midterm Testing Information (page) Midterm Review Document (file)
Test 3 Learning Content (Chapters. . .)	Exact same setup as test 1 but with content that aligns with test 3 material.
Test 3 Graded Material (Homework and Bonuses)	Exact same setup as test 1 but with content that aligns with test 3 material.
Test 4 Learning Content (Chapters. . .)	Exact same setup as test 1 but with content that aligns with test 4 material.
Test 4 Graded Material (Homework and Bonuses)	Exact same setup as test 1 but with content that aligns with test 4 material.
Final Exam Material (Reviews, Homework, and Bonuses)	Final Chapters note and video page (page of links to interactive notes, video playlists, transcripts, and practice worksheets) Final Chapters Homework (embedded in the module) Final Exam Review Information (page with files and links) Final Bonus Options Formative Evaluation (anonymous survey) Final Exam Resource Assignment (discussion board activity when the students discuss what supplemental tool they used, a screenshot and pros/cons of the tool)

REMEMBER

As you build courses and make design choices, approach the course design and work from the perspective of Universal Design for Learning, or UDL. UDL's underlying principle is to anticipate the diversity of learners in order to reduce barriers. A common practice is to provide people with disability accommodations. But why not reduce the need for accommodations by making design choices in your online class that are more inclusive from the beginning?

Creating the course matrix

Chapter 7 introduces the beginning of the process to map the course. Now you will continue to develop the course matrix. Your course matrix will develop over time to meet your students' needs. Often the users will give you the best suggestions to provide them with guidance. In practice, I provide the users with a course matrix that is detailed and has the dates aligned with activities and learning outcomes as well as tools to support their learning route. I also provide the users with checklists that are not as information heavy and are great for quick reference.

Here are examples of headings in a course matrix (not all have to be used):

>> Week/Dates/Due Dates

>> Learning Outcomes

>> How the users practice and show mastery

>> Learning Activities/Assessments

>> How feedback is provided

>> Supporting Content or What you need to complete the work

TIP

The following example is a mockup of information in a course matrix. The entire course matrix model is available for you to access, evolve, and make your own. You can find the file at www.dummies.com/go/creatingcoursesfd.

Biology XXX Fall 2023 Online (Biol XXX-XXX) Schedule

Your final grade is weighted. Adding points together will not reflect your grade in the course. The LMS will give you the grade you've earned with bonus as a running total. When test grades are posted, the grade will only be calculated once the grade is placed in the TEST with BONUS points column. This grade is not posted until the test closes.

Grading Category	Description
Homework (0% of grade)	You have 2 tries per question and there is NO time limit. They are only for review but a great way to gauge your knowledge of the material.
Online Discussions (7.5% of grade)	Discussion questions will be posted for each testing block. Each student is required to research a question (textbook, notes, primary literature — websites that are not .edu or journal based do not count) and answer the question. Each student is to respond with meaningful input (new information, refuting information) to at least 2 other peers. All posts and replies must be APA cited. You have different options on how you can respond — video, tweet, 100 words or less!
Adaptive Practice AP (17.5% of grade) *	AP is a part of Publisher. AP is an adaptive tool that will be unique for your learning needs. All APs are assigned as we move through the semester. You must complete a pretest for each AP chapter. After the pretest, you must continue to practice questions until you reach the assigned number with an 80% proficiency. An 80% proficiency or higher will earn you a 100. I drop the lowest (one) AP grade.
Tests 1–4 (25%)***	Tests 1-4 are a combination of multiple choice, matching, true false, fill-in-the-blank, and short answer. Each test is 50 questions. No tests are dropped. All tests are open notes (no book) and timed.
Bonus and Formative Evaluations	Bonus opportunities are a combination of critical- thinking short-answer questions (like what you may see on the test), crossword puzzles, and online problems. Formative Evaluations are surveys filled out by students to give feedback about the study tools and methods used in the class as well as the learning experience.
Midterm (25% of grade)	The midterm is 100 questions and is all multiple choice, matching, and true/false. Closed notes and books.
Final (25% of grade)	The final is 100 questions and is all multiple choice, matching, and true/false. Closed notes and books.

Add a link to your institution or organization's calendar.

Chapter MasteryPaths lead to the Adaptive Practices.

Students complete the assessment for the chapter.

The score on the assessment determines the path of work. Your path will open once the assessment is complete to reveal one or more activities that you must complete. These are not punitive and do not count toward a grade. However, you cannot be graded until you complete them.

- A score of 0–49 will offer assessments that fill in knowledge gaps and grow understanding of content.

- A score of 50–79 will have assessments that fill in gaps and help develop deeper understanding.

- A score of 80–100 will have the fewest assessments and will deepen the knowledge of the learner.

The capstone for all MasteryPaths is the Adaptive Practice. All paths end in adaptive practice. **Important:** Only the adaptive practice assignments count toward the final grade.

**In class: You can join my virtual classes no matter what type of modality you are enrolled in. Email me at xxx for the link. All classes are virtual at 11a.m. on Tuesday.

***Open Notes Tests: Link to https://collegeinfogeek.com/open-book-exam (a good article to help prepare and understand the idea of open notes). Open note tests are not easier, nor are they a free pass. The test is timed and there is not enough time to look up every answer. You need to organize your handwritten notes or my printed notes with Post-it tabs and headings to help you locate the material that you are familiar with but may need a little reminder.

- Identify key concepts or information.

- Summarize important information.

- Use clear headings.

- Organize notes by topic.

(You can download the following course schedule example at www.dummies.com/go/creatingcoursesfd.)

All assessments close at 8 a.m. on due date unless noted otherwise. How you will be assessed on your knowledge of the material.	What you will be doing during the week to learn the material. All material is in Canvas. Check Announcements for weekly Time Management Suggestions.	Objectives for each chapter, being able to 1) define, 2) explain and 3) discuss these objectives in context will help you perform at a passing level.
TEST 1 material: Chapters 1, 4, 5	Teacher Tools	Course Overview
August 15:	Review Syllabus and Orientation	Review course requirements, course tools, and Publisher
Meet to go over class expectations at 12:30 p.m. If you cannot make it, it will be recorded.	Watch ADAPTIVE PRACTICE How-To Video	Chapter1
	Listen to Online (YouTube) Lectures Chapters 1 & 4	Define Anatomy and Physiology
August 17: Complete Pre-Class Work	Review notes for Chapters 1 & 4	Describe the levels of structural organization
Start Here Module: No Access to Test 1 Notes until it is complete.	Publisher Tools	Outline major body cavities and their associated linings
Optional Introduction Discussion Board	Textbook Ch 1 & 4	List the components of a feedback loop and explain the function of each
August 22:	Animations: All Ch 1 and Intercellular Junctions Ch 4	Compare and contrast positive and negative feedback in terms of the relationship between stimulus and response
Adaptive Practice Chapter 1	Activities Ch 1 & 4: Concepts and Connections/Exercises	Recognize, describe, and provide specific examples to demonstrate how organ systems respond to maintain homeostasis
August 29:	Interactions: Regulation Ch 1	
Adaptive Practice Chapter 4	Flashcards Ch 1 & 4	

All assessments close at 8 a.m. on due date unless noted otherwise. How you will be assessed on your knowledge of the material.	What you will be doing during the week to learn the material. All material is in Canvas. Check Announcements for weekly Time Management Suggestions.	Objectives for each chapter, being able to 1) define, 2) explain and 3) discuss these objectives in context will help you perform at a passing level.
		Chapter 4
		List the four major tissue types
		Contrast the general features of the four major tissue types
		Classify the different types of epithelial and connective tissues based on distinguishing structural characteristics
		Recognize and describe locations in the body where each type of epithelial, connective, and muscular tissues can be found
		Recognize and describe the functions of each type of epithelial, connective, and muscular tissues in the human body and correlate function with structure for each tissue type
		Compare the roles of individual cell types and fiber types within connective tissue
		Recognize and describe locations in the body where nervous tissue can be found
		Recognize and describe the structure, location, and function of mucous, serous, cutaneous, and synovial membranes
		Distinguish between exocrine and endocrine glands, structurally and functionally
		Classify the different kinds of exocrine glands based on function

All assessments close at 8 a.m. on due date unless noted otherwise. How you will be assessed on your knowledge of the material.	What you will be doing during the week to learn the material. All material is in Canvas. Check Announcements for weekly Time Management Suggestions.	Objectives for each chapter, being able to 1) define, 2) explain and 3) discuss these objectives in context will help you perform at a passing level.
TEST 1 material: Chapters 1, 4, 5 **September 5** Adaptive Practice Chapter 5 **September 7:** Complete Resource Learning Activity Complete Discussion Board Test 1 Test 1 opens through Proctoring Tool Bonuses due for Test 1 **September 11:** Test 1 closes online at 11:59 p.m. Optional Test 1 Formative Evaluation **Test 1 is open notes. The notes can be printed or typed. Please review hints for success on open note tests.**	Teacher Tools Listen to Online (YouTube) Lectures Chapter 5 Review notes for Chapter 5 Publisher Tools Textbook Chapter 5 Activities: Concepts and Connections/Exercises Flashcards Testing: Publisher Tools Review ADAPTIVE PRACTICE questions Review Chapter Review and Resource Summary Review Chapter Critical Questions from the textbook	Chapter 5 Describe the tissue type making up the epidermis Describe the layers of the epidermis, indicating which are found in thin skin and which are found in thick skin Describe the basic process of keratinization of the epidermis Describe the functions of the epidermis Explain how each of the five layers, as well as each of the following cell types and substances, contributes to the functions of the epidermis: stem cells of stratum basale, keratinocytes, melanocytes, Langerhans cells, Merkel cells and discs, keratin, and lipids Describe the dermis and its layers, including the tissue types making up each dermal layer Describe the overall functions of the dermis Define the subcutaneous tissue, including the tissue types making up subcutaneous tissue Describe the three pigments most responsible for producing the various skin colors Describe the location and the function of each structure: eccrine and apocrine, sebaceous glands, nails, hair follicle and arrector pili muscle, and sensory receptors (Merkel (tactile) cell, Meissner's (touch) & Pacinian (lamellated) corpuscles, hair follicle receptor, and temperature receptors

Using open-shaped bullets or interactive bullets allows the students to check off the list of work, tools, or objectives to keep track of their progress.

When using bulleted lists, here are some best practices:

>> Keep the text short.

>> Write the bullets to start with the same type of term (verb, adverb, adjective).

>> Be consistent with punctuation.

>> Start with capital letters.

Accessibility and usability

Accessibility was introduced in Chapter 4 but is related to the technical side of creating material for user experience. Usability focuses on the experience of the user when engaging with the content. Material can be accessible and not useable and can be useable but not accessible.

Useability assesses the tasks users are expected to complete using your content. Can users easily complete those tasks? Are the users satisfied with the experience of completing those tasks? Often usability testing does not consider the person with a disability.

Remember to use clear, consistent layouts; use styles in structure headings; use proper alt text, contrasting color combinations, and captions; and transcribe videos and audio content. You want your course to be both accessible and pedagogically sound.

Accessibility checkers are a great place to start in the online courses you build. They can evaluate code, structure, and syntax. They cannot address clarity, relevance, or subjective matter. No matter what, human judgment is required.

Chapter **9**

Factors Influencing Curriculum Analysis

Curriculum design has an impact on students' learning. Analyzing the curriculum can help identify the strengths in the objectives and goals as well as the areas to continue improving. Curriculum provides structure and pre-established competencies, but an analysis allows you to determine other factors that support developing well-rounded citizens. A curriculum analysis can help determine what knowledge, skills, and attitudes should be prioritized.

Curriculum analysis is an ongoing process involving the development of curriculum goals; identifying necessary content, skills, and concepts; and reflecting on what is taught. Curriculum can be considered accredited or non-accredited depending on the institution or program.

What Is the Vision? Curriculum Analysis

A curriculum analysis is a road map for an educational program or a document that reports what the program is about, what you want students to learn, and how you're going to teach them. Think of it as a recipe for a successful education.

The curriculum analysis is like using the scientific method. It focuses on processes through these steps:

1. **Ask questions to explore things you don't know.**
2. **Gather and filter information to collect evidence to support the questions.**
3. **From the evidence, create general guidelines.**
4. **Develop tentative conclusions based on specific conditions.**

TIP

A curriculum analysis looks at how well an educational program is working. It helps you evaluate whether the curriculum design is helping students meet their goals and learn what they're supposed to.

How can you tell if a curriculum analysis is supporting the goals? First, evaluate the students to see whether they are meeting the set standards. This occurs before, during, and after teaching. Have the students achieved what you wanted them to? Teachers measure the data from student assessments to figure out how many students have met the goals. Second, the effectiveness of the teaching materials and the instructor's impact is evaluated. Evaluation of the curriculum helps to determine whether what is being presented, taught, and assessed should be continued, modified, or stopped. Usually, curriculum should constantly be modified to marry content and 21st-century skills.

REMEMBER

The goal of curriculum analysis is to ensure that the educational program is working as it should, and students are learning what they need to learn. The ultimate goal of a well-designed curriculum is student achievement. Since curriculum development drives the course design, development, and delivery, it should be a priority and time needs to be created or devoted to achieving a coherent curriculum.

Assessment, measurement, and evaluation

Assessment is important as it helps show if there is a change in a learner's performance. Measurement determines the level of achievement of a specific student learning objective. You measure student achievement using assessments. Measurements are usually numerical. Some objectives are difficult to measure as they focus on 21st-century soft skills. Evaluation reviews the information gathered through assessment and measurement. Evaluation allows you to determine if the curriculum needs to be altered to support meeting the goals. Is the curriculum relevant, usable, and appropriate? Evaluation is a qualitative factor.

Accreditation

Accreditation is a choice colleges and programs make to have their curriculum reviewed by experts from other institutions. This process includes self-assessment, visits from outside evaluators, feedback and an accreditation decision, and continuous improvement. The goal of accreditation is to meet the standards set by official accrediting agencies.

Accreditation plays a significant role in enhancing the quality of a program's education by offering a structured approach to developing, reviewing, and improving curriculum. It ensures that the design team is following the best practices and standards. Accreditation encourages a student-centered approach to teaching and learning, with a strong emphasis on outcomes, which drives better methods of assessing and evaluating student progress, helping to continuously measure and enhance learning and achievements. Additionally, it incentivizes the institution to continually innovate and improve the curriculum based on feedback and data.

There are numerous accrediting agencies, and many are programmatic-specific. Examples include the American Bar Association, Council of the Section of Legal Education and Admissions to the Bar, Associations of Schools and Colleges divided by regions of the United States, and the European Agency for Higher Education and Accreditation.

The accreditation process

The accreditation process differs depending on whether it is occurring in the United States or an outside country, but the essence is the same. Accreditors access the impact of facilities, equipment, supplies, faculty, curricula, administrative management, admission and student support, and success in the realm of student achievement based on the institution or program's mission.

Following is a dive into the generalized steps of the accreditation process:

>> **Self-evaluation:** The institution or program conducts an extensive self-evaluation to assess its strengths, weaknesses, and opportunities for improvement.

>> **External evaluation:** The institution or program undergoes an external evaluation by an independent accrediting organization to assess its compliance with established standards. The accrediting site interviews stakeholders and reviews reports.

>> **Accreditation decision:** The accrediting organization decides whether to grant accreditation based on the results of the self-evaluation and external evaluation.

>> **Continuous improvement:** Accredited institutions and programs are expected to engage in ongoing evaluation and improvement to maintain their accreditation status.

How curriculum is affected by accreditation

Accreditation includes criteria related to curriculum content, design, and evaluation. The accreditation standards require institutions and programs to demonstrate that their curriculum meets standards for quality and effectiveness. How can this be accomplished?

First, curriculum needs to be aligned to and highlight the student learning outcomes (SLOs) of the program. It needs to articulate the knowledge, skills, and abilities students are expected to gain through the program and training. The curriculum design needs to be rigorous and relevant to the career that is of focus. It should prepare participants for a successful career in the field. Evaluation and assessment must be at the forefront to ensure standards and continuous growth. A comprehensive evaluation and assessment plan must be present to measure SLOs. The dissemination of the curriculum must occur by qualified instructors who have experience and expertise.

REMEMBER

Accreditation provides benefits for institutions, programs, and students.

>> Accreditation provides quality assurance that curriculum meets standards for effectiveness.

>> Accreditation enhances the credibility of educational institutions and programs.

>> Accredited institutions and programs have broader access to private and public funding.

ARE NON-ACCREDITED COURSES AND PROGRAMS WORTHWHILE?

Is it worth your time to create a course if it isn't going to be involved in a program or institution that is accredited? The short answer is yes. As the author, I am not stating whether you should or should not work toward accreditation; I am providing alternate avenues to think about. In general, accredited programs can be very expensive. If you want to offer an avenue for learners to earn some skill sets and knowledge quickly and affordably or in a nontraditional field, non-accredited certifications can be valuable.

Availability

If one is starting from the beginning and needs remediation in both introductory courses and exposure to the field, non-accredited courses are a viable option. Learners who want to start their careers and learn as they go are ideal candidates. Non-accredited courses can allow individuals to test into higher levels or to qualify for credit courses. Employers may opt to fund enrollment for non-accredited courses as they usually cost less. The more affordable price is usually due to lower overhead of administrative budgets and less strict guidelines to maintain business.

The course you design can be a path for the learner to gain practical knowledge that can help define their goals and career.

REMEMBER

You can start designing non-accredited courses; deliver, evaluate, and evolve the courses; and work toward getting the course into an accrediting agency or program.

DO ALL EMPLOYERS ASK FOR ACCREDITED CERTIFICATIONS?

As we continue to move into the 21st century, the working landscape is shifting from degree-based to skill-based. Employees often value your knowledge more than your degree. Many employers look for soft skills such as

- Effective demonstrations of specific knowledge that can be obtained through learning and is not necessarily affected by the course being accredited or non-accredited.

- Experience is often granted for prior learning credit.

- Employers are often more concerned with what you have learned and what you can demonstrate than where you learn from.

Tip: Depending on your discipline interest and the type of course you develop, do research on how the course will benefit the learner and if the careers it supports require accredited certifications.

The Impact of Curriculum on Knowledge, Skills, and Attitudes

When designing the curriculum for your course, you are also creating a learning community. The community you foster will have embedded values and attitudes. This space is tricky because it must accommodate political, philosophical, and ideological differences. The space will also support formal and informal learning through interactions (student-student, student-teacher, student-content), teacher presence, course design, and presentation and delivery of content. Not all outcomes will be measured, and some will be anecdotal, but the knowledge is still valuable for ongoing modifications.

When creating the curriculum, the inclusion of knowledge, skills, and attitudes (KSA) should be present in the learning path for the students. The KSAs are known as the domains of learning. Knowledge is the cognitive domain, skills are the psychomotor domain, and attitude is the affective domain. All three domains incorporated into lessons lend to a well-rounded experience for the learner. By analyzing the type of learning domain or outcome that you want, you can determine which activities, assessments, and modality (face-to-face, online, hybrid, or HyFlex) are optimal based on the learning outcome. With access to technologies, it is possible and desirable to use multiple representational modes to increase the chance that students will attain higher levels of learning.

Knowledge (cognitive domain)

Learning helps develop an individual's attitude as well as encourage the acquisition of new skills. The cognitive domain aims to develop mental skills and the procurement of knowledge. The cognitive domain encompasses six categories: knowledge, comprehension, application, analysis, synthesis, and evaluation.

>> The **Knowledge** category includes the ability of the learner to recall data or information. Example of a knowledge action: Recite the definition of online learning. This occurs as one remembers facts without having to understand them.

>> The **Comprehension** category assesses the ability of the learner to understand the meaning of what is known. Example of a comprehension action: Explain the idea of online presence in your own words. The learner now understands and interprets the learned information.

>> **Application** shows a student's ability to use conceptual knowledge in a new situation. Example of an application action: Calculate the approximate time it

will take to complete each lesson in a 12-week course. In this situation, the individuals use learned material in an experience that is unknown.

>> The **Analysis** category intends to differentiate facts and opinions. Example of an analysis action: Troubleshoot a learning path for a content piece by using deduction. This requires one to break down information into its components.

>> The **Synthesis** category demonstrates the ability to integrate different concepts to help establish a new meaning. Example of a synthesis action: Write a course blueprint for your online course. Synthesis is the ability to put parts together.

>> **Evaluation** shows the ability to come up with conclusions about the importance of concepts. Example of an evaluation action: Explain how the course matrix will support your students' success. Consider it the ability to judge the value of material for a specific purpose.

Learning not only broadens your knowledge but also refines thinking and problem-solving skills, allowing you to apply what you've learned in the real world.

The higher the level of a concept, the more complex it is considered to be in terms of mental cognition. Higher levels are not more important than lower levels of cognitive domains, but higher levels cannot be achieved without the use of lower levels. Teachers should understand the hierarchy of cognitive domains to appreciate the processes and skills needed to learn and master more complicated content in disciplines. Development of learning should be scaffolded, and skills associated with lower levels (knowledge and comprehension) should be introduced in foundational courses and built upon as one moves through course sequences.

As the following sections move into the other two domains, it is necessary to incorporate cognitive domain components because the cognitive domain is the core domain for building curriculum.

COGNITIVE DOMAIN CREATION

ACTIVITY

Design a brief lesson that progressively forces students higher up cognitive levels from knowledge to evaluation.

Choose one topic and create six brief objectives that will guide the production of activities. What must a student know or be able to do to answer the questions relayed by the objectives?

(continued)

(continued)

Some helpful verbs to write the objectives of activities at the different cognitive levels include the following:

- **Knowledge:** Name, list, repeat
- **Comprehension:** Identify, locate, describe
- **Application:** Translate, demonstrate, illustrate
- **Analysis:** Calculate, compare, contrast
- **Synthesis:** Design, organize, prepare
- **Evaluation:** Estimate, value, appraise

Here are some examples:

- **Knowledge:** Identify five parts of the muscle cell.
- **Comprehension:** Describe the metabotropic cell signaling pathway.
- **Application:** If curae poison is ingested, predict what will happen to ligand receptors on a muscle cell membrane.
- **Analysis:** Interpret the EKG to make a diagnosis.
- **Synthesis:** Create a flow chart of the excitation-contraction coupling steps through relaxation.
- **Evaluation:** Estimate how the properties of muscles are translated into activation of muscle force.

Skills (psychomotor domain)

The psychomotor domain focuses on physical skills such as the development of hand-eye coordination and the use of motor skills. Psychomotor skills help people perform physical tasks in daily life and at work. This domain focuses on how individuals use the encoding of physical information with movement to express and interpret information and concepts. Often it focuses on autonomic responses or reflexes. The psychomotor domain contains seven categories:

>> **Perception** is applying sensory information to motor activity.

>> **Set** is the willingness to act.

>> **Guided response** occurs when one copies a displayed behavior or action.

- **Mechanism** is the action of converting learned responses into typical behaviors with skill and confidence.

- **Complex overt response** is the ability to adeptly perform complex patterns of actions.

- **Adaptation** modifies learned skills to meet special events.

- **Origination** is creating new movement patterns for a specific situation.

Table 9-1 lists actionable words to help learners home in on their skills.

TABLE 9-1   **Actionable Words to Incorporate into the Curriculum to Address the Psychomotor Domain**

Psychomotor Domain	Learning Activities
Set	Begins, demonstrates, displays, explains, shows, states
Guided response	Assembles, builds, imitates, traces
Mechanism	Constructs, fixes, sketches
Complex overt response	Builds, calibrates, measures, operates
Adaptation	Adapts, alters, modifies, revises
Origination	Arranges, formulates, modifies, re-designs

Attitudes (affective domain)

The affective domain of learning represents skills that foster appropriate emotional responses. Learning is typically associated with intellectual function, but it's not only cognitive. Individuals can learn attitudes, behaviors, and physical traits. Dealing with emotional things like feelings, values, motivations, and attitudes, the affective domain is divided into five sub-domains:

- **Receiving:** Being willing to listen and be aware to receive knowledge

- **Responding:** Actively participating and engaging to transfer knowledge

- **Valuing:** Finding value and worth in learning and being motivated to continue learning

- **Organization:** Integrating and comparing values; ordering them based on priorities

- **Characterization:** Having value that will control the outcome and behavior

This domain elicits feelings that range from simpler to more complex. These are constructed based on internalization, which is a process where one's affect (feeling) toward something goes from general awareness to a moment that the affect is guiding or controlling your actions. As one moves toward more complex feelings, one becomes more committed and internally motivated.

Table 9-2 presents ways to incorporate the affective domain hierarchy into the curriculum.

TABLE 9-2 **Activities to Incorporate into the Curriculum to Address the Affective Domain**

Affective Domain	Learning Activities
Receiving	Attend focus groups
	Listen to a presentation
	Read articles/papers/textbooks
	Watch a video
Responding	Actively participate in classroom activities
	Brainstorm ideas
	Join group discussions
	Present a session
	Engage in problem-solving activities
	Act out an activity
	Do written assignments (essays, reports, and so on)
Valuing	Debates
	Opinionated writing piece
	Reflection paper
	Self-report
Organization	Analyze and contrast (with charts, tables, Venn diagrams)
	Create a concept map (report formal or informal experiences and identify skills)
Characterization	Critical reflection
	Group projects

Putting it all together

Curriculum maps that are analytical, aspirational, and action-oriented help instructors and students see the big picture of how the curriculum will unfold as well as strengths and areas that need more development in the course's curriculum.

Curriculum mapping begins with the aspirational end in mind (in other words, the knowledge, skills, and attitudes a graduate of the program should have). The teacher needs to be able to articulate the knowledge, skills, and attitudes they want the students to practice in order to achieve the goals for the course and career. The curriculum map is a visual of the course that help students learn the competencies.

Since curriculum is defined in terms of what students must be able to think, do, and feel to achieve program goals, then courses in that curriculum will be designed around the activities that will help the learner process the knowledge and practice the skills they need. The curriculum offers the learner the opportunity to engage in making the knowledge their own so that it will be meaningful. Learner-centered active learning approaches make it easier to assess whether students are meeting and achieving the learning goals. When a curriculum is defined as what students should be able to do, then the content gives students the ability to practice the content. From the beginning, the students know what they are supposed to do as a result of their learning.

The major categories in each domain are found in Table 9-3.

TABLE 9-3   **Each Domain's Hierarchical Categories**

Cognitive Domain	Affective Domain	Psychomotor Domain
Thinking Skills	Attitudes, feelings, and values	Manipulative and motor skills
Knowledge	**Receiving**	**Reflex movements**
Remembering terms, facts, and details without necessarily understanding the concept	Being aware of something in the environment. Beginning to have favorable feelings toward it.	Involuntary response to stimulus (blinking)
Comprehension	**Responding**	**Basic movements**
Summarizing and describing main ideas in own words without necessarily relating it to anything	Showing belief in the values and becoming committed to or involved in them	Combination of reflex movements (walking)

(continued)

TABLE 9-3 *(continued)*

Application	Valuing	Perceptual abilities
Applying or transferring learning to own life or other situations	Showing definite commitment or involvement	Translation of stimuli received through the senses into appropriate movements (jumping rope)
Analysis	**Organizing**	**Physical abilities**
Analyzing, breaking material into parts, describing patterns and relationships	Integrating a new value into one's general values	Basic movements prerequisite to higher skills (weightlifting)
Synthesis	**Internalizing of values**	**Skilled movements**
Creating something new by combining ideas	Acting consistently with the new value. Becomes a way of life.	Complex movements embodying efficiency (dance)
Evaluation		**Nondiscursive communication**
Judging, expressing own opinion based on criteria		Ability to communicate through body movement (facial expressions, gestures)

REMEMBER

When using tables to present information to students, make sure to tag a header row and if necessary, a first column. Do not merge cells in a table as assistive technology is unable to review a table in appropriate reading order.

Chapter **10**

Upping Engagement with a Rolodex of Material

As an instructor, you often are responsible for developing content. And let's be honest, you have your work cut out for you. Between needs analysis, building learning objectives, and managing mandated internal policies and resources, you begin to wonder when you'll have time to create, tweak, and evolve the content required for the course.

Don't worry . . . help is on hand. By following the advice and activities provided in this chapter, you'll be able to produce exceptional content for your course. It starts, though, with getting organized!

TIP

Content development should begin by leveraging content you or others have previously created. Why?

» Already-created content doesn't need to be as heavily vetted as newly developed material.

» Existing content often needs just a little tweaking and refining to fit well with newly designed content.

>> The opportunities for reusing and repurposing existing course modules, text, images, and video are endless, once you know exactly what you currently hold in your repository.

WARNING

Keep in mind that checking and retroactively making already-created content accessible can take more time than starting from fresh.

Inventory: Don't Reinvent the Wheel

To begin determining what you have versus what you need, do an inventory of your materials — documents, slideshow presentations, graphics, videos, assessments, practice material, and other existing content. Having an inventory of the teaching assets enhances your effectiveness when it comes to development and deployment of content. Content development is often more time consuming for online courses because without face-to-face interactions, media that stimulates engagement is necessary. This requires the instructor to have knowledge and skill sets with using technologies.

As one completes an inventory, the scope of work can be determined by a few questions:

>> Are the materials fully developed already? Curating content already present means you are not starting from scratch.

>> Are the materials in digital format already? If not, what content must be revised for an online format?

>> Are the materials accessible and, if not, is there an alternative assignment to accommodate individuals?

>> Are the materials kept in a central repository and organized for ease of use?

Figure 10-1 shows an example curriculum inventory. You can find the template for this document at www.dummies.com/go/creatingcoursesfd.

Content Name	Type of Media	Created By	Date Created	Are they Accessible? If not, what needs to be done?	Copyrighted (can it be used freely)	Purpose	Are the materials complete	Description	Where is the material located?
Chapter 1 Introduction	LMS Page	XXX	Publisher edition X	Yes		Provide students with an overview of what they should be able to accomplish by the end of the activities and materials provided.	Yes	List of LOs for each content section of the chapter.	Chapter 1 Learning Module
Chapter 1 notes	Microsoft Word (passive) and an interactive note program (dynamic)	XXX	Month/ Year	Yes	CC BY-NC-SA 4.0*	Guide students with an outline of the content for the chapter.	Need to check terminology for changes in editions	Document containing outline of notes for chapter 1. Includes images, vocabulary terms, checkpoints.	Chapter 1 Learning Module
Chapter 1 interactive learning videos	WeVideo (dynamic)	XXX	Month/ Year	Yes		Just in time learning. Students go through short content lessons with built in checkpoints and activities.	Need to check terminology for changes in editions	Six videos between 5-12 minutes covering key concepts from chapter 1.	Chapter 1 Learning Module, WeVideo embedded links
Chapter 1 videos	YouTube Videos (Passive)	XXX	Month/ Year	Videos 2 and 4 need captioning cleaned up	CC BY-NC-SA 4.0*	Guide students with visual and aural aids to understand concepts in a deeper manner.	Need to check terminology for changes in editions	Six videos between 5-12 minutes covering key concepts from chapter 1.	Chapter 1 Learning Module, YouTube Playlist (link inserted)
Chapter 1 Differentiated Learning	LMS Feature	XXX	Month/ Year	Yes		Provide students with a pre-assignment to determine their baseline of knowledge. From the performance on the preflight, other assignments to help remediate and expose students will open up for students to complete.		Two to four short assignments will open up based on the students performance on the pre-assignment.	Chapter 1 Graded Module, Differentiated Learning Path

FIGURE 10-1:
Example of a curriculum inventory.

Item	Technology	Publisher/Source	Edition	Date	Accessible	Purpose	Grading Notes	Description	LMS Location
Chapter 1 Resource Exploration	LMS and Publisher X	Publisher X and XXX		Month/Year	Yes	Expose the student to plethora of tools that comes with their publisher material. Goal is to support their learning with different activities.		Choose one resource that is available from the publisher in the chapters on the exam and answer these questions. Pick a chapter from the upcoming exam. Which tool did you use - name of tool and example. A screenshot of the tool as you used it. In 100 words or less or a short video, state how you used it, what it helped you with, and if you would use this same type of tool again.	Chapter 1 Graded Module, Resource Explanation Assignment
Chapter 1 Discussion Board	LMS Discussion Board			Month/Year	Yes	Answer critical thinking questions in a concise manner.	Check rubric for grading requirements	Choose one discussion board question to answer in 100 words or less, a tweet, or a video blog.	Chapter 1 Graded Module, Discussion board
Chapter 1 Worksheets and Chapter 1 Animations	MP4 videos and Microsoft Word	Publisher X	Publisher edition X		Yes	Practice (no stakes) activity for students to check their understanding of fundamental concepts within the chapter.		Fill in the blank, matching, drawing, etc. worksheetsFive worksheets that align with publisher animations. The worksheets help students answer lower level comprehension of content to increase ability to define and explain fundamental concepts.	Chapter 1 Learning Module, practice page
Chapter 1 Practice Activities	Embedded into LMS	Publisher X	Publisher edition X		Yes	Practice (no stakes) activity for students to check their understanding of fundamental concepts within the chapter.		Multiple choice, auto graded, no-stakes assignments.	Chapter 1 Learning Module, practice page
Test 1 Bonus Kahoot	Kahoot! (free)	XXX		Month/Year	Yes			Interactive quiz game provided to students for a bonus.	Chapter 1 Graded Module, Kahoot! Link
Test 1 Bonus Crossword	Crossword Program (free)	XXX		Month/Year	Need to run through a PDF accessibility checker	Practice lower cognitive recall skills with definitions.		Fill in the blank crossword puzzle provided to students for a bonus.	Chapter 1 Graded Module, Crossword Assignment Link

*Attribution-NonCommercial-ShareAlike 4.0 International: This license requires that reusers give credit to the creator. It allows reusers to distribute, remix, adapt, and build upon the material in any medium or format, for noncommercial purposes only. If others modify or adapt the material, they must license the modified material under identical terms.

FIGURE 10-1: (continued)

Content presentation

The instructional content is often learners' first impression of the course and their experience. The ease of navigation allows the learner to focus on content and the learning experience. Consistency allows organization around courses events — a schedule, per se.

>> Use consistent voice in notes.

>> Have patterns in the content structure.

>> Make sure learning objectives align to each content piece presented.

Content patterns

Each time new content is presented in a learning module, make sure there is a pattern in the content structure. Chunk content and repeat the same presentation path for each course module. Start each module off with a description and rationale of how it is presented. Include the learning objectives that will be covered so they are conveniently located to where the students are in the course. Make sure to define what the deliverables are for this module, what resources will be provided to meet those deliverables, and how the user will be assessed on the deliverables.

REMEMBER

Content can be organized like this throughout each module:

>> Introduction

>> Learning Objectives

>> Learning Content (static)

>> Interactive lesson with multimedia (dynamic)

>> Activity (practice and low stakes)

>> Assessment (formative and summative)

Static Content Doesn't Have to Be Passive

Static content is unchanged material that looks the same to all users. The pages do not have elements like animations, buttons, or games. Dynamic content changes as the user interacts with the material. Passive learning is instructor led and relies on a one-way delivery of content through notes, lectures, PowerPoints, and so forth. Active learning is student led and occurs through interactive moments such as teaching others or storytelling. Regardless of whether content will be static or dynamic, passive, or active, the teacher will want to strategically organize and present content to leverage the learners' existing knowledge on a topic while exposing them to the new skills they are going to learn. Using prior knowledge as a foundation often helps the learner associate their current knowledge with new concepts.

To do this well, three steps can be considered when creating either static or dynamic content.

In step one the instructor creates an assignment that pulls out the prior knowledge a student has before introducing new material. Step two occurs when the new information is connected to the prior knowledge, and step three engages the learner in an activity that demonstrates their ability to connect the new information with the prior information.

Notes

Honestly, there is nothing passive about note-taking since it is an activity with material. Note-taking requires students to be attentive. Students need to code, arrange, and sort new information, which can lead to better connections between new content and previously learned content. However, in online classes, faculty often provide students with fully developed notes. While that is fine, and I do that as an instructor, consider providing a skeleton version of the notes. Skeleton notes are partial lecture notes that help students stay engaged while following an online lecture. The notes also provide students with cues and spaces to write facts, concepts, relationships, and questions. They provide students with guidance on how to organize content and see concept connections. This provides the students with an opportunity to engage in the learning process as if they were in the face-to-face course. If skeletal notes are not in your future, no big deal. Why? Because you can make the notes engaging by embedding practice and application into the format.

To create more interactive notes, consider these embedding activities:

>> Embed coloring activities to identify and associate content. Coloring allows students to understand a diagram associated with the content.

>> Associate topics with color. Notes written in one color can become a river of black, white, or blue. Color coding allows content to stick out and stimulates

creativity. You now associate a color with a concept, and this allows you to visualize and recall information. Color makes the notes vibrant and memorable.

>> Embed audio and video links after areas that are considered more complicated. The audio/video links should be brief and enhance the learning, instead of being redundant.

>> Provide a summary section at the end of a content piece to let your students organize their knowledge.

TIP

If you embed materials into notes, make sure that pictures are in line with text so screen readers can recognize them, make sure that alternative text is provided, and if you do use other elements, make sure that the reading order is properly set.

Death by PowerPoint

Many individuals would be happy to never see a PowerPoint or a Google slide again! Overly wordy slides, difficult images, reading directly from the information written on the slide, no contrast, and poorly designed slides are far from engaging. However, what if I told you these tools can become a learning mecca for students as they bring a story to life?

PowerPoint or any slide-based program can become an effective and engaging way to deliver content asynchronously.

Personally, I believe slide presentations are glorified overheads. Do you remember acetates? If not, my age was just revealed. Learners do better when they receive words and pictures combined. Use images that support your story and grab attention. If they can be real images, that is ideal. Consider a cartoon picture of a broken arm versus an X-ray of a broken arm — the latter is more interesting. Videos are a great addition as the video can explain complex issues in a concise manner. However, limit distracting GIFs, animations, and a lot of transitions. In a presentation, quizzes, polls, and games can be embedded to allow for interaction with the student at a convenient time for the student.

Student accessibility is important as many presentations — especially those with graphics, images, and sound — are not accessible to all users.

ACCESSIBILITY HINTS

Use premade layouts as they are designed to be accessible. If you alter the layout, do this in the Slide Master as this ensures the slides retain accessibility.

- Use a sans serif font.

- Use large fonts and avoid wordy slides.

- Colors should be limited. Think about the 60-30-10 rule. Sixty percent of the color should be considered the dominant color, 30 percent should be the secondary color, and 10 percent should be the accent. Often, the institution or business will have already chosen these colors.

- Colors must contrast for accessibility (4.5:1 for 14-point font and below and 3:1 for 16-font and above.) There are some exclusions; for example, 14-point bold font can have a 3:1 contrast ratio.

- All pictures need to have alternative text that describes the visual in detail.

- All videos and audios must be closed captioned.

- Reading order should be hand checked in the selection pane to ensure screen readers can navigate the slides properly.

- Each slide needs a title. This provides screen reader users a table of contents.

Worksheets

Many individuals view worksheets as primary school level work. Whether the worksheet is a printed document or an online activity, there is value in presenting them to students. Similar to skeleton notes, worksheets help guide students through the material assigned, whether it be a reading, a video, or a discussion prompt, and highlight important concepts. Worksheets are essentially step-by-step directions to move through the learning content assigned. The worksheets focus on lower-level cognitive skills but provide repetition, promote attention control, and increase working memory.

TIP

Converting static worksheets to an interactive worksheet in your learning management system can increase student activity, provide instant feedback (in most cases), provide key concept information in one spot, and reduce grading time for the instructor.

A student's engagement in a course can be seen through their actions and their understanding of the content in the learning process. But when students make an active decision to own their learning by applying what they are learning to different scenarios and evaluating their progress, they begin to move from actions (engagement) to accountability (owning). The goal to improve students' ability to take responsibility of their experiences and knowledge can be taught through different strategies (refer to Table 10-1).

TABLE 10-1 **Ways to Encourage Students to Take Active Ownership of Their Studying Approach**

Material and Strategies Presented from Instructor	Passive Approach	Suggestions to Give Students
PowerPoint slides	Print out and follow along with the online lectures.	Print out slides and skim prior to listening to the online lecture. Take notes in your own words. After the video is complete, state how the concepts fit together.
Lecture notes	Review the notes the instructor provides. Look through notes daily prior to the exam.	Summarize key points in your own words. As you write them, say them out loud. Use color for different concepts. The significance of each hue serves as a form of mental shorthand, giving context to the material you mark and helping you to process it more meaningfully and efficiently. Write questions you have in the margins.
Textbook	Read the textbook.	Read one paragraph and explain the material to yourself, summarize the key points, and ask questions. Move to the next paragraph and do the same thing. This time add how the two paragraphs are related. This process of review transfers the information you learned during the readings from your short-term to your long-term memory. It reinforces new concepts and increases confidence.
Studying	Highlight headings and topic sentences as you read.	Brief, intense study sessions tend to be more effective than trying to study for many hours at a time. Successive Studying: By spreading your studying over time, you're studying much more effectively. Spaced practice helps you learn the material because you have more time to process it and see connections. Tell a story to your peers. Do you understand the material well enough that you can teach it to someone else?
Assess	Take practice tests provided by the instructor.	To reinforce the new material you learned during class, and to make sure you thoroughly understand the subject matter being taught, take about 30–50 minutes to review your notes, read your textbook, work problems, make concept maps, or form a study group. As you study, ask yourself "how," "why," and "what if" questions. Don't forget repetition. Create your own study tools through freeware.

Active Content Creates Association

Active learning occurs when the student engages with course material and participates in the knowledge construction process. This approach places more responsibility on the learner to be accountable for their actions. The goal of active learning is to promote higher-order thinking by applying and transferring knowledge and using analysis, evaluation, and synthesis in problem-solving. This may be accomplished through discussion, problem-solving, muddiest points, minute papers, video demonstrations, creation of activities, games, and role playing.

Students may be resistant to active learning because they are used to passive learning and the instructor is relaying the information passively. You might hear statements like "The teacher is not teaching." Reluctance may be seen because the students are unsure of what they should be gaining from active learning. If you clearly explain why they are being asked to engage and highlight the benefits, that will help alleviate some concerns. Also, set clear expectations for each assignment and provide examples and a rubric when applicable.

WARNING

Do not overuse active learning materials as it will lose its impact to engage students, boost curiosity, and improve motivation. I use active learning for bonus, practice material, no-stakes interactive videos, and live class reviews.

TIP

Active learning techniques range in complexity from time commitment to intricacy in implementation. When thinking about a continuum of learning, here is a brief overview of some active learning methods (simple to more complex).

>> **Minute papers:** In X minutes, write in 100 words or less what you learned from the content covered in the content piece.

>> **Discussions:** Prompts are provided, and students watch a video, read a passage, or solve a problem, and discuss the topic in the discussion board.

>> **Think Pair Share:** Students work individually on an assignment and then pair up with an individual in their class to discuss the topic for a common solution.

>> **Peer review:** Students give constructive feedback to their peer's assignment.

>> **Use of technology to build or design:** Students use technology to create a deeper understanding of the content (presentations, videos, infographics).

>> **Interactive lecture:** Students complete work in a prerecorded lecture that supports their learning and competencies.

>> **Gamification:** Students participate in different games that were created by themselves or the instructor (Jeopardy, Crossword, Mindmap, Thinglink).

>> **Role playing:** Students act out a part to gain a deeper understanding of the concept.

>> **Inquiry-based learning:** Students investigate processes to discover concepts. A question guides the student to make observations and tie the activity back to the main concept.

Interactive experiences

Interactive experiences are a technique that has students participating in their learning process, often via the use of technology. Some examples are augmented reality (AR), virtual reality (VR), artificial intelligence (AI), and gamification. If time and finances permit, integrating technologies in student experience can help students practice, refine skills, and synthesize new experiences. (Refer to Tables 10-2 and 10-3.)

TABLE 10-2   **Brief Definition of Interactive Experiences**

Interactive Experience	Brief Definition
Augmented reality	AR uses a real world setting and the user controls their presence in the AR world. AR can be accessed by a smartphone.
Virtual reality	VR is completely virtual, and the users are controlled by the system. VR requires a headset and enhances a fictional reality.
Artificial intelligence	AI allows machines to learn from experiences and adjust to new inputs. AI mimics problem-solving and decision-making capabilities of the human mind.
Gamification	Gamification allows learners to apply game design in education settings by using objectives, competition, scoring, awards, role playing, and creativity.

AR applications in education can increase engagement and interactivity. AR can allow students to interact with lessons on their devices. AR brings a layer of interactive technology into your personal space — a layer on top of what you see. There are many free VR educational applications that are available for educators in disciplines such as language, mathematics, biology, art, history, geography, and more. VR is an experience that is created through a computer to generate a new environment. Users leave their real world and enter a new space. Glasses need to be purchased if VR is used, and the glasses vary in price. Many brands offer affordable versions.

Both AR and VR can create more immersive and participatory experiences. AR and VR increase access to information, contextualize learning, and provide a more inclusive experience. Students can visit historical sites, explore equipment, and go to outer space. These realities can become virtual laboratories and replace dissections, use of expensive microscopes (scanning electron), and dangerous chemical experiments.

AI tools offer increased efficiency and convenience. An AI tool is a software application that enables machines to perform tasks associated with human intelligence — think perception, reasoning, and decision-making. AI can generate text, images, and videos with instructions. Since the directions are given in a spoken language, not requiring coding, teachers can personalize their classes and the instruction can be tailored to meet the students' needs. A teacher can create a tutoring program by having each lesson end in a short quiz. The AI tutor can allow the student to move forward if they answer it correctly or AI can explain the concept using a different approach. This provides a personalized learning path for students and immediate feedback to meet them where they are.

Gamification is not new. It has been used in the business world with loyalty programs and enhances education by offering badges and achievement awards. Gamification can improve student curiosity. Introducing an innovative or creative way to learn helps the students relate to something they identify with. In addition, gamification increases attention span and can provide immediate feedback. These outputs help reinforce positive behaviors and encourage a continuation in learning.

TABLE 10-3

Examples of Interactive Learning Experiences

Interactive Experience	Examples of Tools and/or Software
Augmented reality	ARize
	Assemblr Studio
	Halo AR
Virtual reality	Oculus
	Meta Quest
	Google Cardboard
Artificial intelligence	ChatGPT (Open AI)
	Grammerly (checking grammar)
	Designs.ai (creative content design)
	Descript (audio and video editing tool)

Interactive Experience	Examples of Tools and/or Software
Gamification	Blooket
	Flippity
	Fun with Factile
	Kahoot!
	Quizlet

WARNING

While it's important to push boundaries, try new techniques, and deploy new tools, things can and will go wrong. Don't try to change everything or integrate five new tools at once. The course is still focused on the learning objectives and not learning endless new technologies.

Alternative assessments

Alternative assessments are known as authentic assessments. They provide a means of assessing valued skills that cannot be directly assessed with traditional tests. Alternative assessments provide a way to evaluate and measure a student's proficiency in an area instead of their level of knowledge. This approach provides a more realistic setting on student performance than traditional tests because it allows the learner to demonstrate their ability to execute actions. Alternative assessments focus on student performance and the quality of work performed and are easily aligned with learning outcomes.

User creation of content

When students are the content creators, it helps increase engagement and makes the content more relevant and authentic. When students have the opportunity to choose the way to express their knowledge, they will be accountable for their actions, their tenacity, and their skill proficiency. Self-directed learning allows students to use a variety of learning preferences, empowers ownership, and gives them the ability to inspire, create, and design their path.

In classes, I thrive on choice. Not just for the benefits it brings to the students, but let's be honest, I don't want to get bored either. I want to see variety, laugh, and enjoy what I am reading and grading. I want to be inspired by my students' creativity. I do not want to hinder their growth to fit them into a multiple-choice knowledge box.

I use alternative assessments in two major ways: discussion boards and bonuses.

DISCUSSION BOARDS

Discussion boards are usually the last assignment students want to participate in, and they are not a lot of fun to review as an instructor, either. There is a lack of passion and a view of "get it done to get it done." The students know the drill: post once, reply twice. Yet, discussion boards play an important role in learning, exploring, researching, writing, and being succinct. So I still include them as part of my teaching repository of assessments.

I give students the choice of how they create their content. I provide prompts that may be focused on a reading, a video, a case study, a current event, and so on, and then I provide them with multiple ways to answer the question(s). There are written directions as well as a rubric that guides and supports them with my expectations of their performance. Students can choose from the following:

- » A written post consisting of between 90 and 100 words
- » A brief video or audio of the answers; limited to 1.5 minutes
- » Two tweets at 180 characters or less for each tweet
- » A drawing with bullets to explain the processes

BONUSES

Who doesn't love bonuses? Many teachers do not, but students will move a mountain for a bonus. I don't believe in bonus work that is frivolous or easy. The bonus assignments I create are intended to create a relationship with the content but entail deep diving and engaging with the material. Most of the bonuses I use are creation based on the student side.

Here are some examples:

- » Create a Thinglink (freeware). Take a static picture and create a story with tags, videos, hyperlinks, images, facts, quiz questions, and so on. The student posts the Thinglink to a social thread so it can be viewed by all students for review and study.

- » Post to Padlet (freeware) and create a repository of pictures or links related to a specific topic. Students take pictures or post relevant links for the entire class to study.

- » Create a presentation that is an analogy of anatomical structures or histology (tissues) to everyday structures, often food. In the presentation, there will be five chosen anatomical structures with information on function, location, and specific structure description. The analogy requires the student to compare why the everyday picture and structures are analogous to the real structure or tissue. (See a direction example at `https://create.piktochart.com/output/a12490a134a6-histo-info`.)

REMEMBER

Not all companies that provide software and tools, whether they are paid or free, ensure their tools are accessible for all users. The responsibility is on the individual deploying it to ensure it is going to meet the needs of their users.

IDEAS FOR ALTERNATIVE ASSESSMENTS

Since students have diverse abilities, providing a variety of assessment types will help a broader range of individuals demonstrate their abilities and knowledge. Some ideas to help students apply their knowledge creatively or spurs them to think in a unique manner are below:

- Creating concept maps to represent how different ideas/concepts are intertwined and connected. These can be drawn with pen/paper and uploaded or use freeware such as coggle.it to make it interactive and digital.

- Creating an infographic using freeware such as Canva or Piktochart. An infographic is a visual representation of content including pictures, charts, icons, or diagrams that present alphanumeric information. Infographics require learners to analyze information and create a product explaining the concept. Students create a repository of resources to share as they are actively working with the content, increasing their engagement.

- Designing a treasure hunt using freeware such as Padlet or Jamboard. Learners create clues and post them on a digital wall. The users then use the clues and upload pictures to the clue to complete the tasks.

- Telling stories using pictures that turn interactive. Freeware such as Thinglink allows for immersive learning by interactive media with images, videos, simulations, and more.

- Developing study guides using games for competition. Students practice writing test questions and understanding Bloom's taxonomy and a deeper understanding of the content. There are multiple tools that allow hosting of individual or team play such as Kahoot!, Factile, Flippity, Quizlet, and Socratic.

Community building

Learning is an active, complex, and individual process shaped by many influences. Student learning can be influenced by the learning environment that helps put information being presented into context. When learners feel safe, seen, and included, they are more likely to participate. A lot of community building is based on instructor presence and opportunity for feedback on experiences. Instructor presence increases perceived learning and course satisfaction, and learners feel the course is more robust and fulfilling.

Flip, formally known as Flipgrid, is one of my favorite freeware tools to use, and it has amazing built-in accessibility features. Flip is a video discussion tool that allows individuals to have conversations without being in the same place at the same time.

Jamboard is a free online interactive whiteboard that can be used in both synchronous and asynchronous learning environments. Think outside the box using group drawings, fridge magnets, Things, and what is on your plate metaphors.

>> Group drawings occur when a prompt is given, and students have X amount of time to add to the Jamboard. An example prompt might be "What is your favorite food?" and each student draws, to their best ability, their favorite food.

>> Metaphors can be found online, but one example is "What is on your plate?" The picture has a plate, a fork, a knife, and a spoon. On the plate you list what you are working on, on the fork you post something you want to take a stab at, on the knife you post what is cutting into your time, and the spoon is what you may be fed up with.

>> Fridge magnets start with a prompt on the Jamboard and then each participant finishes the thought. Consider it a grown-up version of MadLibs.

>> Things is a silly game in which the facilitator posts a note that states things we want to do on vacation or things we like to watch on TV or things that the chapter made you feel. The only rule is that it has to start with "things." The community then responds, and it helps get people talking.

CONVERT A PASSIVE LESSON INTO AN ACTIVE LESSON

ACTIVITY

Create an activity using a tool you have access to or a tool that is considered freeware.

Traditional education has long been focused on didactive methods with a one-way flow of information. To help limit the amount of passive learning that may occur, adopting active strategies can help create a more engaging experience.

Remember: Freeware is free software, but most have a paid version that will unlock more features. I encourage you to use the free version for a bit to determine if you would find the paid version an effective use of finances.

This activity requires you to think outside the box. Ideas to think about:

- How can something you do in class be moved online?
- How can something that is solitary work be made into a community project or a collaborative project?
- How can you take a mundane task and create an engaging activity?
- How can something that requires memorization be made into a game?
- How can a traditional measurement of knowledge be converted into an alternative assessment?

Following are the steps to take to convert a lesson from passive to active or from face-to-face to online:

1. Identify the activity's learning objective.
2. Determine whether the student will choose their activity or the facilitator will give them choices.
3. Create a rubric with grading expectations for the user. Try to make the rubric generic enough to cover many alternative ideas but have enough details to provide ample guidance on student expectations.

IDEAS FOR ALTERNATIVE ASSESSMENTS

Need help coming up with alternative assessments? Maybe the following ideas can help:

- Creating concept maps to represent how different ideas/concepts are intertwined and connected. These can be drawn with pen/paper and uploaded or created using freeware such as `https://coggle.it` to make it interactive and digital.

- Creating an infographic using freeware such as Canva or Piktochart. An infographic is a visual representation of content including pictures, charts, icons, or diagrams that present alphanumeric information. Infographics require learners to analyze information and create a product explaining the concept. Students create a repository of resources to share as they are actively working with the content, thereby increasing their engagement.

- Designing a treasure hunt using freeware such as Padlet or Jamboard. Learners create clues and post them on a digital wall. The users then use the clues and upload pictures to the clues to complete the tasks.

- Telling stories using pictures that turn interactive. Freeware such as Thinglink allows for immersive learning by enabling interactive media with images, videos, simulations, and more.

- Developing study guides using games for competition. Students practice writing test questions and understanding Bloom's taxonomy and gain a deeper understanding of the content. There are multiple tools that allow hosting of individual or team play such as Kahoot!, Factile, Flippity, Quizlet, and Socratic.

4
Measuring Success

Chapter **11**

Assessing Learner Outcomes

As a teacher, a course designer, and a course creator, you want to be able to say that your course provides users with the skillsets they will need to be successful in their chosen field or in their new hobby. To do this, you must align the curriculum with learning objectives, provide develop assessments that improve student learning, and be able to measure results in a meaningful way. Analyzing the results will help plan curriculum revisions and course iterations as well as guide you in deciding where to allocate your resources.

Diagnostic: Where Are the Users?

Learners enroll in a class for a multitude of reasons, and when they enter the classroom, they have a broad range of pre-existing knowledge, skills, beliefs, and attitudes, which influence how they participate in the class and how they interpret and organize the information. Their ability to process and interpret information affects how they remember, understand, apply, analyze, evaluate, and create new knowledge. Knowledge, skills, and abilities (KSAs) are dependent on pre-existing information. Finding out what students know and can do when they come into the course or before a new topic is introduced can help instructors develop activities that build off student strengths and acknowledge and address areas that need work.

To improve the quality of the learning process and teaching experience, students' learning gaps must be identified during teaching, and remediation needs to be interjected. Gaps in knowledge affect not only the students' path to success but also the achievement of the learning process and the experience of the teaching process.

The phrase *educational diagnostic* refers to measuring and interpreting efforts that identify knowledge gaps and their underlying causes for individuals or classes.

Instructors can use assessment methods to answer these questions: "How do I know where the learner is?" "How do I know learning has taken place?" "What material can I modify, and how, to best support student learning?"

Information about student KSAs and learning can be assessed through both summative (direct) and formative (indirect) measures. Summative measures include homework, quizzes, exams, reports, essays, research projects, and presentations, to name a few. Examples of formative measures include pre-tests, self-assessments, course evaluations, student surveys, retention data, and interviews/focus groups. The next sections focus on formative assessments, which help teachers and students identify areas of strengths and weaknesses to target where efforts should be focused.

Pre-tests

Pre-tests are assessments that allow a teacher to determine the students' knowledge of the subject matter. In my opinion, they should be non-graded. If you want to keep them anonymous, you'll want to have the students create a personal identification number (PIN) to compare a post-test in the future. Pre-tests, when given prior to the first real lesson in the course, give the instructor a way to gauge student knowledge and prepare content that will appropriately challenge students while meeting course requirements. In addition, they help understand any gaps in the students' learning, allowing one to support student needs early in the course.

TIP

Post-tests are the same assessment, usually graded, that allow the instructor to measure how much knowledge the student acquired in the course. Being able to measure student improvement quantitatively is very helpful in reporting and funding. In addition, some post-tests may be aligned with industry-based credentials or certifications to validate the skills the students earned.

Pre-tests provide clear standards, so students know the expectations when beginning the course. Pre-tests can prime students for learning because they are more aware of the type of content they are expected to know at the conclusion of the course. In general, it may help them pay more attention during learning at each level because they have a preview of content and testing format. For instructors, the pre-tests show them where to focus the teaching for reviewing concepts, emphasizing new content, and when challenges may occur.

As we know, data drives decisions, and this is a wonderful way for instructors to gather information to improve instruction to benefit students. Pre-tests help tailor the material in the beginning, but the post-tests help determine the changes to improve students' ability to understand content in the future.

REMEMBER

Pre-tests verify what students need to learn; post-tests exhibit what they have learned.

The following is an example of a pre-test:

> First day of a higher-level course that required General Biology I as a prerequisite. The questions can be short answers, matching, multiple choice, or cloze types.
>
> What do you remember from General Biology I for Science Majors?

1. What is an ion?

2. What is a cation?

3. What is an anion?

4. What is the difference between a polar molecule and a nonpolar molecule?

5. Four dialysis tubes have a 7.1 percent salt solution. They are placed in beaker 1 (5.4 percent salt solution), beaker 2 (7.1 percent salt solution), beaker 3 (9.3 percent salt solution), and beaker 4 (11.2 percent salt solution). In which beaker will osmosis cause expansion of the dialysis bag?

   a. Beaker 1

   b. Beaker 2

   c. Beaker 3

   d. Beaker 4

Self-assessments

Gathering feedback on students' prior knowledge, skills, and abilities by asking questions to assess a topic is a type of self-assessment. Self-assessments give instructors an idea of the range of knowledge and experience the students believe they have, or the class attains. Self-assessment allows the learner to reflect and comment on their level of knowledge, skills, and abilities across a range of items.

These items can include topics that are considered prerequisite information for the course or the material that will be delivered in the course. Question feedback allows the instructor to adjust the course content appropriately or provide appropriate direction on how the students can access supplement materials to help fill in gaps of knowledge and information. In addition, the questions can help students address the course content and access prior experiences and knowledge that can be applied to the course.

TIP

Self-assessment promotes reflective practice and self-monitoring. This can increase self-directed learning because the student understands how to recognize their learning progress, which can increase motivation. Also, self-assessment can transfer to numerous areas of their life outside of academia, such as career and personal growth.

Advantages

Self-assessments are easy to create, and the data is easy to review. They can be done via a survey feature in the Learning Management System (LMS), and students can be awarded points for completion. In addition, if they are done anonymously, they are usually low anxiety for the learner.

Disadvantages

Self-assessments may not represent student KSAs because students may not be able to assess their SKAs accurately if they are not answering for right or wrong. This disadvantage can be counteracted by the questions being well written and tied to specific concepts and behaviors, so that students can reflect on a task, a term, a concept, or an experience.

WARNING

Be careful not to confuse self-assessments of their knowledge with self-assessment activities that help students judge their performance (exam wrappers as an example) and their peers (peer review with rubrics). These topics are addressed in Chapter 12.

The following are some examples of self-assessment questions for a statistics course:

1. How familiar are you with Analysis of Variance (ANOVA)?

   a. Have never heard of it

   b. Have heard of it but don't remember what it is

   c. Have some idea what it is, but not too clear

   d. I know what it is and could explain what it's for

   e. I know what it is and when to use it, and I could use it to analyze data.

2. Have you designed or built an Analysis of Similarities (ANOSIM)?

   a. I have neither designed nor built one

   b. I have designed one, but have never built one

   c. I have built one but have not designed one

   d. I have both designed and built an ANOSIM

3. How familiar are you with a t-test?

   a. Have never heard of it

   b. Have heard of it but don't remember what it is

   c. Have some idea what it is, but not too clear

   d. I know what it is and could explain what it's for

   e. I know what it is and when to use it, and I could use it to analyze data.

Interviews and focus groups

In online courses, interviews and the focus group options will most likely be a synchronous virtual session as students and faculty (or evaluators as necessary) are not always in a common location.

Interviews are one-on-one dialog with students to discuss their experience in their course. In these interviews, their motivation, perspectives about the course, and their KSAs from the course can be discussed. It should be a reflective and positive experience, and the interview structure should be informal.

Focus groups are small groups where the learners answer questions and discuss their experiences, motivations, and perspectives about a course. These allow students' behavior and thinking about how the course curriculum can be effective and support student learning. Often, it is good to do focus groups more than once during the course length, especially when a course and the content are new. When developing the questions, it is important they are open-ended to create extended answers rather than "yes" or "no" response. In follow-up, have probing questions ready to go in case the responses are too short or too general.

In both scenarios, you want to make sure you have written consent to record the conversations. Ensure you allot enough time for the participants to answer the questions but be flexible if there is some deviation from protocol due to opinions or examples being provided. At the end, give a summary and thank the participant or the group and remind them how the results are being used to support future learning. As always, ensure that their anonymity is of top importance. For the example that follows, interview questions can be written or oral. The questions can focus on specific information to gain from course content but can also focus on student reflection on their approach and experience.

List the departments or institution's mission statement and the main goals for the course.

A few key areas to ask questions can be:

1. Why they chose the course, to understand their decision-making

2. How they rate their own confidence in subject knowledge

3. How they rate their own confidence in assessments

4. What they enjoyed about the class format and what can be improved

5. What their next steps are with the discipline moving forward

If the exit interview needs to have a written component or be transferred to an asynchronous format, a Likert scale can be placed with strongly disagree, disagree, neutral, agree, strongly agree.

Goal 1: Learning the content of Course X

Through Course X, I have gained an appreciation for the content.

Goal 2: Critical Thinking

Through Course X, I have learned to analyze, construct arguments, define, and solve problems.

Goal 3: Communicating

Through Course X, I have learned to communicate my ideas, written and oral, in a clear, organized, compelling way.

Agreement forms

Agreement forms are learning agreements that promote student engagement, leadership, and accountability, and lay the foundation for a successful course experience. The agreement form can help students adhere to the best practices and goals as well as establish learning behaviors. The agreement form should be completed early in the course. Consider having it as a gateway assignment to open access to course content. The assignment does not have to be graded, but it is a required component of the course.

Learning agreements provide perspective and direction to students when looking at their course path and experience. Hopefully, it can help motivate them to become owners of their own learning.

Are there different approaches to learning agreements? YES. Is there a right or wrong way? NO.

TIP

Throw in a funny question or ask them to provide a "dad" joke. Learners want to know you're human, so humor, done tastefully, can carry a lot of positive vibes for the teacher. Here are a few examples:

>> When does Friday come before Thursday? In the dictionary.

>> What did the tree say when spring finally arrived? What a re-leaf.

Example Agreement Form 1

This agreement form is very specific to the course guidelines. The purpose of these types of agreements is to ensure the students understand their responsibilities based on course rules, guidelines, and instructor expectations.

These questions may be a graded or ungraded assignment, but it is graded for completion and accurateness.

The following answers may be in a discussion board format or essay/short answer questions.

1. What will be your backup plan if you lose internet at your house?

2. Please explain where you will go and how you will still complete the class work on time. (Loss of internet and computer technical issues are not valid reasons for not submitting work on time.)

3. What will be your backup plan if your computer breaks? Please explain how you will still complete the classwork on time. Public libraries do not allow you to download software that may be required for your work.

There is a laptop loan program whereby you can apply for a computer at XXX. (Loss of internet and computer technical issues are not valid reasons for not submitting work on time.)

Find the time management schedule and fill it out. You do not turn it in, but it will be extremely helpful in making you realize how busy you really are.

These questions are usually multiple choice, auto-graded questions.

1. How many tests, including the midterm and final, do you take this course?

   a. Below the question, the instructor should provide the distractors or answer choices.

2. Each testing block has graded assignments assigned. What are those assignments?

   a. Below the question, the instructor should provide the distractors or answer choices.

3. I understand that I am in a class that requires use of a computer, reliable internet, a webcam to take tests, and knowledge of how to download and upload files. I am aware that I have to download X (which is free) through the LMS.

    a. Yes (This should be chosen as the correct answer by the user.)

    b. No

4. I understand that this is an online course and thus requires basic knowledge of the use of office suite programs (like Microsoft Word — free for students), the internet, and email. This course is not designed for those with little or no computer experience.

    a. Yes (Should be chosen as the correct answer by the user.)

    b. No

5. How do you meet me, the facilitator, to discuss any concerns or for support?

    a. Below the question, the instructor should provide the distractors or answer choices.

6. What email is used to contact you throughout the course? (The instructor will choose the correct answer for the activity, prior to deploying it in the LMS.)

    a. Personal email

    b. Institution email

7. Are your grades averaged on the LMS throughout the course? (The instructor will choose the correct answer for the activity, prior to deploying it in the LMS.)

    a. Yes, it is always exact based on completed assignments.

    b. No, the gradebook only is used to post the grades.

8. I understand that my instructor will email me at the email address I registered with the school. This will be the address that my instructor will contact me with. I understand that it is my responsibility to check emails regularly and to make sure that they do not go to the junk/spam folder. Emails should have a professional tone.

- Include a salutation (Hello Professor, Mr. Ms., Dr.).
- No text messaging language (do not use R, U, thx, 2, and so on).
- Use complete sentences.
- Use proper spelling and grammar.
- Do not type in all CAPS (denotes yelling).
- Always sign your name and include the course.

a. Yes (This should be chosen as the correct answer by the user.)

b. No

9. I understand that assignments have specific due dates. Due dates can be found on the course calendar and the schedule. I am responsible for being aware of the due dates.

   a. Yes (Should be chosen as the correct answer by the user.)

   b. No

10. I agree to abide by the academic honor code, which includes but is not limited to refraining from cheating, collaborating, lying, and plagiarizing on all graded material.

    a. Yes (Should be chosen as the correct answer by the user.)

    b. No

Example Agreement Form 2

This agreement of understanding should be completed only after thoroughly reading the course syllabus and course introduction documents. Please initial each understanding statement. Sign, date & return this document to the instructor.

This assignment can be completed via auto-graded using initials or "Yes, I have read this statement." The last question can be an electronic signature and a date.

1. I understand that I must complete an X assignment to remain enrolled in the course or the instructor will drop me from the course. ____

2. I understand that the standards in this course are set and explained in the course assessment area and that I am responsible for monitoring my own schedule. ____

3. I understand that critical reading/writing are expected in this course. ____

4. I understand that I am responsible for completing assignments by the assigned due date. A suggested time management for each learning piece is provided. ____

5. I understand that no late work or emails with assignments are accepted in this course. ____

6. I understand the basis on which the final grade will be determined (listed in the grading rubric). ____

7. I understand that all exams will be administered on the dates listed on the schedule. ____

8. I understand the course grade is weighted so total points are not an accurate reflection of the grade I have earned. ____

Any other statements can be added and tailored to the course needs.

CREATE A SELF-ASSESSMENT

ACTIVITY

Create a self-assessment 3-2-1 exit ticket for your students to complete at the end of an online activity (an interactive video, a reading, a document presenting information). This activity can be done in an essay format, an assignment that students write out or fill in and then submit, or even through a discussion board or Flip video they share with their peers

3 things I learned in this X*	
2 things I found interesting in X*	
1 question I have about X* OR 1 area of X about which I am still confused*	

X = chapter, learning objective, video, and so forth

EVALUATING TESTS

ACTIVITY

Review your course's matrix that was addressed in Chapter 8. Look at your course objectives for each unit, chapter, or learning piece. A valid test occurs when there is unity between the test questions and the objectives of the course. As the instructor, you want to make sure the learning objectives and your assessments overlap.

- Start exams with easier questions to reduce anxiety.
- Have a variety of question types.
- Have a variety of easy, medium, and difficult questions.
- Questions should address one skill type at a time.

The test should be piloted, edited, and reviewed through iterations. Use your colleagues to help clear up language; ask past students or teaching assistants to review it for typos or formatting issues.

The learning objectives should offer a blueprint for test design to ensure that one is accurately evaluating student performance.

Example Learning Objective: Explain a ketogenic versus a glucogenic amino acid. Describe how a ketone body can be used as fuel.

Instructional Activity: Text reading on amino acid metabolism. Video review of amino acid metabolism. Case study on amino acid metabolism.

Assessment: Essay, multiple choice.

The following is an example of a multiple-choice question to address a learning outcome:

Question: Can a ketogenic amino acid be used to synthesize glucose?

Multiple choice questions can assess higher level cognitive skill. Students will make choices based on scenarios.

Answer: Include distractors that will address a reasoning that justifies the answer and a description about a ketogenic versus glucogenic amino acid.

Summative Assessments (Low and High Stakes)

Very similarly to indirect measures, direct measures should start with the course's goals. Knowing what you want the students to be able to do is helpful when creating assessment type and may affect how they will submit the assessment. In the future when students are expected to apply their KSAs, whether it be via collaborative work in a team, making a presentation, or completing computational problems, can the assignments mimic what they will be asked to do beyond the classroom?

TIP

Design assessments that require the learner to exhibit their thinking, not simply produce an answer.

Promoting thinking through action can also promote academic integrity.

REMEMBER

When writing assessments, being aware of the question's validity and reliability is important. Assessments can be versatile and assess many LOs to help determine whether students can organize and articulate cognitive levels of thinking and performing.

Is a test reliable? Reliability is the degree at which a test measures the LOs. The more questions that target a single LO, and the more results are replicable, the more reliability is enhanced.

Is the test valid? Validity is if the test measures the learning outcomes it implies to measure. Does the assessment accurately measure the skills it intends to measure?

Examinations

We have all rolled our eyes, shrugged our shoulders, and had the look of impending gloom and doom when it comes to taking exams in a course, especially when they are a large portion of your grade. But the fact is they are still around because they are a tried and true, efficient method of assessment to help the instructor determine whether your knowledge of the content satisfies the course level. Exams also help show how individuals react and perform in controlled conditions. Notice I did not state that exams are an effective method of assessment. Exams are only effective and can be a fair and impartial method of evaluation if they are well-designed. In general, exams give the students an opportunity to display their KSAs without bias or favoritism.

These types of assessment can be very valuable as they can provide feedback that may influence the course's future development and the student's future career path. For example, a student may change their career path if they do well in a new discipline or if they do poorly in classes that are critical to their profession's success. The feedback from exams helps a student understand whether they are prepared for higher level coursework in a discipline. Knowing one's strengths and weaknesses helps to make better informed decisions on a career path.

So, if exams are this helpful, why do a majority of people dislike them? Well, exams are often not well designed and focus more on rote memorization than demonstration of abilities. Testing brings extreme anxiety and stress, especially to those who have outside commitments and responsibilities. A student whose job is to go to school versus a student who is a caretaker, works, or has children often approach testing differently. The time available to commit to studying is different. This does not mean the students who have other responsibilities are less committed, but they may not be able to express their KSAs the same.

Since exams are not going anywhere, it is important to learn basic tips on designing and writing fair, challenging exams that gauge student learning accurately. Following are some strategies to help design exams and best practices.

Multiple choice questions

Multiple choice questions, or MCQ, are teachers go-to question type. A simple internet search will have hundreds of websites dedicated to best practices in designing MCQ and the need for guidance and support in well-designed questions.

Here are the basic rules for creating an MCQ:

>> Have a well-written stem (the question portion) that can be aligned with a learning objective that was taught or assigned.

>> Stems should not contain "fluff" or irrelevant content as it can decrease the reliability and validity of student performance.

>> Stems should be a full question and not a partial sentence when possible. Partial sentences often result in students just placing the answer options into the blank.

>> Create the correct answer first but randomize the order when being asked.

>> Create distractors, the incorrect answers.

>> All distractors should be plausible.

>> Try to avoid "all of the above" and "none of the above" because if one can identify more than one answer as correct or incorrect, regardless of their knowledge of the other alternatives, they can eliminate a distractor.

>> Distractors and the correct answer should all be similar in length, phrasing, vocabulary, and style.

Here are some examples of multiple-choice questions:

Relevant material.

Stem: Amanda has trouble making ATP in her cells. Which organelle is not functioning normally?

A. Mitochondria (correct answer)

B. Ribosomes (distractor)

C. Nucleolus (distractor)

D. Golgi Apparatus (distractor)

E. Lysosome (distractor)

Irrelevant Material: The sentence before the question is irrelevant to the question being asked.

Stem: Mitochondria have double membranes, their own genome, and divide independently of the cell in which they are located. What is the function of mitochondria?

A. To produce lipids (distractor)

B. To produce RNA (distractor)

C. To produce ATP (correct answer)

D. To produce glucose (distractor)

True/False questions

True/False, or T/F, questions are composed of a statement. They are popular because they are quick to create and quickly assess familiarity with course content. But there is a 50 percent chance of guessing the right answer. One way to address a student's guessing is to have them change a word or statement to correct the false statement. When writing T/F statements, avoid long and complex sentences and focus on one main idea.

Example:

False Statement: Mitochondria package lipids for the cell.

Correcting the statement can be done in multiple ways:

Option 1: Mitochondria create ATP for the cell.

Option 2: Smooth endoplasmic reticulum package lipids for the cell.

Matching questions

Matching questions are great for having students order information either logically or chronologically. When creating matching questions, it is important to give clear directions, keep the sets of homogeneous items aligned, and have more responses than premises.

Example:

Column 1 would be events such as names of wars.

Column 2 would be the year or specific span of years the war lasted plus three to five extra responses.

Here's an example matching question:

Column 1: War Name	Column 2: War Years
The Revolutionary War	1775–1783
War of 1812	1812–1815
Mexican-American War	1846–1848
American Civil War	1861–1865

Column 1: War Name	Column 2: War Years
Spanish-American War	1898
World War I	1914–1918
World War II	1939–1945
Korean War	1950–1953
	1943–1946
	1853–1855
	1878

WARNING

When using pictures in question types, alternative text (ALT TEXT) for accessibility must be used. Be thoughtful on how you describe the picture. You do not want to ask for the identity of an animal and have the ALT TEXT state Panda. Instead consider describing the animal: "black and white fur that resembles a bear with four paws, and eats bamboo." ALT TEXT is not just important for the visually impaired but also supports learners with internet and bandwidth issues. Not loading pictures allows a system to run faster.

Short answer and essay

Short answer questions can evaluate a student's problem-solving skills, knowledge of facts, and opinions of events. Usually, they can be answered in one to two words or short sentences. Essay test items are like short answer questions but are longer and more complex. Often, essay questions have multiple parts, so it is important for the grading scheme to be clearly defined to manage student expectations. Often a rubric is helpful in delineating the grading guidelines.

Both short answer questions and essays give the students an opportunity to explain their understanding and exhibit creativity. These options make it difficult for students to bluff, but they do show whether they know how to express their knowledge.

WARNING

Just as in writing MCQ, you do not want fluff. I like to help students understand the statement TBI: True But Irrelevant. Learn how to narrow down your thoughts and express the knowledge in a structured manner. It allows them to express higher levels of cognitive skills.

The following are tips for writing short answer and essay prompts:

>> Make sure enough time is allotted on the exam for the students to plan, write, and edit.

- » Communicate whether punctuation, grammar, and spelling are evaluated.

- » When possible, provide the rubric or grading scheme to the students prior to the exam.

Alternative forms of short answers and essays are computational questions that require students to perform calculations to solve for an answer. This helps students express their ability to apply techniques to solve questions.

Papers

When you teach higher-level educational classes, problem- or work-based learning classes, or classes that students can use for portfolios, essays can promote their ability to think critically and show higher-level cognitive skills.

A well-designed term paper assignment can provide meaningful learning and authentic assessment; writing clearly and organizing ideas about a topic are an important part of "real" work. When students write, they are practicing for future career situations such as memos, proposals, reports, or health histories.

Because papers can cause anxiety for students, are time consuming for students and teachers, and require multiple skill sets from researching to academic citations, grammar, structure, organization, and time management, scaffolding the assignments into management tasks helps everyone. Taking one step at a time is sequencing or scaffolding. These structured assignments with due dates give students a systematic way to support their course goals. Students may state that small assignments are busywork. Frame it differently: SELL the idea by sharing how it is organized differently to reduce stress, focus on LOs, allow early feedback, and is based on the rubrics. Grading guidelines may be pass or fail for early drafts or smaller sections.

Scaffolding allows you to be creative to focus on smaller steps. A single "doom and gloom" paper can be broken down into five, six, or ten smaller assignments.

Example:

Selection of topic: Working statement that can be freely written or a proposal or sales pitch.

Research: A literature review and a reference page of supportive research or material to support the body of the paper.

Evaluation of sources: A critical review of the material to build toward analysis, a business plan, or a lap report. Drawing concept maps to show relationships between the sources may be helpful for students.

Draft(s): Outlines first; then class length will determine the number of drafts. It is helpful during the outlines to ask for a short statement on what may still confuse them.

Revisions: Peer review, and facilitator or instructor review feedback helps guide smaller revisions.

TIP

If a student has a disability and writing or typing is difficult, consider having them complete an alternative assignment (more about this follows) and do an oral paper or make a video.

Project-based learning (PBL)

Project-based learning (PBL) is the process of addressing real-world conditions that often have no direct solution at the present time. PBL helps students learn how to ask the right questions rather than focusing on answers. Students gain important skill sets such as managing time, interpreting data, resolving issues, respecting different opinions, communicating results, and managing real-life scenarios. Students have various learning preferences and build their knowledge based on their backgrounds and experiences. Most students have a broader range of abilities than normal examinations will promote usage of. PBL can heighten the use of these abilities as students use many modalities in the process of researching and solving a problem and communicating the solutions.

The value of PBL over exams is long listed, but with all great tools, disadvantages accompany advantages.

Advantages:

>> Applying theories to solve real problems. The application of these ideas helps students increase retention of knowledge.

>> Students increase motivation for success due to the authentic experience of solving real problems. In addition, communication skills (oral, written) can increase employability.

>> Similar to papers, projects are usually scaffolded to allow feedback as they move through the timeline. The feedback, if it is timely, gives students a better connection to the subject and helps improve their performance outcome.

>> PBL allows students to express creativity and show their abilities in alternative manners.

>> PBL can provide the students practical value of the course and its relevance to industry careers.

>> Compared to the exams, student performance is often higher due to the time to complete the steps and the access to learning resources usually not allowed during exams.

Disadvantages:

>> Designing a PBL takes time and resources and can require teachers to develop multiple versions of the project to diminish like projects.

>> Developing feedback requires time and thought, which can be difficult in large classes or in small classes where teachers have multiple sections and other responsibilities.

REMEMBER

PBL can provide students with many skill sets that companies want to see. Many companies state they can teach them how to do their job, but they cannot teach these skills, which is often a huge portion and outcome piece of PBL:

>> Personal and social responsibility

>> Cross-cultural understanding

>> Planning, critical thinking, reasoning, and creativity

>> Strong communication skills, both for interpersonal and presentation needs

>> Visualizing and decision-making

>> Knowing how and when to use technology

Example:

Application development for a platform.

Students in the beginning of the course state their goals and how they may achieve these goals (vision).

Students submit a document that summarizes the project, its purpose, and the development process of the app.

The faculty compares the student's goals to their submission document. This step is to help the student stay on track and reformulate goals based on obstacles.

Students create a story board, and an elevator pitch is given (video synchronously or asynchronously).

Peers give feedback to the storyboard and video.

Create a final iteration based on feedback.

Create a short reflection on how the feedback and obstacles allowed them to evolve the project.

WARNING

While PBL is phenomenal, it may not fit in all disciplines. Do not force it, but do not dismiss it. Use your peers and your students to help determine whether it is a viable approach in the discipline and course level you are teaching.

ePortfolios (electronic portfolios)

An ePortfolio is a collection of work (evidence) in an electronic format that showcases learning over time. These platforms or products encourage students to take responsibility for their learning and showcase that learning with others. Students organize, document, and display significant learning experiences in the digital platform. ePortfolios produce a dynamic product that makes learning visible to the viewers. The ePortfolio can show growth over time, promote student's KSAs, and allow a product (artifacts) and a process (reflections) to be seen.

ePortfolios are popular in promotion packets and evaluation packets for faculty but can be used in the same manner for students in the arts, sciences, engineering, computing, technical, languages, marketing, communication, and business classes or degrees.

ePortfolios allow students to have a better sense of themselves as a student and monitor their growth and development over time. Good practices in using ePortfolios are to have the students reflect on an essay, a project, or an art piece and discuss the challenges, their growth, and the impact it has had in their academic or career path.

There are many ePortfolio tools to choose from. Some are free and some are subscription based.

ePortfolio sites include, but are not limited to, these options:

>> Google Sites is a free tool that allows one to create a website for an ePortfolio with templates, themes, and widgets.

>> WordPress is a free platform that allows one to create a blog or website with themes, plug-ins, and widgets. There are ads, and storage is limited.

>> Mahara is an open-source platform that allows one to create a portfolio, resume, and personal learning environment.

>> LinkedIn is a free and paid for professional platform that allows one to create a profile, resume, and network.

>> Journo Portfolio is a free and paid for platform with a live preview editor, built in analytics, prebuilt themes, and contact forms. It is mobile friendly.

>> Adobe Portfolio is free if one has a Creative Cloud membership.

>> Portfolium is a free academic portfolio network that allows one to connect with people and companies and also discover and apply for jobs.

TIP

ePortfolios can be used to curate all different types of information as detailed in the following lists.

Academic information:

>> Coursework samples

>> Writing samples

>> Certificates

>> Clubs and extracurricular activities

>> Demonstrations of specific skills, such as design, drawing, and so forth

>> Lab research and experiment results

>> Awards you've received

>> Academic honors

>> Internships

>> Transcripts

Professional information:

>> Resume

>> Sample reports, papers, and projects you worked on in a professional capacity

>> Letters of recommendation

>> Personality type assessments

>> Current or previous reviews from your manager

>> List of references

>> Processes or procedures created

>> Sample forms or templates created

>> Evidence of specific soft skills

>> Evidence of specific technical skills

>> Certificates of completion for professional development

>> Workshops, seminars, conferences attended

- >> Degrees
- >> Certifications
- >> Licenses

Personal information:

- >> Volunteer work
- >> Hobbies
- >> Nonprofit work
- >> Community service
- >> Professional affiliations
- >> Personal/professional mission statement
- >> Public speaking opportunities
- >> Social media content (as appropriate)

Evidence-based instructional practices (EBIPs)

Evidence-based instructional practices (EBIPs) are instructional practices that have been empirically demonstrated to support student learning. Research supports EBIPs improving comprehension of concepts, improving performance, improving course and program retention, and decreasing failure rates. EBIPs have been linked to how people learn so focusing on prior knowledge can influence current and future learning. How do you learn about students' prior knowledge? Indirect assessments, of course. Students' motivation can direct and sustain learning concepts. Helping students organize content and knowledge influences how they learn and how they apply what they have learned. Targeted feedback helps learning. Emotional, social, and intellectual factors influence learning and may not be areas a teacher can be in tune with.

There are many types of EBIPs. Many are not as easy to adjust for the online environment but are worthy of mentioning due to synchronous online classes still being a large part of the online community.

Small group work:

- **Think Pair Share:** Students are provided think time and then asked to discuss ideas with a peer partner and then share with their peers.

- **Process-Oriented Guided Inquiry Learning (POGIL):** A lecture-free instructional method that relies on processing skills and guiding inquiry. POGIL uses communication, problem-solving, and self-assessment. POGIL is based on exploration, concept development, and application of concepts to the situation at hand. Instructors are facilitators, not lecturers.

- **Cooperative learning:** Students work together on a common task and each member's contribution benefits the group.

- **Collaborative learning:** Although similar to cooperative learning, collaborative learning focuses on each student homing in on a single subset of the content and when they meet, they are responsible for teaching their peers in the group.

- **Flipped instruction:** Content is presented prior to class, and class is used for active learning via POGIL, cooperative or collaborative learning, or game-based activities, to name a few possibilities.

Formative assessments:

- **Concept maps:** Students create diagrams to demonstrate relationships between concepts.

- **Minute paper:** Students do an exit ticket to state what they understand versus what they still struggle with.

- **Just in Time Teaching (JiTT):** Web-based activities guide the instructor to tailor a remediation activity that helps with misunderstandings (great synchronous and asynchronous).

- **Exam wrappers:** Students are allowed to identify their strengths and weaknesses, reflect on their preparation for studying, and reflect on and recognize recurring patterns in their approach to preparation. These can be called homework wrappers, paper wrappers, a mid-semester wrapper, and so forth.

Here's an example of an exam wrapper for any discipline:

- Did the content on the exam reflect the topics covered in material presented?

- What percentage of studying occurred alone versus with peers?

- How much time was spent

- Reviewing notes/videos
- Working problems
- Reading the textbook
- Add distractors as appropriate

» Estimate how many points were lost due to
- Not understanding a concept
- Not being careful (careless mistakes)
- Not being able to figure out the proper approach
- Other reasons (please specify)

» Based on the information provided, what will you do differently in preparing for the next exam?

» What can the instructor do to help support your learning in the course?

The following is an example of a paper wrapper for a writing assignment:

» How much time was spent:
- Reading for the assignment
- Planning for the assignment (outlining, mapping)
- Writing
- Revising
- Asking for support

» What strategies were helpful in drafting the assignment?

» What are two things you might do differently in drafting the assignment?

» What can the faculty do to support your preparation of the assignment?

Scenario-based content:

» Problem-based learning: Students are presented with a problem, and they create a process to identify information needed to address the problem.

Alternative assessments

To end this chapter, I focus on alternative assessments, also known as authentic assessments. An alternative assessment allows students to apply what they are learning or have learned to a new situation. The assessments can require judgment, design, and effective and efficient use of skills to complete a task.

The reason this is the caboose of the chapter is because many of the formative assessments, PBLs, and EBIPs described alternative assessments already. Alternative assessments can require more time and effort to develop and grade, but the repository of material allows the instructor to create many opportunities for students in face-to-face, online, hybrid, and HyFlex classrooms.

When creating alternative assessments, outlining the process can eliminate confusion and establish project scope. Here's the general process for alternative assessments:

1. What is the challenge you want to introduce to students? Figure out the content and practice material to create or make available to support student learning. Often, creating a small blueprint or storyboard can help with assessment vision.

2. Designing the assessment requires clear outcomes and LOs. What is being assessed by knowledge checks and what is being assessed by performance?

3. What type of feedback will be required to help the students meet the LOs?

4. If multimedia is being used, determine whether students can access the technology and have the knowledge to navigate the technology.

Benefits of alternative assessments may include reinforced learning through immersive, interactive content. Increased cognitive thinking types occur with diverse instructional methods. Students are now responsible for their learning and their work. This approach reinforces the importance of organization, time management, and communication skills. Due to the higher cognitive engagement, students can navigate more complicated processes. Students can learn through their hiccups because when creating and using new technologies, trial and error occurs.

TIP

Most LMSs support alternative assessments because they can be integrated deeply or assigned as an assignment. These processes can lead to gradebook integration and feedback directly in the LMS. They can be graded as no stakes, complete/incomplete, bonus, low stakes, and high stakes. Peer reviewers can often be assigned, taking some of the grading time and effort from the instructor and giving students opportunities to evaluate constructively.

Here are some examples of alternative assessments that were not previously mentioned:

>> **Analogies:** Comparison of two things to provide explanation and clarification.

>> **Study guides through gamification:** Have students create games such as Jeopardy, a Kahoot!, a Quizlet, a crossword puzzle, and more to share with their peers or practice content organization and delivery. Rubrics can be created to properly help guide students on expectations.

>> **Treasure hunts:** Students create content treasure hunts using hints, pictures, scenarios, and case studies.

>> **Infographics:** These use design applications to explain a concept in a visual manner.

>> **Social media posts:** Great for marketing a single concept.

>> **Podcasts:** Audio narratives that capture analytical skills in a creative manner.

>> **Case studies:** Create or complete a case study. These require critical thinking and analyzing situations to present a potential solution.

Table 11-1 lists some discipline-aligned alternative assessments.

TABLE 11-1   **Discipline-Aligned Alternative Assessments**

Discipline	Alternative Assessment
Nursing	Case study provided and students create a care plan.
	Students write a case study and have peers create the care plan.
Computer science/ Information Technology	Troubleshoot code.
	Develop an application.
	Find the bug and propose a solution.
Sciences (chemistry/ biology/physics)	Provide students a diagram, table, or lab results and ask what happens in a specific situation.
Marketing	Provide the students with a short brief on a product and have them create an audio, video, or social media commercial.
Any discipline	Songs and short films.

WARNING

With any assignment, something can go wrong, but when relying on technology, the chance for something to go wrong increases with variables such as internet, device health, and student savviness with technology. Be prepared for tech issues and be adaptable.

TIP

If there is one takeaway for alternative assessments, it is that ownership of the assignment and development and creative freedom within the assignment increases student engagement and accountability.

TIP

If you want to deter violation of academic integrity when high-stakes assessments are given, consider these approaches:

>> Creating tests as open-book formats can alleviate student anxiety but still assess how students prepare and organize their knowledge of content.

>> Essays are open-ended questions and can assess critical thinking rather than information retention, such as applying what they have learned to a scenario. The students can analyze short texts or data to explain the relationship between ideas. In addition, have them annotate how they approached the problem.

>> If essays are not doable due to time constraints or a large number of learners, having the students explain why they chose a single multiple-choice answer may be more feasible.

>> When calculations are needed, require students to submit their work.

Chapter **12**

Evaluating your eCourse

E valuations are necessary in any class for comprehending what works for the students, for the instructor, and most importantly, what can be improved. There are many types of evaluations, and incorporating different types will help the instructor enhance their teaching, improve learning outcomes, improve retention rates, and allow students to increase accountability.

Formative Evaluations

Formative evaluations or *formative assessments* or *formative feedback* can be used to measure learning to provide feedback to the student or to the instructor. In the lens of the student, it helps them to see how well they are grasping the content and communicating their knowledge, skills, and abilities (KSAs), and improve their learning process. For a teacher it is essential to continue growing, improving, and evolving the course both through curriculum adaptation and course design, navigation, and delivery.

Formative assessments help determine if learning is occurring as the material is being taught. This instructional strategy is the day-to-day information that helps the teacher identify how to guide instruction and helps the learners develop their skills and their confidence.

Summative assessments are usually taken after students have completed the curriculum for the learning unit. They are considered formal and a sum of the student's progress and knowledge. They can be thought of as one way to check and measure the student's progress in formative assessments. Table 12-1 summarizes the differences between formative and summative assessments.

TABLE 12-1 **Difference Between Formative and Summative Assessments**

Difference Between Formative and Summative	Formative Assessment	Summative Assessment
Purpose	Improves learning via frequent checkpoints and feedback.	Measure of attainment after learning units.
Frequency	Occurs frequently throughout lessons.	Occurs after many lessons or units are covered.
Type of Assessment	These assessments are no-stakes or low-stakes.	These assessments are usually high-stakes.
Outcome	Improves learning because of frequency. Nonjudgmental and supportive feedback promote growth and reflection.	Outcome is a grade on a large unit or course to represent mastery of learning objectives. Assesses how and why a student achieves a grade.

In Chapter 10 and more so in Chapter 11, many diagnostic and summative assessments are discussed. All can be used as a formative assessment, but here I discuss some new ones and delve deeper into those in earlier chapters.

Muddiest points

The term "muddy," according to Merriam-Webster, is not clearly defined. Muddiest points are just that — areas in which students struggle to find clarity and understand the content. They are not confident in their ability to describe, explain, or engage in a discussion on the muddiest point. In general, using muddiest points as formative assessments gives the learner an opportunity to state what area of a lesson they are still confused about. For teachers, the preparation time is low, and the investment from students to complete the assessment is low. Reviewing the muddiest point responses and analyzing the content takes a bit longer but can be glanced over to gain an overall picture of student confusion with content.

In online classes, it is best to employ formative assessments, like a muddiest point, after shorter lesson chunks. Consider presenting the learning content of one to two LOs and then have the muddiest point available. Muddiest points can be given to the learner in a variety of ways.

The muddies point can be deployed directly in video platforms that allow interactions to be embedded. An assignment can be assigned to students after the content is presented. The instructor can decide to make it a required or an optional assignment; if required, the muddiest point assignment must be submitted before future content appears or is available in the Learning Management System (LMS). In addition, the assignment can be anonymous, and most LMSs support graded surveys (points for completion or check marks for completion). We know students are motivated by points as it puts value on their bandwidth, time, and ability, so many instructors may assign points to the assignment (low-stakes or bonus points) to encourage thorough participation.

As an instructor, when processing the assignment responses, skim through all responses looking for themes that can be assigned. Take these themes and group the responses so you can create a pile of similar muddy points and curate a one-of-a-kind response, video, or activity to help clarify the muddy point.

If the class is very large, take the responses and paste them in a word cloud. Many are freeware, and they can determine common keywords with high occurrences to decrease instructor response time.

TIP

These can be assigned to a class to be completed prior to the next chapter/unit/LO beginning. Have the students identify a concept they struggle to grasp or a gap in knowledge through an assessment such as a quiz, discussion board, or homework activity. Make sure the directions explain the types of answers you are looking for — words, fragments, sentences — and when they can expect feedback from you (timeliness and presence).

If the class is virtually synchronous, the next lecture or in-class activity can be tailored based on the current muddiest point information provided.

Here's an example: New chapter/unit/LO pre-work is due on a Tuesday at 8:00 a.m. The muddiest point of the previous chapter/unit/LO can be due on Monday at 8:00 a.m. This provides time to analyze and formulate responses to remediate any misunderstood or confusing information.

Surveys

Surveys are effective in teaching for multiple purposes. Surveys help instructors gather feedback on their teaching, feedback on student learning, and assess student knowledge. Most survey tools, whether in the LMS or a third-party tool, allow anonymous and non-anonymous options, as well as graded and non-graded options. Surveys are a quick, timely way to attain educational feedback.

There are many survey tools. Some survey makers are free like Google Forms, and some have free versions that one can choose to upgrade such as SurveyMonkey.

Here are some recommendations for creating surveys:

>> **Anonymity:** When creating survey questions, anonymity is often important, so place a statement in the survey reminding them it is anonymous if that's the case. However, instructors need to use their best judgment on whether surveys should be anonymous. What is the goal and how will the data be used?

>> **Question length:** When questions are short, the student is more likely to answer the questions and complete the survey.

>> **Iteration:** Keeping the questions iterative and asking learners to respond to different question types may help clarify areas of confusion.

>> **Question type:** Mix it up to make the survey less repetitive for students. By mixing question types (such as Likert scale, multiple choice, and open-ended questions), you give students different ways to share their experiences.

>> **Survey length:** The shorter the survey, the more likely students are to complete it. However, giving an approximate time to complete the survey and offering points may increase the completion rate.

The subsections that follow provide examples of survey questions.

Example course material questions

What tools did you use to study? (Select all that apply.) This is specific to your class and your publisher material.

>> Tool through publisher

>> Practice materials through publisher

>> Homework through publisher

>> Videos by publisher

>> Textbook

>> Interactive notes or notes

>> Lecture videos by instructor

- » Practice assignments by instructor
- » Crossword bonus
- » Discussion boards
- » Quizlets/Flippity/Kahoots!/Jeopardy/other freeware

How much time did you spend in preparation for the test (homework, studying, reading)?

- » 0–3 hours a week
- » 4–7 hours a week
- » 8–10 hours a week
- » 11–15 hours a week

What part of the class (notes, interactive notes, textbook, pre-class work, practice assignments, lectures, and so on) helped you the most? This question allows you to focus on course specific tools/publisher tools, and the like.

In terms of learning, what tool(s) do you believe is/are most beneficial to your success? Why?

Example teaching questions

In terms of assisting you in learning, what can I, as your professor, spend more time doing?

Do you have any suggestions or advice for other students on what helped you learn the material or what you wish you had done differently to learn the material?

What would you suggest to enhance the course?

What are your thoughts/experiences on your professor's lecture style?

Do you think you would have studied more if there were more or less homework and weekly activities during the course? Please explain.

Would you continue to use XXX Tool in future classes if the instructor did not make their use part of assignments? Please explain.

Make any comments about the course/professor you want to share.

Example technology questions

Do you find the LMS helpful?

>> No, I was too overwhelmed with the options.

>> Yes, I did use most of the tools.

>> Yes, I figured out what was best for me and used those tools.

Was course organization clear to you?

What suggestions would you give to improve course organization?

Has any of the technology used been a barrier to your learning in the course?

Just in time teaching

For this formative assessment, *just in time teaching* (JiTT) can be done in a synchronous online environment or in an asynchronous environment where feedback is created once a week based on learning content information. JiTT is a teaching and learning strategy comprised of two elements: activities that promote active learning and World Wide Web resources that are used to enhance learning. Students complete these individually, at their own pace, and submit them electronically. Following student submissions, instructors adjust and organize their lessons in response to feedback from the student submissions, "just-in-time" for the next lesson or before moving on to the next activity.

In an online synchronous environment, JiTT is relatively easy to implement. Interactive engagement, such as Jeopardy games or Kahoot! is a student's activity in the learning process. This requires the student to actively engage with the material, their peers, and their instructor and make meaning of the content being discussed. As students engage, they will receive formative feedback about approaching the content and increasing their understanding. The feedback is specific to the coursework areas that help students fill their knowledge gaps. There is reinforcement throughout the experience, which focuses on what they did well or need work on — hence, ongoing formative feedback. There is flexibility in how and when the students learn in preparation for the interactive engagement. This is through mastery learning and differentiated learning, which allows the instructor to vary the content to support their needs and give them due date choices.

TIP

JiTT is great to implement in a *Hybrid Flexible* (HyFlex) class modality, which is discussed in detail later in this chapter. Whether online synchronous, hybrid, HyFlex, or another modality is employed, quiz questions in polling tools or Jeopardy! type games are great because JiTT remediation can happen based on student response. In online asynchronous classes, adaptive practices, pre-assessment assignments, or any auto-graded assignment, the instructor can use assignment analytics to tailor material to support student learning and needs.

Don't take it personally: Student feedback

Asking for feedback is scary as course creation and delivery is a work of art. And while we all have a desire to evolve and improve, constructive feedback is important to improve instruction. The material we create is for the students and their opinion is important. But just because everyone has an opinion, it doesn't mean it's the right one for your vision or student needs.

Feedback opens us up to the good, the bad, and the ugly. Asking for feedback in the first place leads to two major outcomes — improved instruction and meeting the needs of the students.

You will receive many comments that praise your teaching, presence, course organization, course materials, and course design, but the one or two critical responses are the ones that are hard to forget. Do not let this rain on your parade upset you. It is totally understandable to be sensitive as this feedback is about your work and effort in developing the material. Use those critiques as a time of reflection to determine whether they can help improve the course, the delivery, or the content.

Your job is not to please everyone, but to make an equitable, accessible, and inclusive learning experience for all students.

TIP

Ask for feedback often to potentially use it to implement small changes in the course as you teach it. If the feedback suggests a course redesign and material creation, that obviously most likely won't happen mid-course, but if the changes are feasible, such as clearer guidance on assignments, then that should be incorporated immediately.

WARNING

How and when the feedback is requested may affect the responses. Choose deployment time frames and types of questions with intentionality.

Reflections Are Not Just a State of Mind

Reflection allows one to contemplate, analyze, and speculate on different aspects of teaching. For teachers, keeping a reflective journal is a practice that serves multiple needs. Personally, it allows you to share your thoughts, feelings, and ideas in a confidential way and to get them off your chest. Academically, it can help you keep a log of areas to improve based on feedback from students, instructor experiences through the process (what went well and what did not go smoothly), and an overall documentation of areas to consider improving and problem-solving ideas.

FAIL really just means First Attempt In Learning!

What does a reflective teaching journal look like?

Teaching journals are specific to the individual and the content may be a diary, a narrative, or a teaching log. How the experiences and observations are recorded personal in nature and captures successes and areas that need further exploration or modification. The teaching journal is an archive of personal experiences in the classroom and provides an opportunity to reflect critically on steps taken, or not taken, to deliver content. This opportunity can allow one to recognize biases and improve the environment to be more inclusive by focusing on diverse and equitable experiences.

Benefits or bogus: What do reflective journals offer?

If a teaching journal is practiced consistently, it can improve the overall teaching experience and student learning experience because it helps the instructor develop a knack for recognizing issues in delivery, content, organization, and assessment. The personal investment of time increases motivation to ensure the class is well designed for both teachers and students.

What can a reflective journal assist teachers with?

>> Recognizing that their job is more than teaching

>> Identifying gaps in the curriculum

>> Evaluating materials that were used

>> Acknowledging strengths and identifying weaknesses for points of improvement

>> Outlining successful activities and ones that need sharpening

>> Developing a personal teaching philosophy and learning philosophy

>> Aligning learning objectives more effectively and efficiently

>> Recognizing the importance of decision-making and seeing patterns in the process

>> Accessing student learning strategies

>> Noting new strategies that may be innovative and more engaging based on feedback and experiences

ACTIVITY

DIPPING YOUR TOE INTO REFLECTIVE JOURNALING

There are different approaches to begin journaling. Are you going to keep it digital or handwritten? If handwritten, purchasing office supplies is always a fun motivational start!

To begin, here are examples of ways to get started. Consider trying to complete one of these examples based on your experiences in the classroom or a foreshadow to what you want the experience to bring to the students.

Example 1: Write your responses these prompts:

- What I did or what I want to do.

- How I prepared.

- What I learned from the experience or What I want to reflect upon once the content unit is completed.

You can use the Rolfe Framework for Reflective Journaling as a guide:

Descriptive level of reflection: What is the problem/difficulty?

Building the reflection: So what does this tell me/teach me/mean about the content/course design/template/assessment?

Action based on reflection: What needs to be done to improve, maintain, or change what is being done or to resolve the experience?

Example 2: Answer these questions or questions of a similar nature.

- Record an experience/event and describe it.

- Reflect: Contemplate the experience. What are your initial thoughts and what are the positive and negative aspects?

- Conclusions:

  What can be concluded from this experience?

  What will you do differently or the same to support the experience?

TIP

When using reflective journaling, keep these tips in mind. Make the journal your own, be honest when writing, use your own words, be kind to yourself but still dig deep, and write as soon as possible after the experience. Be lenient with yourself as you begin and be open to trying different approaches that support you.

Reasons to keep a reflective journal

If the previous sections didn't convince you to keep a reflective journal, it is simply a mirror of your actions and an archive of your daily/weekly activity. Consider the following quantifiable list. If any of these catches your attention and inspires you to try journaling, then a success occurred.

>> **Talk to yourself (no, really):** A reflective journal is your inner dialogue and voice being recorded, on paper or digitally. Private thoughts and issues can be documented so reflection can occur at a later time without judgment or harsh criticism from oneself immediately during or after an incident.

>> **M&Ms:** Mapping and monitoring learners allows you to determine how they acquire knowledge as an individual or a class. Is the content best assessed as a reflection, low-stakes assignment, group interaction, or some other form of assessment?

>> **Decision fatigue:** Teachers make many decisions in a day — thousands or more when interacting with content, an LMS, student questions, and whatever else is thrown at them. Reflective journaling can help with more efficient and effective decision-making. Based on experiences over time, the teacher can predict what obstacles the students might face and create a path to increase successes with a specific method or approach. The more exposed the teacher is to student learning preferences, the less time and preparation they will need to adapt (in most cases). Spontaneous and flexible!

>> **Thinking about thinking:** *Metacognition,* awareness of your own thoughts and knowledge, aids to deepen reflection and increase self-regulation. As a teacher, you make an observation, ask questions, form a quick hypothesis, make a prediction, and test it out until you find a process that either helps the students or helps create a better learning path.

Example: The students didn't answer the question in the discussion board? An announcement (email) is sent out asking if they understood the question. Based on the replies such as the directions were not clear or the topic was confusing, you try out another approach — clearer directions or more supplements supporting the topic. Based on the students' responses, the process begins again.

WARNING

>> **Curiosity and connections:** Reflective journaling can improve critical thinking and observational skills if completed daily when the experience is still fresh. Yes, it is an ongoing process, but if not done frequently, the experiences will not be able to support your decisions in an unbiased manner.

Colleague, family, and friend support is great, but often if reflection occurs prior to discussing incidents or thoughts with them, your experience will not be swayed by opinions, comments, and suggestions. Always try and complete reflective journaling prior to discussing it with peers.

>> **Safe space:** Griping, venting, and elating can all be captured in reflective journaling. But this is your safe space and a way to dump the day but not lose the memories. It allows for a storage area to improve short- and long-term memory, declutter, and promote creativity. Less clutter = less stress = more space to review the problem and take steps toward a solution.

>> **Qualitative queue:** Reflective journaling is a written record through a day or an experience in the classroom. Recording personal assumptions and subjectivities allows you to look back and consciously acknowledge values, experiences, and rationales, and how they can change, continue, or be tweaked based on the analysis from the archived content.

TIP

What does reflective journaling allow you to gain? Self-reflection helps you experiment, so the teaching is relevant and impactful. You can better understand your learners by placing yourself in their situation and seeing it through their experiences. Most importantly, humility keeps you centered and honest about choices, mistakes, and personal growth. As a famous country artist once sang, "Stay humble and kind."

Thinking Ahead for Modality Shifts (Face-to-Face, Hybrid, Online, HyFlex)

Based on experiences of life, natural disasters, and the COVID-19 pandemic, recognizing the different course modalities and designing for all at one time can help you transition during times of needs. The four main modalities are face-to-face (on-campus or brick-and-mortar), hybrid (blended), HyFlex, and online. This does not completely encompass virtual synchronous, but it is also addressed. All teaching modalities have benefits and restrictions, but the overarching goals of any modality are to maintain rigor of content, engagement of students, support of students, and the ability to meet the students where they are at.

"Where students are at" is meant to be taken both geographically and educationally.

>> **Geographical location** should not limit opportunities for students to participate and experience a topic, a major, or a pastime they find interesting. Education can be designed for students living anywhere and can be delivered with finesse when done well.

>> **Educational experience** (or lack thereof) should not deter a student from participating in topics they are interested in. Of course, many courses have prerequisites and pathways designed to ensure success, but all courses, especially ones at the entry level or for personal interest and gain should offer alternative approaches to help all students learn. Inclusivity should provide all students equal access to opportunities in the learning environment.

TIP

Inclusive learning allows students with diverse backgrounds, ethnicities, races, socio-economic statuses, learning abilities, and experiences to create meaningful learning throughout a unit. Allowing students to express their knowledge, skills, and abilities in multiple ways helps create authentic learning experiences.

The most glaring obstacle, in my experience, has been having students accept, adapt, and immerse themselves in instructional methods different from their primary and secondary schooling experiences and even their higher education, professional learning, and personal learning experiences.

WARNING

No matter the modality, appropriate access to tools and content is the first component to student inclusion and success. Ensure that guidelines for accessibility are being acknowledged and implemented. Guidelines set by IDEA, the Americans with Disabilities Act, Section 504, and Individualized Education Plans (IEPs), to name a few, must be followed. For digital support, the Web Content Accessibilities Guidelines (WCAG) can help you meet requirements (refer to Chapter 4).

This section explores the main modalities, and online-type formats are the stars of the chapter. Throughout these next sections I reference building content once and deploying that material to many modalities. The goal is to work smarter, not harder. But be realistic that tweaks will be made through the iterative process of building, analyzing, implementing, evaluating, and evolving.

I'd be remiss not to mention face-to-face as most instructors begin in this modality, and this is usually the material and curriculum that is converted to digital format for online delivery.

Face-to-face (sage on the stage or guide on the side)

Face-to-face education is tried and true and provides familiarity as we have learned in this manner for hundreds of years. Sometimes this modality provides intimacy, and other times it may create isolation due to course size. When discussing face-to-face, brick-and-mortar or in-class lessons may also be referenced. For this section, face-to-face refers to material being presented and provided in the classroom, not a web-enhanced face-to-face modality. In face-to-face courses, instructors are often labeled as sage on the stage or guide on the side, but a combination of both is a better description of instructors. So what do these catchy sayings mean?

Sage on the stage is referencing the teacher-centered approach and didactive method, where the instructor uses one-way communication. This is considered the traditional approach. In this approach the instructor often imparts knowledge to the student to remember. In general, even if there are video lectures in an online course, this method does not lend itself to online modalities for teaching because students need to have the agency to inquire, think, act, and do.

Guide on the side focuses on a student-centered approach and is often compared to facilitating and coaching. This approach does not mean that teachers don't lecture, but it is usually focused on small pieces of content to help students build a foundation to explore the content further on their own or in an activity. In a sense this is constructivism because learners are building knowledge by discovering and transforming information they have been given or gathered. Table 12-2 compares the sage on the stage and guide on the side approaches.

TIP

Certain skills need to be practiced so students need direct involvement. Considering the learning objectives to be met guides approaches to deliver the content. Content can be told, but skills must be practiced. This statement may help determine the best practices on creating curriculum and delivering it.

Hybrid: Innovation begins

Hybrid courses have also been referred to as blended courses. Some researchers distinguish between the two terms, but in this book, they are used interchangeably.

TIP

Hybrid formats are designed to deliver content online for specific material and in-person for other activities.

TABLE 12-2   Sage on the Stage versus Guide on the Side

	Benefits	Hiccups
Sage on the Stage (teacher-centered)	Teacher being in control allows better pacing to cover content.	Teachers may not be story tellers, so students get bored.
	Students know where their attention should be focused.	Work is often siloed so opportunities to discover and share thoughts is minimal.
	Learning may be more focused due to organization.	Fewer opportunities for students to develop soft skills.
Guide on the Side (student-centered)	The learning experience is shared among students and the teacher.	Student interaction can be overwhelming and distracting due to noise.
	Soft skills such as communication and collaboration are developed.	Classroom management can become more difficult.
		Some students need more pointed guidance and may miss out on key content pieces.
	Students often are more engaged.	Students may have difficulty focusing due to the setting, and it doesn't take introverts into consideration.

Hybrid courses are a percentage of time in a designated location (on-campus, office building, or a virtual synchronous setting) and an online environment to support the live class time. Students attend a class in-person or virtually synchronous at a designated time and engage in other activities online on their own time. How the instructor chooses to deliver the information is a personal preference. Some instructors use the online environment for pre-work to prepare students for active learning in the classroom. Other instructors may lecture in-class over content the pre-work data designated as areas of struggle.

TIP

When designing the curriculum and determining what will be delivered synchronously versus asynchronously, consider which LOs are best supported by synchronous or asynchronous delivery.

Synchronous and asynchronous experiences occur in hybrid courses. See Table 12-3 for a summary of their advantages. The synchronous, or live session, whether virtually synchronous or in a physical classroom, can host discussions, polls, questions and answers, active learning, breakout rooms, gaming, and more. Variety is the spice of life, but make sure that the directions and expectations are clear and the focus is on taking advantage of having people present at the same time. Live classes offer unique opportunities for lively interaction, community building, and just in time teaching (JiTT). Asynchronous experiences are used to present material for exposure and learning. Keep this material chunked so it is smaller and more palatable; use a variety of tools to hold the student's attention as it helps the learner remain engaged.

TABLE 12-3   **Activity Types and Asynchronous and Synchronous Advantages**

Activity Type	Synchronous	Asynchronous
Lectures	Read body and facial cues for immediate feedback. Ability to answer questions and elaborate content. May digress and move to nice-to-know instead of need-to-know content.	Reusability Focuses on need-to-know and there are fewer distractions Concise, and pace control
Self-assessments	Monitor class as whole for remediation. Answer questions live.	Automated grading and feedback Many attempts Pools of questions
Activities	Monitor class as whole for guidance and remediation. Collaboration and communication with peers (soft skills).	Students choose an activity that meets their learning needs Increased opportunities for alternative assessments/activities Allows for reflection, evaluation, and growth during a single activity
Testing	Allows for monitoring high-stake assignments. Can reduce academic integrity violations.	Can use proctoring software and deliver exams with policies (for example, timed, one question at a time, no backtracking) to deter academic violations Frees up class period for valued learning opportunities or review of exam Allows for automated grading when appropriate and allows plagiarism detection to be used automatically
Technology	Allows students opportunities for live help as needed to learn about the technology or for the teacher to clarify technology issues.	Creates an opportunity for a more engaging experience Want to ensure the focus is on content and not technology use if the course is not technology-based content

When moving material from a face-to-face format online or designing material for online delivery, take the following into consideration:

>> What material makes students passive participants?

>> What material can be effectively and efficiently replicated to be delivered online? Use class time for interaction, engagement, active learning, collaboration, and communication. Good examples of what to move online include

- A quick lecture
- Notes (interactive or static)
- A quiz

» Can a case study or a journal article be introduced for in-class work or group work?

In hybrid courses, one begins to convert curriculum and activities to an online, digital format. This includes documents, video lectures, online assignments, quizzes, and activities. It begins the process of building a repository of material online instead of all of it being presented in hard copies for face-to-face delivery.

Online: Avoiding out of sight, out of mind

If you are fortunate to go through the modality style development of a face-to-face course, hybrid course, and then an online course, your experience should be relatively seamless as you have been working toward the online modality, whether you were aware or not. However, you can design for any modality type at any time.

Online courses are the most flexible to develop but require the most attention to detail. Online classes offer advantages of virtual learning — convenience to learn anytime, anywhere, and hopefully on any device. The courses are self-paced but usually have due dates. One drawback is it is more difficult, but not impossible, to create hands-on activities.

REMEMBER

Online learning considerations must be considered with accessibility of technology and tools — internet access and device access that is compatible with tools being taught. Rural areas and socioeconomic status can affect the student experience or access to successfully complete an online course.

With online course delivery, especially if you have been teaching face-to-face and hybrid course modalities, you can use the student feedback on course delivery, design, and navigation to help develop the course. Involving the learner, whether through past feedback or present feedback, helps to incorporate authentic activities with real-world relevance. Also, the learner recognizes that their input matters and can influence their experience, and it brings accountability to the experience.

Course mapping is important in all course modalities but especially in online courses because the teacher isn't always available. Course mapping is covered in detail in Chapters 7 and 8, but here's a brief recap:

» Use a table to list the LOs.

- List the activities for each LO.
- List the assignment and assessments for each LO.
- Dates and time management suggestions can be added for guidance.

When this is complete, an analysis can be done to help recognize whether there are missing LOs, missing important activities, or assessments that are not being addressed. This exercise helps determine nice-to-know versus need-to-know, which facilitates prioritizing the goals. Doing this early and often (before each course begins or once a year) allows you to make adjustments to assist students in reaching their goals.

WARNING

As you transition to hybrid and online formats, it is important to remember that all digital documents need to be accessible via assistive technology or alternative formats. This requires thoughtful development of videos, documents, presentations, assessments, and more. Remember to keep the Web Content Accessibility Guidelines 2.2 in mind (see Chapter 4). Quick tips for accessibility: Use a sans serif font and dark text on a light background, and incorporate a heading structure, transcripts for video, and descriptive transcripts for video.

HyFlex: Teaching of one class via three modalities

What do the following words have in common?

- Alphanumeric: Alphabetic and numeric
- Athleisure: Athletic and leisure clothing
- Botox: Botulism and toxin
- Webinar: Web and seminar

They are all portmanteaus, which is the result of smooshing two or more distinct parts of words together.

HyFlex — Hybrid and Flexible — is a portmanteau. HyFlex modality is relatively new, being introduced in the mid-2000s, but the modality did not become well-known until the pandemic in 2020. Hybrid flexible or HyFlex is a combination of a live-meeting option and an asynchronous option. Basically, it combines face-to-face, virtual synchronous, and asynchronous learning. The students are given flexibility regarding the mode and time of participation. The key is flexibility, but this can pose difficulties to instructors as they have to design for the flexibility.

In brief, HyFlex is the teaching of one class via three modalities. Students are allowed to choose participation paths and when they participate (within prescribed boundaries set forth by the instructor). The following are the three participation paths:

>> Face-to-face synchronous sessions in a classroom

>> Synchronous sessions via a webinar platform (Zoom, Teams, WebEx, Google Meets, or the like)

>> Fully asynchronous through the LMS

Students in theory can change the participation by meeting based on their needs, life circumstances, and comfort with content.

When designing a HyFlex course, there are four values or pillars on which the original creator, Beatty, 2007, based the modality: Learner Choice, Equivalency, Reusability, and Accessibility.

>> **Learner Choice** provides students with a meaningful mode of participation the student can choose daily, weekly, topically, or however the course meetings are designed.

>> **Equivalency** provides activities that meet the LO's goals in an equivalent manner regardless of how the student participates.

>> **Reusability** means that the curriculum developed can be used for all students regardless of participation mode.

>> **Accessibility** focuses on students having access to all modes because they have technology and internet access providing equitable experiences regardless of mode. It's important to note that accessibility to digital technology and content based on laws such as the Americans with Disabilities Act (ADA) and the Rehabilitation Act must be abided by to ensure all individuals can participate and use the materials, and there is no discrimination toward individuals with different abilities.

Learner choice

In my opinion, the HyFlex Learner Choice principle is the reason HyFlex works. HyFlex works because of life — in spite of natural disasters (flooding, fires, hurricanes, tornados, earthquakes); world pandemics; geographical limits; work, family, and caretaker responsibilities; or just a bad day. Without choice, there is no flexibility. Students are now accountable for making decisions based on their immediate needs. They are not penalized for their life events. The instructor must be amenable to providing choice, so the learner makes the decisions.

Equivalency

Equivalent learning is important because designing for an inferior experience is poor design and delivery. Students' instructional materials, activities, and assessments should challenge them to reflect on content, develop ideas, and contribute to a discussion (asynchronous or synchronously), and perform tasks regardless of the mode they chose to experience the content.

A way to do this is use a template to outline the development and delivery of a lesson (similar to the one in Chapter 7 but in more depth). A blank form is provided online at www.dummies.com/go/creatingecoursesfd.

Here is an example of a HyFlex course template for one section.

COURSE:	Human Anatomy and Physiology I Lecture
INSTRUCTOR:	XXX
LEARNING OBJECTIVE(S): Overview — specific LOs are listed in the LMS	Describe the skin and the accessory structures and their role in helping maintain homeostasis. Compare the cells and tissue types in the skin and the composition of the skin structures and layers.
CHAPTER:	4: The Integumentary System

PRE-WORK (BEFORE CLASS)

>> Students complete an online differentiated learning path. All students' capstone is an adaptive assignment.

>> Students review interactive notes, interactive videos, and can participate in practice assignments provided by the instructor and the publisher.

IN-CLASS	OUT-OF-CLASS Equivalent
Live Activity: Gaming: Kahoots!, Flippity, Family Feud, or another game. Games usually contain 20–25 questions.	Students receive a recording of the live class.
Time Limit: Classes are usually 75 minutes once a week.	Students receive notice that since they did not attend the live class, they need to complete the in-lieu-of-class assignment. This assignment is due X hours later. (In my personal classes it is 61 hours later (two and a half days).)

IN-CLASS	OUT-OF-CLASS Equivalent
Location of teacher: Meet in classroom with technology that supports virtual synchronous broadcasting and recording. Students may be present in the classroom or attending virtually. Recording is being transcribed live. A camera is filming instructor (if they want) and recording the computer screen.	Location: Online in the LMS: Students receive two to four options of assignments to complete, but they only need to complete one. Grading scale for in-lieu-of-class 75–100% = 100 points 60–74% = 75 points 20–59% = 50 points 1–19% = 25 points
The live in-class activity is based on differentiated learning (preclass work); the results from the pre-work guide the questions presented in the game. The game is tailored to meet student's needs.	Options: Worksheet Submit a drawing with specific guidelines. Rubric is provided. An interactive game that presents different questions presented from the one hosted in a live class.
The first question presented in the game is always a polling word cloud to request topics that were difficult.	At the end when the activity is submitted, students provide this information: No matter which option you complete, when you submit your in-lieu-of-class, please tell me in minutes how long this took. You can leave it in the comment box. 0–30 minutes 31–60 minutes 61–90 minutes 91–100 minutes 101–120 minutes
Game. Students receive credit for participation (not right versus wrong; top five students are awarded bonus points toward the in-class grade).	
Based on game question results, the instructor stops and gives short lectures over areas needing clarification (JiTT).	

>> In the course the homework is the pre-work.

>> There are ample practice assignments that are presented in different manners.

>> Students have a variety of bonus assignments ranging from crosswords to discussion boards, resource reviews, games, drawings, and more.

QUESTIONS/ISSUES

>> Creating equivalent assignments — consult with instructional designer.

>> At what point does the instructor discuss students attending if the online option is not supporting their needs?

>> How to offer student options and what that means in terms of incentivizing class participation, grading complexity, and so on.

So to recap, if a student chooses to attend a face-to-face session, they can still join online discussions during the same content piece or week. Online students can still review the face-to-face material (recording from session). Students are supported no matter their location, any time, and sometimes, at any pace. HyFlex courses are designed to provide a means by which most students will engage with content, peers, and the instructor regardless of participation modality.

Reusability

It is often stated that HyFlex is best approached by experienced teachers, but the principle of reuse can help manage the workload. Build an assignment or curriculum piece once and use it multiple times in multiple modalities. One should not build separate versions of the class. The content must be in the same area to support and serve the learning needs of all students. Building an online path may require a greater time investment if the online course is not already built. If it is, this process will not be as difficult as starting from an empty vessel. Most of the course is built if you have an online or hybrid course modality ready. Approximately 75–90 percent of the material is reused.

REMEMBER

You can find an efficient and effective way to build a HyFlex course. The more you develop digital tools and content, the more reuse you will get from course to course. Remember that instructional content is delivered via the LMS no matter the learning mode once it is class time (face-to-face, virtual synchronous, or asynchronous).

Here are a few examples of reusability

>> A Jeopardy template from PowerPoint, Flippity, or Jeopardy Labs (to name a few) can be made once, copied, and then new questions can be imported to provide a variation of the same game. PowerPoint and Flippity versions are freeware, and a template for PowerPoint Jeopardy is provided in the appendix.

>> Kahoot! allows one to combine questions from previously built games and to pull questions from a public repository (functionality depends on licenses).

>> Creating a common, succinct way to grade multiple assessments with one rubric is a great way to minimize workload, support students with consistency, and make it easier to remember course design.

TIP

No teacher would use this approach if it were truly two to three times the workload. It is a learning curve and there is some extra work on the front end, but once built, tweaks and changes are no more difficult than any other course one teaches.

Accessibility

Accessibility through alternative assessments is not helpful if students can't participate in class activities outside of face-to-face. If geographical constraints are present and technology is not available, then participating face-to-face, virtual synchronously or asynchronously is not an option.

Students need access to technologies, hardware and software, internet, and skill sets in order to enact their right to participate in alternative modes. This principle may be the hardest to meet as many of these aspects are financially out of your realm of control.

TIP

Provide students with any information on school, public libraries, regional, and state lending programs (laptop and hotspot loans). Reduced pricing on internet through affordable connectivity programs may be offered via internet providers as well as state and federal initiatives. List any free training and support offered to students to support their use of technology (LMS, software).

My favorite topic is digital accessibility, which is covered in depth in Chapter 4. However, it is important to be proactive and build with accessibility in mind from the beginning. Being reactive and fixing an issue after it is built is often not time efficient or possible. Consider Universal Design for Learning to help guide you on best practices to present content that is usable for most, if not all, students.

WARNING

While equity is a goal, there may always be some inequity in a course. Some students learn better hearing, doing, or watching but attend a modality that is not fully meeting their needs. Showing effort, flexibility, grace, and presence can help meet the student's needs on a one-on-one basis when issues arise.

What if class is a ghost town?

If no students show up to face-to-face or virtual synchronous classes, what do you do? Class goes on. Students' lack of presence doesn't mean they don't value the learning experience, but that the online modality is meeting their needs. HyFlex was designed to support the students' needs with flexibility, both in attendance and time. Helping students know what is being delivered in each class can help inform their decision on attendance. You can ask if they will attend to help plan accordingly, especially if you are only a few content pieces ahead of the students.

Many schools require faculty to still teach from the lecture room regardless of whether students attend face-to-face. This information is something to discuss with your team to determine best practices and policies for the institution.

Taking steps to move to HyFlex

Here's the process you should follow to move your course to HyFlex:

1. Consider how the normal environment and experience will change for the students and the instructor.

2. Ensure opportunities across modalities offer equivalent experiences.

3. Adjust activities and lessons for each modality.

4. Adjust assessments for each modality.

5. Reuse material created from previous course modalities when possible (face-to-face, hybrid, and online).

6. Create material that is accessible to all learners.

7. Practice with the technology and be able to perform basic troubleshooting for students.

WARNING

Based on experience, I believe that HyFlex is best for experienced instructors who have a larger repository of materials created over time. The material available to you can be altered to meet other delivery formats. Having taught more modalities provides already made content for face-to-face, hybrid, and online formats. This does not mean that it is not doable for a first-year instructor, but the time investment may be considered overwhelming or immense on the front end. One should have all delivery methods for units ready to go prior to the time of the class meeting.

STORY TIME: TEACHING HyFlex FOR THE FIRST TIME

My first time to teach HyFlex was in an accelerated semester that happened to be Spring 2020, COVID-19. Even though I have taught all modalities for almost 20 years, I still ran into hiccups and should-have-known-better and oh-no moments. I had my entire course ready no matter the modality the student chose to attend, but my directions were not clear, execution was not seamless, and the feedback of the students, my logs (reflection journal), and patience allowed me to tweak on the go, evolve for future courses, and invest more time in seeking outside training. Remember, anything that can go wrong will go wrong. How you react will determine if it can be turned into a success or slay or remain a crash-and-burn experience.

5

Sharing Your eCourse with the World

Chapter **13**

Marketing your eCourse to the Masses

As a teacher or facilitator of knowledge, marketing your course to increase enrollment and sales is often not on the to-do list. You built the course and designed it to show off insight only you can offer. It will sell itself, right? Unfortunately, probably not.

Before selling work that you may have created for a company or institution, check to see whether the contract you signed states that the creator maintains ownership of the materials created. Many materials used in a classroom are considered work for hire and are owned by the employer. Copyright law in the United States will allow the teacher/author to own the rights to the original work if it was created outside the scope of their employment.

Once you know your rights to intellectual property (IP), you can move forward with marketing your course, and essentially, yourself.

First, there is an abundance of free content on the internet to explore. But the time invested in finding information deemed worthwhile can be immense. When marketing your course, consider why someone would want it. All the information comes organized. And use the fallacy of purchase power. If someone pays money for it, then they will use it and actually be able to learn, grow, and give feedback.

Displaying Your Authority in the Field

Teachers have teaching experience. Sounds simple. Many teachers have a lot of experience, even when they are new, due to the dedicated schooling and training they receive in their major — think student teachers in an education program at a college. These individuals are earning career training in the art of teaching. In contrast, many teachers are hired for content mastery and being subject matter experts (SMEs). These teachers often have a steep learning curve to combine content knowledge with pedagogical knowledge. Yet, they often do have the opportunity to enroll and participate in teacher training programs via professional development. Regardless of how one is trained, informally or formally, many teachers have a natural ability to disseminate information to others.

Anyone looking to earn money by teaching and selling their courses usually enjoys sharing knowledge. In addition, the personality with traits of patience, passion, and a naturally positive attitude really helps improve the experience, and hence the reception, of the online course.

As you move toward the monetizing aspect of building online courses, knowing educational best practices is essential. In Chapter 8, a course matrix and blueprint were discussed. Putting together a course plan and knowing what the curriculum should be, how it should be presented, and ways to assess the process of learning is going to help the learners achieve their goals.

There are many other areas that are important to helping the course you want to sell be profitable and helpful to the learning community.

Is the content special?

When creating your course, make sure to do an in-depth search of what is already available for free on the internet. If there is a lot of information on the internet, is it easily navigable? Are the sites providing the content complementary or contradictory to each other? Is the material presented basic or advanced? These findings will help you determine whether the course you have in mind to design is worth it. If there is ample material on the beginner's level, then focusing on a more advanced level would be more beneficial for sales.

An important question to ask yourself is about your success in the field. Do you have awards, accolades, or sites supporting your knowledge and success in the field, helping learners trust that you are an SME? A positive online presence is helpful in marketing yourself and your course. Allowing influential individuals access to the course to experience and review it can help promote the product.

Selling yourself

Selling yourself as part of the product is important and makes the course unique because there is only one you. The biography, or bio, is usually the first place others look to find out about you. Being creative can compel potential customers to dive deeper and learn more about you and your products as a brand. Your backstory gives readers insight into your role in their life. Your personality can be seen and help readers connect with you.

Bios can follow a formula focusing on what are you known for, unique characteristics, interests, mission statement or call to action, and even themes and topics you focus on. You don't need to include everything, but be intentional about what you draw attention to. Specifying the problems you can solve is always a good idea.

If room permits, a skills or service checklist can be brief and informative. Personal bios should be on your website and your social media platforms.

TIP

Your website is where people go to access the course, but social media is how people find you. Follow people on social platforms in your niche and introduce yourself to them.

REMEMBER

Different platforms have different restrictions. Having a prewritten bio that is able to be reworked swiftly can help you stay on brand for different opportunities and platform uses. Following are space limitations for some popular social media sites:

>> **Instagram:** 150 characters

>> **Pinterest:** 500 characters

>> **Facebook:** 101 characters

>> **TikTok:** 80 characters

>> **X** (formerly Twitter): 160 characters

>> **LinkedIn:** 2,600 characters

WRITING A PERSONAL BIO

ACTIVITY

There are no right or wrong ways to write a personal bio, but for this activity, short examples are presented for you to fill out so you can begin crafting a catchy yet professional bio that will propel you to success.

Here are example ideas for sites with shorter character limitations:

- Use emojis and one or two words.
- Use fragments and hashtags as taglines.
- Include your mission statement, website link, social media accounts, and email.
- State why one should use your services, your website and social media links, and your email.

For longer bios, you may want to use one of the following combos of information:

- Name and title, expert in or niche area, accomplishments (personal/work), skills, contact information
- Name and title, proof of success, services offered, contact information
- Name and title, core values, pain points solved for users, contact information

Try to write two bios. One bio should follow a shortened character limit, but challenge yourself to use all characters. The second bio should be more informative, but keep it lighthearted, approachable, and professional. Humor is welcomed, but keep it clean.

Being device agnostic

When designing the course, the most valuable thing you can do is make your course device agnostic so learners can start their work on one device and continue on another. Device agnostic design promotes functionality across software and devices. A device agnostic application is compatible with Android, Apple iOS, and Microsoft Windows. Creating device agnostic content can be difficult, as it's hard to determine how content will appear on various screens. But designing for the consumer make it possible for users to access applications and websites on any device. In addition, agnostic development aids in responsive learning. Responsive learning adjusts the content to be optimized on any device — desktop, laptop, tablet, or mobile.

TIP

There are free websites that can allow one to preview how content will look on different devices. Responsinator can check responsiveness of websites via different device resolutions (www.responsinator.com).

The goal is to allow users to focus on learning. This means that the design should get out of the way. Having the flexibility to learn via alternative devices such as tablets and mobile devices is better for those in remote locations or for some with different abilities.

Providing Customer Service

As a creator, you should look at customer questions as opportunities, not burdens! Keeping in contact with your customers can assist your business and help your students benefit from your online course.

Learners are customers. Their opinions matter, and their questions and feedback are opportunities for growth. Since you are going to be viewing your course as a business, understanding customer service is a must.

Getting feedback: The good, the bad, and the ugly

Learners, also known as customers, chose your online course for a reason. Even though your content is complete and should fulfill the learners' needs, inevitably, there will be more questions and guidance will be needed. Their goals, their results, may occur regardless of your support, but it may be delayed until after course completion. This may lead to negative experiences and reviews. Being present (Chapter 6) helps learners feel supported and their experience perception is often more positive.

The learners' feedback is the best growth currency for the course. Online courses are not static, so implementing change is easier and usually instant. The beginning feedback is very valuable as it is insight to your customers' first impressions and experiences in the course (think navigation and intuitiveness).

Having meaningful interaction

Any interaction is a positive addition to an online course because it shows effort to create a community.

Being available and open to students' opinions of their experience increases student gratification, even if the solution is not exactly the requested outcome. The online feedback space can be anonymous via surveys, one-on-one via online meetings, or asynchronously social such as a discussion board. Asking questions shows initiative to the students and indicates that their thoughts and experiences are appreciated (see Chapter 12 for more on getting feedback).

Meeting the learners where they are

An important aspect of support is making it easy to contact you. You need a dedicated contact page with information such as email, phone, and office hours. In addition, providing timeliness for return time is important. If hundreds of learners are enrolled, the timeline for returning contact should be stated so their expectations are not unrealistic.

Take it a step further: Insert a contact form, an email link, or provide access to instant messaging, all of which can be set up within the Learning Management System (LMS). If you are open to communicating via social media, provide the links to your pages.

Offering Frequently Asked Questions (FAQ)

Often, learners don't read the information that is provided, but if it is conceivable, many questions can be avoided by providing as much information as possible, and this page should be public facing. In the FAQ, the course content can be described, what the learner should expect by purchasing the course, what the results should be, and any type of equipment or tools that may be needed. FAQs grow the more the course is taught. As you receive questions, especially if they are repetitive, it profiles two aspects: 1) This information is not clear in the directions, and 2) this would be a good FAQ.

Think about all possible questions and try to answer them clearly on the FAQ.

Never assume something is clear or understandable by future or potential learners.

TIP

Using Badging and Certifications

Digital badges represent the skills, knowledge, and abilities (SKAs) of learners. The digital badges represent accomplishments. With the metadata attached to them, it is an easy, affordable way to honor significant achievements such as completion, accreditation, and certifications. Badges need criteria (metadata), which determine how users receive the badge. This criterion is a guide for all receiving or viewing the badge; in addition, it gives context to employers to better understand student SKAs. Badges motivate individuals to complete actions because they represent accomplishments.

The standard metadata needs required information, and optional information can be included. Required information includes the badge name, description, and criteria. Optional infarction includes evidence, standards, and tags.

>> Badge Earner: Identified via email.

>> Badge Name: Skill or achievement.

>> Description: Details of achievement usually with completed tasks, assessments, and context.

>> Criteria: Tasks completed.

>> Issuer: Organization, company, institution, or private entity. When entities issuing the badge are verified, it improves credibility.

>> Evidence: Information that enhances the achievement.

Badges work well if used properly. There are three psychological reasons that badges can improve engagement and completion: 1) ownership, 2) social influence, and 3) fear of loss.

Ownership occurs because learners want to show they have reached key milestones in the course. These can be awarded for using specific skill sets or completing a challenging activity such as a project or high-stakes exam.

TIP

Make the badges special. Don't award them at the completion of every activity, especially those that are no-stakes or low-stakes.

Social proof is a powerful influencer. When learners earn badges for skillsets that are perceived as more difficult, they are proud to flaunt it. Whether this makes the student more knowledgeable or more senior in their path, it shows commitment. This may influence or give motivation to others to challenge themselves to earn the same badge.

Fear of loss plays off ownership. When a learner puts in a lot of time and effort, they are invested and more likely to stay involved in the community. People do not like walking away from what they have earned via hard work. This psychological phenomenon is tricky though. The learner needs to remain motivated and invested to stay and not overwhelmed or defeated to walk away.

There are many badging platforms, both paid and free, and there are many design tools that can be used to design badges. But when looking at badging programs, a lot of features and functionality need to be considered to make informed decisions on what is best for your needs. Table 13-1 provides some comparisons.

TABLE 13-1   Brief Comparison of Some Badging Companies

Badge Name	Free Option	Pricing ($: 0-99; $$:100+)	Templates	Social Media Sharing	Analytics	Integration in LMS
Open Badge Factory (www.openbadgefactory.com)	Yes	$	Yes	Not instantly	Yes	No
Credly (info.credly.com)	No	$$	Yes	Not instantly	Yes	Yes
Open Badges Openbadges.me	Yes	$-$$	Yes	Not instantly	Yes	Yes
Canva (www.canva.com)	Yes	$	Yes	Not instantly	Yes (not as robust)	No
Canvas Credentials (www.instructure.com/higher-education/products/canvas/canvas-credentials)	No	Contract based	Yes	Yes	Yes	Yes
Badgecraft (badgecraft.eu)	Yes	$$	Yes	Not instantly	Yes	Yes

Being Multilingual and Catering to a Global Audience

Inclusive design strategy takes into account how each learner can reach their full potential. Inclusivity depends on intersectionality, which focuses on individuals' identity and is made up of a multitude of factors such as age, class, race, language, disability, gender identity, and more. Inclusive design and intersectionality consider how people access material, how they participate in learning, and the diversity of their needs. One approach to inclusive design strategy can be done most effectively if the content is delivered in the learner's preferred language. Learning in one's native language reduces cognitive barriers and provides equal access to learning. Translating is not simple, and it is a design aspect of the course. This action needs to be planned from the beginning of the course design and development as it will affect production. Professional translators, SMEs, and designers need to be onboarded early to ensure a smooth collaboration and timeline deadlines.

Is translation enough? Usually, no. Having an expert to help with localization is a necessity. Localization allows the content of the course to be culturally and linguistically accurate. Often content, including imagery, will be altered.

In addition to translation and localization, design elements such as page and design layout may be changed to suit the language, especially if is a right-to-left language. The number of changes depends on the language and the type of content being addressed. Documents include video, audio, date formats, currency, measurement system, wordplay, and imagery, as well as supportive technology for games, learning activities, and assessments.

TIP

Translating courses is not only for international business models. Online courses translated into different languages encourage more learners from pockets of nationalities and backgrounds. But this can also boost brand recognition to an audience throughout the world.

WARNING

When translating course information, make sure to research law compliance within the area. Some countries require material presented in the country to be presented in multiple languages. In translated courses, the material should reflect the local rules and regulations.

Selling the Product

When creating a course, thinking long-term is of utmost importance. What will the course offer to the learner that will convince them to purchase your product instead of a competitor's. The following sections detail what you need to consider when creating, marking, and selling the course.

First, the course needs a landing page that has the FAQ, a contact area, and a compelling reason why this course will help one accomplish their goals.

Building a great landing page

The landing page for your course is the first point of sale. On this page, the FAQ should be available. Can you convince potential learners what the course is about verbally (video, aural, visually) in addition to or in lieu of offering a free trial? This page should provide catchy text, learner testimonials, and an introductory video to give a preview of the product — a sneak peek per se. Videos increase purchasing and this is an opportunity for the learner to meet the facilitator, creator, and SME, and to begin forming their relationship with you. A contact page with an embedding contact form, email address, or other contact methods should be easily seen.

The headlines should be what you are promising the learner. What solution are you providing to the problem they want to solve? The results should be reasonable and not something the course cannot deliver. Ensure the text provides an insight as to what you are selling, why it is different, and who it is for. The ideal customer should be defined (working parents, gamers, graphic designers, coders, and so on). What is the value proposition that makes your course unique, different, and a better fit for the consumer?

Giving free trials: Yay or nay

Free trials help convince cautious consumers that the course is the right fit. If you are hesitant to provide a free trial, a refund policy can be considered. Both are great marketing strategies and can have an impact on profit. The education being offered is not strictly tangible, so the learners need to be able to achieve the end goals promised via the course.

When giving a free trial, where you may not collect credit-card information, there is a chance that the desire to use your course for learning will be diminished. If it is too easy to access in terms of availability, then it is not as exclusive. A free minicourse that informs learners how the content and full course can help them is a great way to invite students to purchase the full course. A free mini-course is a teaser to entice the students your course serves an important purpose. They are not completing a section and paying to continue. They are paying to access the course as it brings a potential solution to their problems.

Discounts are an effective marketing tactic. This opportunity produces revenue more swiftly and provides an opportunity to gather feedback early on. The money earned can be placed into future marketing. Do not sleep on QR codes. These dynamic images can bring individuals to the free mini-course and landing page, making exposure and course registration fast and simple.

Offering a refund policy as a market tool

Refund policies should be lenient and clear. Less strict policies help avoid bad press and disputes. Placing a time limit on the refund is a simple, yet effective marketing strategy.

A common policy seen is a 30-day no-risk money-back guarantee. If for any reason the program is not a proper fit for your needs, alert us within 30 days and you will receive a 100 percent refund. This time frame allows ample time to investigate the course platform, course design, course content, and the learning communities. Include completion requirements for refund eligibility. Have a set percentage of course material that a user must complete, for example, a minimum of 50 percent completion, as this encourages the learner to gain knowledge, pick up new skill sets and complete the course prior to requesting a refund. The more invested users are, the more likely they will not complete the refund process. Just keep in mind there will always be individuals who will want a refund regardless of the experience.

WARNING

Choose the search engine optimization terms carefully to ensure you market to those you believe will represent the ideal customer profile.

Doing cost analysis

There are many purchasing methods, which are discussed in more detail in Chapter 14, but you need to decide whether you're selling a one-time purchase, a monthly/yearly subscription, or lifetime access with or without updates. These are not easy decisions as the customer's lifetime value needs to be analyzed to predict which direction may be best for your business. A customer's lifetime value is how much profit the company can generate through their relationship with the company and product.

When creating the pricing for the course, it is important to complete a cost analysis to understand expenses associated with creating and maintaining the course.

Following are questions to answer in a cost analysis to create and maintain the course. These answers can help you determine the proper business plan.

Initial creation cost:

>> What are the hours spent on creating and designing the course multiplied by your hourly rate?

>> How much does the website or LMS initial setup cost?

>> What are your initial hardware investments such as webcam, microphone, lighting?

>> What software programs were considered a business investment to develop the content?

>> How much will it cost to set up a payment processing service?

>> What is the investment in initial marketing costs?

>> Outsourced work needs to be budgeted for. Some potential areas of cost are

- Localization and translation

- Accessibility compliance in abidance with the law

- Professional video/audio production

Maintenance cost:

>> What is the number of hours you spent maintaining and updating content in the course multiplied by your hourly rate?

>> How much does the website or LMS hosting service cost?

>> What are the monthly/yearly software subscription costs?

>> How much will it cost to maintain the payment processing services?

>> What are the ongoing marketing costs?

>> Is there a budget for continued outsourced work?

Social presence is a present

Having a community for the learners in your courses is helpful. Regardless of your business model, the community should be ongoing and accessible for the learners. These communities can be on social media or specific social type platforms.

There are many social media platforms (Pinterest, TikTok, Discord, Threads, X (formerly Twitter), Reddit, Quora, and Snap Chat, to name a few), and you do not need to be on all of them. But your topic, your age, and your target audience can all help determine which platform(s) you want to leverage. Best strategy is to focus on one or two platforms and become really good at them. Work on a couple of strategies at once to meet the goals.

Other ways to market the courses are live webinars, guest blogging, and guest podcasts. Offering expert knowledge in your field to bloggers and podcasters can expand your visibility. In these settings (webinar, podcast, or blog), you have an opportunity to share some of the content for free. Cover one interesting topic to catch the learners' attention. From the webinar and podcast, create catchy short videos to post to social media.

Facebook

Facebook allows you to create a community that focuses on the content you are presenting. In Facebook, there are groups and pages.

Groups are communities that promote engagement among members. Administrators can delete and pin posts, but for the most part, everyone has an equal opportunity to see, visit, view, and participate.

Pages are usually focused on a product, and the administrator or owner controls what is being shared. A scheduler is built in, which creates a presence consistently through scheduling material weeks in advance.

Pages promote content, and groups engage a community.

TIP

LinkedIn

Like Facebook, a LinkedIn group is an opportunity to target professionals. This can lead to opportunities such as guest appearances on podcasts, webinars, blogs, and speaking engagements.

Instagram

Instagram allows for visual engagement with content. Being engaged on Instagram can grow the brand. This requires active liking, following, commenting, and producing and posting high-quality content.

YouTube

To generate buzz quickly, YouTube can be integral. If you are creating content that is meeting needs of the world, then YouTube's search engine can help you become recognized quickly. You can determine unmet needs by searching your keywords and seeing whether the results show irrelevant or relevant videos. If relevant, check out views and comments on the videos or playlists.

Branding

Social media branding is important, and for the most part, free. The brand identity should consist of the visual elements, colors, fonts, and appeal. The brand voice should align with your values and messaging but should be tailored to the platform.

Create a plan for content delivery on the social media platforms so the brand's message and voice are consistent. Remember that audience engagement is key, and this should provide opportunities to learn about the content and interact with you and the content. Inform, entertain, educate, and add value for the community.

WARNING

Accessibility for color contrast and graphic imagery compliance guidelines are different for logotypes, large text, and incidental imagery. Make sure to review the proper guidelines for your brand and logo to ensure you are reaching all potential customers in your advertising.

IN THIS CHAPTER

» Comparing different payment structures

» Dipping your toes in search engine optimization

» Dabbling in pricing and payment methods

Chapter **14**

Making Money from Your eCourse

aking money selling your online course will depend on many factors such as the demand for your course, the price you charge, marketing, and value perceived and received from users. As a course designer and deliverer, you determine the course value by conducting market research, planning the marketing strategies, building an online community, and setting the right price.

Online courses can bring some creators tens of thousands of dollars per month, but others may only earn a few hundred dollars. As an example, Rob Percival created "Complete Web Development Course" on Udemy, and with over half a million students, it is estimated he has made almost $3 million dollars.

Monetizing Your Work

Earning a paycheck is important. To ensure your livelihood is sustained, there are many models to consider when selling your online course. Is a membership model or a one-time payment model best for your goals? Each model has pros and cons. There are other factors to consider as well, such as type of content, target audience, and pricing.

The type of content being delivered plays a role in determining the proper payment path. If the content is dynamic and constantly evolving based on world events, the material will need ongoing updates, lending it to a subscription-based model. If the course content is self-contained and doesn't change often, a one-time purchase may be ideal.

The pricing of the course is dependent on the audience being targeted, and the quality and depth of the content. If the course provides foundational knowledge and targets beginners, and is considered entry level or basic, the price tag will not be as high. The price should reflect the expectations and value to the consumer. Learner ability should be addressed. Do you offer 24/7 support, live sessions, and community-based groups? If so, this may increase the price.

Pay as you go (one and done)

Paying for a course one time has advantages and disadvantages. Picture easy-to-handle transactions, low customer interaction, and potentially higher, yet static, revenue.

Setting up a one-time payment method is easier to manage and track. You can successfully make investments for future courses because the revenue is upfront. Revenue may be limited as the course is only profitable one time from a single customer, not on an ongoing basis. The price set can reflect the course value. Once customers have interacted with the product, it may be easier to upsell since they have a sense of the process and can trust the experience. Yet, the customer may lose motivation as the product is paid for, and the ongoing engagement may suffer, losing critical data points. Often the value of a one-time payment is seen as less than because there is no ongoing support or access to updated content.

TIP

For first time sellers, one-time payment options are easier to manage and market but the payment method you choose truly depends on your business goals.

Subscription based

Subscription-based learning is when the learner, also known as the customer, pays a monthly or yearly fee to access content from courses, certificates, tools, and other resources. There are numerous benefits of subscription-based learning including flexibility, access to vetted material, cost-effectiveness, ongoing learning, and community.

If the content created is vast and high quality, learners have access to a wider range of material for a monthly fee. Each item purchased individually is usually more expensive than bundling. This model produces revenue that is recurring. While it may not provide as much money upfront, it is more stable and easier to determine budgets. The number of tools provided to learners allows them to choose what they want for their current needs. The variety of material provided encourages more interaction among learners. They remain piqued by new additions of content and experiences. They are designing their education and learning to represent their interests and needs. This allows for continuous improvement of oneself through ongoing education — whether formal or informal.

If certifications or continuing education is important in a chosen career path, having the ability to choose high-quality resources to support learners' needs is of a high value or as some people state — priceless. Because of ongoing updates, customer service will be a larger investment, but it can improve customer retention. The experiences of customers via testimonial increases credibility, which affects retention of current learners and attraction of new ones.

Because there are options, different tiers of pricing can be presented with subscription-based plans — monthly, yearly, or lifelong service. Consider marketing strategies to attract new customers such as free mini-courses, refund policies, and creator presence in the market and consumers' view (Chapter 13 tells you more about this). Of course, there is a cancellation risk that affects funding and revenue, which drive ongoing marketing efforts and content development.

Examples of successful online learning platforms are Coursera, Udemy, and LinkedIn Learning:

>> **Coursera** (coursera.org) is a massive open online course (MOOC) platform with a repository of courses from top entities (industry and universities) around the world. Coursera offers individual course purchases and subscription-based options. Coursera courses are reviewed upon submission for consideration.

>> **LinkedIn Learning** (linkedin.com/learning/) is a professional development platform that offers courses on characteristics and skills that one wants to improve their impact and trajectory in their chosen career. LinkedIn Leaning offers subscription-based options, but LinkedIn vets all industry and professional experts that create the courses.

>> **Udemy** (udemy.com) is an online course platform for professional skills and hobbies. Anyone can publish a course on Udemy, but this allows all to share their expertise niche. Udemy courses range from affordable to more expensive for individual purchase, but a subscription can be purchased.

The types of subscription-based learning vary. The following sections review the different types — monthly and lifetime.

Monthly membership subscription

Monthly membership subscriptions are popular because the customer has access to legacy, new, and future content for a flat monthly fee. The monthly fee is a recurring income and most often offers customers an affordable price that doesn't seem too steep. Because you want to maintain the customer base you have, customer support must be more robust, new content needs to be continuously produced to maintain interest, and the initial investment will take longer to recover as the marketing budget must remain large to account for new market and loss of market.

TIP

Because customers often only stay for a few months with memberships — research states it is around three months — keeping customers longer profits your business. Discounts for longer subscriptions should be offered upfront and in case of cancellation, on-the-spot lifetime discount memberships can be automated. Ensure the community groups are active and engaging, and request feedback and testimonials to show the customer they are valued. Have a strong, consistent, marketing plan via email, social media, and platform/course news.

Lifetime access

As I mentioned, this pricing model is beginning to take off. And for good reason. It's simple to understand, you recoup your investment quicker, and you're not continually stressing about membership churn and the cost of acquiring new customers.

Lifetime access offers a sense of relief because money is paid upfront, and you have less stress about losing customers. You can create a budget more easily based on membership numbers. While the price is high because it's a one-time purchase and may thus scare customers away prior to investigating the produce, it also adds value to the product, especially in unique niches. Payment plans or installment plans can initially alleviate the sticker shock of a higher upfront price.

WARNING

Charging an ongoing subscription price doesn't translate to getting paid forever. Customers need reasons to stay with the subscription, which translates into continuous work, improvement, and additions of content.

TIP

To keep lifetime members feeling valued or that their investment was worthwhile, offer exclusive content or exclusive live events.

Using Search Engine Optimization (SEO) to Get Discovered

Search engine optimization (SEO) means that you optimize your website to rank better in search engines like Google. When people search for things related to your course, the website will be on the results page. This is dependent on how the website is set up, too. In the case of Google, Google uses a crawler called Googlebot to crawl the web looking for new or updated web pages. Googlebot discovers URLs and indexes them. Indexing is the process of taking the URL and storing the content description and URL. If your site is not on Google, it may have been missed for numerous reasons. There are documents in Google that can help you create the best search elements. There are ways to view your site on Google to understand how the crawler reads it, and there are help pages on promoting your site via Google. Many tools, paid and free (my favorite), are available to assist you in researching best keywords, such as Google Adwords.

WARNING

There are other search engines, and each search engine performs similarly with crawlers and SEO, but there are nuances for each one. Alternative search engines to Google are Bing, You.com, Yahoo, and DuckDuckGo. There are international search engines like Baidu, and specialized search engines that concentrate on specific topics.

TIP

Check if your URL is on Google by typing "Site:URL." If you see your site in the results, you are in the index.

When thinking about SEO, keep these ideas in mind: keywords, title, URL, meta descriptions, and header 1 text:

>> **Keywords:** Choose keywords and phrases that are relevant to your course and what you want students to learn or do in the course and as a result of the course. Have a spreadsheet but try and focus on a single keyword and any semantically relevant words (creative writing, writing course online, online creative writing course, creative online writing course, writing creatively online, and so forth).

>> **Titles:** Use keywords in titles of file names and page titles.

>> **URL:** Use the keyword in the URL name. The slug portion of the URL is a great place to put a keyword. Here's an example of URL reading, or how a crawler

"reads" the URL `https://blog.website.com/blog/creative-writing-online-course`.

- **https://** is the scheme, and this states what protocols to use when accessing a page.

- *Blog* is the subdomain, which can be like a store in a mall.

- **Website** is the second-level domain, which is the website name.

- **.com** is the top-level domain, which states the type of entity the organization is registered as.

- **Creative-writing-online-course** is the slug or subdirectory, which is the keyword the crawler will identify.

>> **Meta descriptions:** These are HTML attributes that crawlers may use to find information about the course.

>> **Headings:** Keywords in headings are helpful as search engines pay attention to headers. Place the keywords strategically, in header 1 especially, but also consider headers 2, 3, and so on.

When growing the business, analytics are important to improve decision-making. Keep track of keywords and use webmaster tools to search traffic and queries to determine whether the keywords being used are increasing visitor traffic.

Since SEO is made up of so many elements, understanding how to properly choose the keywords and phrases to connect your potential customers with your product. In addition, the content posted is essential as it is your angle into the users' life. Content is varied from the web page you may build, videos, blogs, social media, infographics, and pictures. Having a great SEO strategy can increase your product's awareness enabling use to grow.

As you continue to learn about SEO optimization and its benefits, it is important to plan ahead and understand terminology and types of changes (onsite and off-site changes) that may need to be made to the website and the course. On-site changes and tweaks are made on the website and are considered technical. Off-site changes are ones that do not occur on the website. These include the brand, social media, and marketing.

TIP

Install analytics to determine traffic and monitor SEO progress. The data will help make decisions about marketing and targeting audiences.

SEO EXERCISE

ACTIVITY

In this activity, you will use your course idea or a potential idea and begin to think about your SEO strategy.

Questions to ask yourself about SEO relevancy:

- Do the pages in your website or course contain unique titles and meta descriptions?
- Do the page URLs have good slugs?
- Does page content include relevant keywords?

Online Advertising

Free marketing strategies such as social media, blogging, being on a podcast, and speaking engagements can all improve brand awareness (see Chapter 13 for more on these methods). But investing in advertisements (ads) on search engines and social media can funnel traffic at a faster pace to your online course. Paid ads can focus on a specific audience, therefore providing a quick way to attract customers. Ads have built-in analytics to provide data that track your return of investment. This data can direct you to change the target audience if needed. There are many types of ads: native advertising, display advertising, social media advertising, and search engine advertising.

Here are the types of advertisements you generally see online:

» **Native ads** blend in with the page content and are not intrusive. Examples are the ads that play on YouTube for a few seconds prior to the video you intended to watch. The ad blends in with the content.

» **Display advertising** is flashier and appears in the form of banners and pop-ups. These ads intend to be visually appealing to catch the customers' attention. This type of advertising helps increase brand awareness and focuses on users' interests.

» **Social media advertising** is great to capture a younger demographic and run on social media platforms such as TikTok, Facebook, and Instagram. The data from these platforms is available for use to determine the audience to target based on age, location, interests, and website use, among other criteria.

» **Search engine advertising** allows you to bid and pay for placement on a web page based on users searching for specific keywords. Every time a user clicks on an ad connected to the keyword, you are charged a fee.

The goal is to target learners with relevant content in ads, which improves the likelihood they will become paying customers.

It takes money to make money.

Examples of ads:

>> **Google Ads** is Google's pay-per-click platform. With Google Ads, there are different types of Ads such as display and search ads.

>> **YouTube Ads** reach large audiences that are highly targeted based on demographics, topics, and website search traffic history, and their metrics are easy to measure. In general, YouTube Ads are cost effective compared to others.

Ads provide fast results as they are easy-to-track successes, and the audience can be targeted at granular levels chosen by you. But make sure to research the targeted audiences' time spent on the platform you choose to advertise. If it is low, it may be a poor investment. With social media, users are there for interactions and not necessarily purchasing. Make sure the ads are compelling enough to lure them to your landing page.

>> **Banner ads on other websites, blogs, or podcasts:** Websites or other platforms that serve your target audience can be a place for advertising. You can offer to pay them to post a banner for your course. Associate a discount code with each banner to trace which website visitors respond to the and make more informed decisions on where to advertise in the future.

You can pay an individual to design the banner for you through sites such as Fiverr (Fiverr.com), a freelance service marketplace, or you can use freeware design sites (many are free with paid options) to design your own banner. Common sites are Canva (www.canva.com) and Piktochart (www.piktochart.com).

As you can see, there are many different areas on the Internet where you can place ads, and all have different processes, but I think it would be helpful to focus briefly on Google Ads. In Google Ads, it takes six steps to setting up and launching your campaign:

1. Create a Google Ad account at https://ads.google.com/home.

2. Add your business information. Linking websites is optional.

3. Select your campaign goal such as company awareness or increasing sales.

4. Create the ad and preview the format.

5. Define the audience and budget to ensure you are working within your means.

6. Finalize and approve the launch of the campaign.

From Pricing to Paying

Determining the price tag is difficult as this decision determines your progress to achieve your goals, promote your brand, and make the course appealing. The course value is usually more than you recognize because you are not just providing education but your knowledge and experience as well.

Research your competitors but don't let their price be your limit. Use the information to guide your decisions and validate your ideas.

TIP

When starting off, don't oversell yourself, the course, or your knowledge. Perfect a single course first. Focus on the course that will help customers see results relatively quickly but is not terminal in knowledge.

Making sure the price is right

People will pay for what they value. People will pay to have access to exclusive information, especially from an expert.

In general, the time invested is part of the cost analysis and price point. A rule of thumb is to price more in-depth courses above $100 depending on the end results (certifications, business development, business launches). Smaller courses covering content nuggets can be sold for a lower price point. When you think about education, price tags increase with prestigious universities. The image of the course is reflected in the price of the course.

The education being provided is an experience that encompasses different learning artifacts to keep the learner engaged and improve learning experiences.

WARNING

Charge too little and the perceived value deteriorates, opportunities to grow through advertising and marketing may be stunted, and a lower price may attract a different type of audience. Charge too much and sales are dismal, requiring you to reduce the price, which also looks bad to the audience.

TIP

Due to individuals' responsibilities in life, courses may be considered a luxury item or a discretionary expense. Consider offering a payment plan to sell the course over an extended period. Instead of a one-time purchase at $300, they may pay $50 a month for six months.

Choosing a payment platform

Processing the payment is one of the most important aspects of the whole process. If you don't have a payment platform set up, then you cannot earn sales. Payment processors provide the ability to add a payment button to the website. They secure credit card transactions and enable the delivery of the product.

Consider different aspects of the numerous platforms on the market:

>> **Customer experience:** Making payment should be easy and intuitive, and a support aspect should be in place in case there are issues during the check-out process.

>> **Security:** The Payment Card Industry Data Security Standard (PCI-DSS) optimizes the security of credit and debit transactions and removes you from providing additional security measures via card payment.

>> **Transaction fees:** While they may not be avoidable, they should be reasonable based on the features offered.

>> **Payment methods:** These should be varied, meaning all major credit cards should be accepted.

>> **Support and analytics:** These should be included in the price.

Here are some examples of processing systems:

>> **PayPal** (paypal.com) works on all devices. This service is trusted and simple to use. The button permits quick, click buys for customers, but there are numerous pricing structures for users when purchasing their platform.

>> **Gumroad** (gumroad.com) is included because it allows you to set up payment plans and is great with promoting more original items.

>> **Stripe** (stripe.com) works on all devices. Stripe offers many features and is intuitive to use for customers, but setup entails a learning curve for the seller.

>> **Square** (square.com) works on all devices and allows in-person sales too (think conferences and workshops). In addition, if you don't have a website, it provides you a website builder.

6

The Part of Tens

IN THIS PART . . .

Explore low- and no-cost tools for your course.

Create a free account with freeware of your choice.

Search educational repositories.

Take important steps toward success.

Chapter **15**

Ten Freeware (or Low Cost) Tools to Spice Up the Course

Freeware is software that is free of charge but cannot be modified. It is different than free software, which is proprietary software available to the public, but the free software's copyright determines how it is able to be modified and redistributed. If you can program, the best software to use will be free software without copyright available to the public. In this chapter, the software focus is primarily freeware.

Freeware that is popular often becomes open-source software (software with a source code that can be modified), but the freeware that has been referenced in the previous chapters is software that is copyrighted and cannot be modified or distributed. Usually this is perfect for faculty members creating curriculum.

Some freeware is *shareware* too. Shareware allows individuals trials that provide the program with certain features disabled. If one finds the program suitable for their students and teaching, they can choose to purchase a version. Freeware should never require payment, but oftentimes shareware will, after the free trial ends.

The particulars are important when you invest a lot of time in developing material for your students, but don't let that stop you from exploring. If you see good reviews and others have had positive experiences, review the agreement to ensure there are no hidden fees.

TIP

I use many freeware programs that have fees to unlock advanced features, but if I find it extremely valuable and my students' feedback is positive, then I consider purchasing it for more in-depth use. There are many I have invested in personally only to influence a larger entity to purchase it for the masses. Explore, engage, experience, and enjoy.

Educational Support and Content Sources

Educational content is often created by educators and can help students engage and interact with content. Educational content that is used to support students should be versatile, accessible, and vetted.

Khan Academy

Khan Academy (khanacademy.com) provides videos, text, and basic assessment practice questions to help learners improve their knowledge in dozens and dozens of subjects for all ages. Instructors can set up classrooms and assign content to students as well as collect analytics.

Price: Free

Features:

>> Accessible on desktop, mobile devices, and tablets.

>> Interactive lessons, quizzes, and progress tracking for a personalized learning journey.

>> If an account is created, the content one interacts with will sync across devices.

>> Can be integrated in many LMS via specific integration tools or Google Classroom, and can be embedded into LMS. Integration is when a tool is functionally part of the LMS while embedded objects are attached to a portion of the LMS.

Learning Labs for your courses

Open educational resources (OERs) are a great option to use as a supplement to your personal curriculum. The resources available are created by museums, government agencies, and non-profit organizations.

The platforms can provide videos, lessons, readings, presentations, instructor resources, interactive simulations, and often offer customizable textbooks. Many platforms have LTIs and apps for LMS integrations, and many can be directly embedded.

Price: Free

Features:

>> OpenStax (openstax.org) is a platform providing free college textbooks with instructor resources.

>> Smithsonian Learning Lab (learninglab.si.edu) has millions of digital resources that teachers can use for instructional activities with students.

>> Smithsonian History Explorer (historyexplorer.si.edu) provides teachers and students resources for American history. Lessons and activities are available along with a repository of audio, video, and interactions.

>> National Archives (archives.gov/education) hold historical United States government documents that can be used in online activities to help students experience real-life examples of civic concepts.

>> PBS LearningMedia (pbslearningmedia.org) provides an array of content for all grade levels and interactive lessons are provided for teachers to use for students.

>> CSPAN Classroom (c-span.org/classroom) provides video materials for social studies, and the videos can be embedded into LMS. Lesson plans are provided for teachers.

>> OER Commons (oercommons.org) contains educator-created lessons in many disciplines that include games and assessments that do not rely on a specific textbook.

>> US Government Open Data Set (data.gov) provides data sets to create applicable lessons and activities for students.

>> The Library of Congress (loc.gov) provides classroom content that guides teachers to use primary resources.

>> Multimedia Education Resource for Learning and Online Teaching (MERLOT) at merlot.org provides discipline-focused material, exercises, and content

builders for web pages that are curated for faculty and students by higher education institutions, industry, professional organizations, and teachers.

>> Technology, Entertainment, Design, otherwise known as TED, has spin-offs such as TED-Ed and TEDx (ted.com). This tool promotes learning through short talks and presentations. TED provides listening, reading, and viewing content. The videos offer relatable information that's engaging. TED offers an immense variety of topics, and you don't know what you don't know, so this format encourages exploration and reflection.

>> Google Arts and Culture is a mobile-based app that allows VR tours of museums, street views of artwork, and search features based on colors, subjects, and location.

YouTube EDU

YouTube EDU (www.youtube.com/edu) features thousands of videos from teachers and partners such as TED, PBS, National Geographic, and more. The videos range from academic to inspirational and provide quick lessons from subject matter experts around the world.

Price: Free

Features:

>> Accessible on desktop, mobile devices, and tablets.

>> Allows learners and teachers from around the world to learn, collaborate, and communicate.

>> Global classrooms can be built by an individual or an institution.

>> A community of practice formed by teachers that can help incorporate content into lessons.

>> YouTube for schools is available to be integrated into LMS via an app or embedded videos.

Study Tools

Study tools can help improve online student experiences. Student use study tools to help reinforce concepts they need more exposure to, understand concepts they did not grasp when first introduced to it, and to grasp the bigger picture. By interacting with study tools, you can reinforce their learning and help take control of their experiences. Study tools can take material from static to dynamic and keep students entertained and engaged.

Quizlet

Quizlet (www.quizlet.com) is a popular study tool that allows students and teachers to create flashcards that can be converted into quizzes and interactive games.

Price: Free; premium upgrade option

Features:

» It's accessible on desktop, mobile devices, and tablets.

» It allows teachers and students to create flashcards and quizzes that can be used in study or game mode.

» Flashcards can be printed for offline studying.

» Users can create custom study material tailored to their needs.

» Teachers can create classrooms to track student data.

» Material can be shared publicly to be used by a wider audience, but the sets are not vetted for accuracy and quality.

» Quizlet can be embedded into LMS, and many LMS have apps and can use the Quizlet LTI integrations.

Brainscape

Brainscape (www.brainscape.com) allows one to create flashcards or can provide premade flashcard sets from an extensive library covering many disciplines. Adaptive learning and confidence ratings are used to help gauge students' mastering of concepts.

Price: Free; premium upgrade option

Features:

» Accessible on desktop, mobile devices, and tablets

» Allows students to rate their confidence in their knowledge

» Uses spaced repetition and interleaving practice to improve active recall

>> Focuses on working memory and self-awareness

>> Allows instructors and students to build flashcards or use flashcards from the public repository

>> Makes it possible to add sounds and images to flashcards

Photomath

Photomath (https://photomath.com) can simplify and explain step-by-step solutions to math equations.

Price: Free; premium upgrade options

Features:

>> Uses a smartphone or webcam to take a picture of a printed equation and the solution appears with individual steps

>> Steps are not explained, so it supports learning but doesn't teach process

>> Contains a scientific calculator

>> Covers numerous topics including geometry, algebra, statistics, trigonometry, and calculus, to name a few

Creation through Communication, Creativity, and Collaboration

Communication and collaboration are soft skills employers want to see in employees, and they are very important in teaching. Many teaching tools support communication and collaboration in a fun, engaging, active manner. These tools may offer communities of practice, tips for teaching, and ideas for activities.

Flip

Flip (info.flip.com) is a Microsoft tool that provides video discussion and sharing with fun tools and features to enhance the videos created by students and teachers.

Price: Free

Features:

- Accessible on desktop, mobile devices, and tablets.
- Allows recording, editing, and sharing of video content.
- Includes automatic closed captioning that can be edited.
- Directions can be text and video to prompt student experience.
- Interactions can be via text, audio, or video.
- Repository of discovery content.
- Training is in English, Spanish, and Hindi.
- Flip certified trainers are available for free.
- Can be embedded into LMS, and there are LMS LTI integrations.

Thinglink

Thinglink (thinglink.com) allows you to create interactive images and videos by adding tags. Tags can link to videos, audio, images, maps, social media pages, and more. Thinglink encourages using multimedia to engage with the content, peers, and teachers. Teachers and students can create and share interactive images, videos, and 360-degree/virtual-reality images.

Price: Free (limited trial); eLearning plans

Features:

- Accessible on desktop, mobile devices, and tablets
- Mobile app facilitates notes, text, and audio
- Desktop allows editing and creation of new materials for assignments
- Immersive reader overlays the product and can read text, read video hotspots, and translate words to over 60 languages
- Content engagement statistics
- Virtual walk-throughs of real-world environments
- Can be embedded into LMS, and there are LMS LTI integrations

Gaming

Gaming can create an exciting learning environment. Usually it incorporates points, badges, and leaderboards to help motivate student interaction. If students are enjoying the content and experience, they are more likely to retain information. Gaming helps with cognitive development as it engages brain processes, employs learning by doing, and stimulates the imagination.

Kahoot!

Kahoot! (kahoot.com) is used to create fun content and games for students. Kahoot! provides a platform to build quizzes that can be customized with videos, diagrams, and images. Students participate in the game by using a QR code and a pin and accessing it on their device.

Price: Free; premium upgrade options; eLearning plans

Features:

>> Access on desktop, mobile devices, and tablets.

>> Use predesigned templates or create interactive lessons.

>> Duplicate and edit existing Kahoots from a repository or personal Kahoots.

>> Collaborate with peers (known and unknown).

>> Use spreadsheets to import questions.

>> Use videos and images in questions.

>> Employ different question types — quiz, true/false, poll, puzzle, word cloud, fill in the blank, open ended. Timer and point options and multiple selection options.

>> Live games (synchronous or asynchronous) and student-paced challenges for homework and practice.

>> Individual or team play. Personalized learning available.

>> Reports via spreadsheets.

>> Can be embedded into LMS.

Blooket

Blooket (blooket.com; pronounced blue-kit) is a game-show-type platform that allows themed game modes that can be competitive or used for solo practice or even just fun. Teachers create questions but there is a repository available to search and use questions. Originally, Blooket was developed as a formative assessment tool.

Price: Free; premium upgrade options

Features:

>> Accessible on desktop, mobile devices, and tablets

>> Live games (synchronous or asynchronous) and student-paced challenges for homework and practice

>> Points-based game to earn rewards and character progression

>> Adjustable game speed to reduce anxiety and pressure on students

>> Allows students and teachers to track their progress, collaborate with peers, and work in teams

>> Provides immediate feedback and tool can be used to help students demonstrate what they know via game modes

>> Use a repository of questions or create your own

Flippity

Flippity (www.flippity.net) uses a Google spreadsheet to create cool games such as flashcards, matching, escape rooms, spelling quizzes, memory games, interactive timelines, and more.

Price: Free

Features:

>> Accessible on desktop, mobile devices, and tablets

>> Uses premade template Google Sheets you can personalize for your needs

>> Easy to share across platforms and devices because it is URL based

>> Demos, instructions, and templates provided for each type of interaction

>> Templates available:

- Flashcards

- Quiz Show

- Random Name Picker
- Randomizer
- Scavenger Hunt
- Board Game
- Manipulatives
- Badge Tracker
- Leader Board
- Typing Test
- Spelling Words
- Word Search
- Crossword Puzzle
- Word Cloud
- Fun with Words
- MadLabs
- Tournament Bracket
- Certificate Quiz
- Self-Assessment

LAGNIAPPE (SOUTHERN FOR "A LITTLE SOMETHING EXTRA")

Lagniappe (lan-yap) is something good that is extra and free.

Libby (`libbyapp.com`) allows teachers and students to use their library card to access e-books and audio books for free.

Make Beliefs Comix (`www.MakeBeliefsComix.com`), **StoryboardThat** (`storyboard that.com`), and **Canva** (`www.canva.com"www.canva.com`) allow students to create comic strips for storytelling, language development, history reenactment, and timelines. Students can use visual elements to express events, emotions, and drama. All have free versions and offer premium upgrades.

Crossword Labs (crosswordlabs.com), **JeopardyLabs** (jeopardylabs.com), and **Bingo Baker** (bingobaker.com) allow you to create crossword puzzles, Jeopardy games, and Bingo cards without any software download. You can search repositories if you don't have time to create your own. The games can be played on any device.

Artificial Intelligence (AI) supports teachers by helping to create activities in a fraction of the time. Yes, the activities often need to be vetted, but the bulk of the content is present and only needs tweaking. It's the difference between spending hours writing and formatting 25 Jeopardy questions versus three minutes using AI. Many different AI tools are available that support classroom activities, so don't be afraid to explore. Here are a few to consider:

- Gibbly.co is free and allows you to create game-like quizzes by giving criteria and then producing a game that can be hosted with a leaderboard.

- A suite of gaming tools that can be created instantly based on criteria can be created via Almanack.ai. The free tool allows you to make games like Jeopardy, word searches, Battleship, and Bingo.

- Questionwell.org takes a reading or a video and creates questions that can be instantly imported into Blooket or Kahoot!

- Eduaide.ai also allows you to create Jeopardy and Bingo cards.

Tip: When choosing an educational freeware tool, make sure the app supports the grade level you are teaching and is usable on a variety of devices. Learning apps facilitate a variety of preferences for learning, such as reading, watching, doing, listening, or a combination of these. You want the apps to be interactive to increase engagement but remain user friendly.

For more ideas, check out my personal Padlet (padlet.com/amanda_h_rosenzweig/freeware; freeware with paid versions). Here, I post all freeware and shareware that I have used as a student or use in my classes.

Chapter 16

Ten Checklists for a Great Start

The checklists in this chapter will help you transition from a face-to-face course to an online learning course. No finger snaps or magic wands will convert your material to a digital format but hopefully these ideas and tips will help support your journey.

If you are building an online course without a face-to-face course as a template, no worries. No preconceived experiences will restrict your creativity.

Fans of a Plan

Have you heard this statement: "If you fail to plan, you plan to fail"? Planning is a critical component in being successful as it helps clarifies goals, and objectives, increases efficiency and effectiveness, helps improve communication and can reduce stress.

» Plan by identifying the topics, resources you want to create, resources you have already, resources you need to convert, and type of assignments you want the students to submit.

- » Use a course matrix (Chapter 8) to manage time, expectations, and design of the course. This document will be your gold and your guidance.

- » Determine the tools you want to use for communication and delivery.

- » Test out technology; try new technologies prior to creating activities and content.

TIP

Have your communication plan front and center. Having a communication plan ready to go helps learners know what is expected. Provide it on the landing page of the course so learners can easily find the information, know your availability, and see the best ways to contact you.

Moving and Grooving

First impressions can be lasting and make a huge difference in an online environment. The elements in your course help student get where they need to go, so make sure it is consistent, logical, and efficient.

- » Simplify course navigation to minimize student confusion.

- » The landing page is the first impression of the course, so its design and directions are important to consider (see Figure 16-1).

- » Create a walk-through video to welcome students and guide them to best practices in navigating the course and understanding the design and expectations.

- » The course blueprint (see Chapter 8) acts as a guide to properly set up the course layout, design, and projected movement and journey.

TIP

Use visuals to engage students and provide important information.

Accessibility is important, so ensure that your visuals have alternative text and the welcome video is captioned and has a transcript.

WARNING

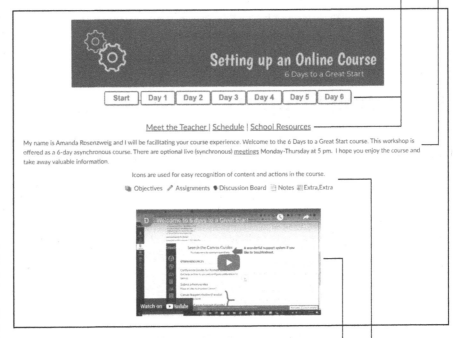

Brief Introduction

Easy Navigation Links

Setting up an Online Course
6 Days to a Great Start

| Start | Day 1 | Day 2 | Day 3 | Day 4 | Day 5 | Day 6 |

Meet the Teacher | Schedule | School Resources

My name is Amanda Rosenzweig and I will be facilitating your course experience. Welcome to the 6 Days to a Great Start course. This workshop is offered as a 6-day asynchronous course. There are optional live (synchronous) meetings Monday-Thursday at 5 pm. I hope you enjoy the course and take away valuable information.

Icons are used for easy recognition of content and actions in the course.

Objectives Assignments Discussion Board Notes Extra,Extra

FIGURE 16-1:
A landing page provides users a welcome message, important information that is easy to locate and navigate, and a guide on how to get started.

Welcome Video on landing page

Repetition and easy recognition of information

Cultivating Resourcefulness

Finding creative solutions to problems and navigating difficulties are wonderful skills. Knowing what you have to work with, understanding your LMS and being familiar with your learning objectives allows you to be successful.

>> Knowing how to harness the components of Learning Management Systems (LMS) is important in order to use the tools that are present, integrated, and will support curriculum delivery.

>> Take time to review the LMS offerings from folders or modules, pages, assignments, built-in assessment type tools such as quizzes, discussion boards, Wiki pages, surveys, rich content editors, apps, LTI capabilities, linking abilities, and more.

>> Invest time in becoming familiar with the support material, help page, and community of learners when available.

>> Align your learning objectives from the course matrix with the tools that will present and assess the content.

Providing Support

Remember that support equals success.

>> Create a module/unit that provides learners with information such as system guides, LMS help, information technology help (email), student services, and software services.

>> If available, include links to technology support such as laptop loans, computer labs, disability/accessibility services, library resources, and tutoring and writing support.

Welcoming the Learner

Creating an environment that helps the users feel welcome and have all the information to be successful from the start is important.

>> Create a clear course matrix (see Chapter 8) that includes LOs, assessments, timelines (tentative or set), and tools needed.

>> Include a syllabus addendum to support the syllabus. The syllabus addendum should represent your personal course desires such as grading rubric, class guidelines, policies on late work, timeliness with communication and grading, and anything else necessary to help students understand the expectations.

>> A welcome letter and video are great tools to bridge the gap between the unknown and trust. These tools and efforts ease anxiety, allow students to e-meet you, and set the tone for the course duration.

- » Provide an activity such as a discussion board or Flip to help students recognize they have allies in the experience and build a community.

- » Offer synchronous meeting times to help students believe that you are a human teaching the course.

TIP

Aesthetics is important. Fonts, color, and style should be consistent but not used alone to signify importance. Colorblind and low vision users may be unable to perceive color nuances and assistive technologies don't always announce colors or style to users.

Starting in Style

An introduction experience sets the tone for your course and gives the user an idea of what to expect. The beginning of the course will pique the users' interest and set them up for success. Many elements can be involved in a successful beginning.

- » A welcoming module, which I lovingly call the "start here" module, is a clear indicator of where the students should begin their journey. This area is the entry point for students, no matter the modality, and helps students figure out how to engage in a course.

- » In a robust, but not overwhelmingly long, start here module, there should be basic components including, but not limited to the following:

  - An instructor introduction can humanize your course. Include contact information such as email, phone number, and conferencing meeting tool, email return time, office location, and a welcome message or video.

  - Course documents such as the syllabus, syllabus addendum, a schedule, testing information, and technical documents should be included.

  - Census assignments ensure the student logs on early and completes activities. Often these are paired with a proctoring solution to verify student identity, ensure technology is working, and provide time to address issues early prior to high-stakes assignments.

- » Consider adding prerequisites and requirements on objects (files, pages, assignments, assessments) to help guide the students through a structured, scaffolded, learning journey.

Organization Is Key

Organizing courses in a clear, consistent manner benefits the user and the teacher. Organization makes the process of building the course more manageable, which improves how the student will access, communicate, interact, and submit materials.

>> Using the blueprint to guide the structure means a plan is in place so the design is predetermined and systematic. The building process is now more manageable.

>> A well-designed course leads to intuitive navigation, so material is found with ease.

>> Organization leads to an easier time focusing on work, completing assignments, and improving performance, all in a timely manner.

>> Don't hesitate to provide a road map to help create a sense of direction to facilitate the students' learning.

Design to Delivery

Design and delivery are not static and will continue to improve and change with each course offering and iteration of the course.

>> The course design has been developed in the course blueprint and the course matrix. Now it's about looking at the course goals, course activities, and course assessments.

>> Keep the material relevant, clear, concise, and engaging.

>> Content should be well-structured, logical, and effective.

>> Use various types of content — text, audio, video, quizzes, case studies, polls, chats, discussions, games — to foster collaboration and a community.

TIP

Instructions for students should be clear. Provide tips on how the previous material connects to the new material. Provide steps via bullets. Consider completing these tips last, after everything is complete, so it is a holistic view of the actions needed.

Assessments in Action

Assessments serve many purposes such as monitoring student progress and performance. Based on feedback from the assessments, students can become accountable for their learning.

>> Use numerous, no-stakes or low-stakes assessments to help students assess their progress.

>> Align LOs to the assessment.

>> Create assessments that measure skill sets, not just knowledge.

>> Incorporate feedback throughout the course not only for students' learning but also for the growth of the course design, delivery, and development.

TIP

The actionable, measurable verb in the LO can help define what the student should be able to do because of the content and lesson.

Accessibility Is a Requirement

Intentional, thoughtful design and development are critical to creating a great course. Digital accessibility matters because it supports the fundamental objective of providing equal access to all learners. Following are a few key factors to consider and address when creating digital documents:

>> **Table captions:** Tables should include a caption describing the contents of the table.

>> **Table header scope:** Tables headers should specify scope and the appropriate structure.

>> **Table header:** Tables should include at least one header.

>> **Sequential headings:** Heading levels should not be skipped (for example, H2 to H4). However, the tool does not check whether the first header starts with H2 or whether the headings are sequential with the rest of the content in the page. Tables do not begin with H1, which is designated for the page title.

>> **Heading paragraphs:** Headings should not contain more than 120 characters.

>> **Image alt text:** Images should include an alt attribute describing the image content.

>> **Image alt filename:** Image filenames should not be used as the alt attribute describing the image content.

>> **Image alt length:** Alt attribute text should not contain more than 120 characters.

>> **Adjacent links:** Adjacent links with the same URL should be a single link. This rule verifies link errors where the link text may include spaces and break the link into multiple links.

>> **Large text contrast:** Text larger than 18 point (or bold 14 point) should display a minimum contrast ratio of 3:1.

>> **Small text contrast:** Text smaller than 18 point (or bold 14 point) should display a minimum contrast ratio of 4.5:1.

WARNING

Accessibility is not just to meet compliance. Accessibility allows all individuals to acquire the same information, engage in the same activities, and enjoy the same opportunities. Compliance is the beginning but not the end goal.

TIP

You don't need to be an accessibility expert. But learning about the accessibility essentials and implementing accessible practices is the responsibility of all educators. It allows the work created to be used by a larger group of learners.

Index

bonuses, as alternative assessment, 166–167

boundaries, setting, 80

Brainscape, 255–256

branding, 9, 17, 238. *See also* marketing eCourses

building eCourse as you go, 104

bulleted course outline, creating, 100–101

bulleted lists, in course matrix, 140

businesses, as target audience, 40–41

BY license (Creative Commons), 64

C

Canva, 232, 260

Canvas Credentials, 232

Canvas platform, 74

captions, accessible, 56–57

case studies, alternative assessment through, 197

CC (Creative Commons) licenses, 63–67, 68–69

CCO (Creative Commons Public Domain), 64

census assignment, in course outline, 100

certifications, eCourse, 230–232

characterization, in affective domain, 149, 150

cheat sheet, explained, 4

choice, in HyFlex courses, 216

chunking, 14, 125–126

closed captioning, 56–57

CMS (Course Management System). *See* learning management systems; platforms

cognitive domain, impact of curriculum on, 146–148, 151–152

cognitive learning objectives, 119

cognitive presence, 84

collaboration
  freeware tools for, 256–257
  learning techniques encouraging, 84–85
  Open Education Resources as providing, 63

collaborative learning, 194

college students, 39, 94, 118

color
  in course blueprint, 130
  in notes, 158–159
  in slide presentations, 160
  tips for accessible use of, 57–58

combination searches, 13

comic strips, 260

communication
  freeware tools for, 256–257
  planning, 82, 264
  preplanned, 103
  skills, analyzing, 88–90

community, building
  asynchronous and synchronous options, 81–82
  collaborative and engaging learning techniques, 84–85
  establishing presence and immediacy, 84
  expertise, providing, 84
  feedback, creating document for, 83
  meeting synchronously, 85–86
  optimizing student engagement, 25–26
  overview, 9, 81
  planning communication, 82
  through alternative assessments, 86–87, 168
  through social media, 236–238
  welcoming users by, 116–118

Community College Consortium for Open Educational Resources, 68

commuting, benefits of avoiding, 26–27

company vision statements, 10

compassion, 26

complex images, 53

complex overt response, in psychomotor domain, 149

comprehension, in cognitive domain, 146, 148, 151

concept maps, 167, 170, 194

concise hyperlinks, 56

connection. *See also* community, building; presence, establishing in eCourse
  as optimizing student engagement, 25
  with others, tips for, 87–88

consistency, in blueprint, 130

consumers, focusing on when picking topic, 13–14. *See also* students

contact page, 230, 234

content creation, as alternative assessment, 165–167

matrix, course
  creating, 134–140
  evaluating tests against, 182
  mapping course with, 98–99
  overview, 14, 264, 266
  role in efficient development, 104
MCQs (multiple choice questions) in exams, 184–186
meaningful interaction, providing, 229–230
measurable learning outcomes, 96
measurement, in curriculum analysis, 142
mechanism, in psychomotor domain, 149
meet and greets, 114
meeting synchronously, 82, 85–86. See also synchronous courses
MERLOT (Multimedia Education Resource for Learning and Online Teaching), 253–254
Merlot II, 67
meta descriptions, in search engine optimization, 244
metacognition, 208
micro credentialing, 40–41
micro learning, 41
Microsoft products
  accessibility and, 59
  Accessibility Checker, 51, 59
  adding Alt Text to images in Word, 53–55
Midterm Exam Material module, 133
minute papers, 162, 194
MIT Open Courseware, 68
modality shifts, thinking ahead for
  eCourses, 214–215
  face-to-face, 211, 212
  hybrid courses, 211–214
  HyFlex, 215–222
  overview, 209–210
modules
  alignment, achieving, 105
  chunking, 125–126
  in course outline, 99, 100
  to include in blueprint, 128–134
  lesson plan, designing, 102
  organizing blueprint around, 125

patterns in content within, 157
  scaffolding, 126–127
monetizing eCourses. See also marketing eCourses
  online advertising, 245–246
  overview, 9, 27, 239–240
  pay as you go, 240
  payment platform, choosing, 247–248
  pricing, 247
  search engine optimization, 243–245
  subscription based, 240–242
monthly membership subscription, 242
Moodle, 74
muddiest points, assessments for, 200–201
multilingual design, 233
Multimedia Education Resource for Learning and Online Teaching (MERLOT), 253–254
multiple choice questions (MCQs) in exams, 184–186
music playlist getting acquainted exercise, 117–118

N

names, community building by sharing, 116
National Archives, 253
native ads, 245
navigation
  accessible design, 47
  intuitive, 106–107
  links on LMS home page, 128–129
  reviewing, 90
need-to-know versus nice-to-know
  overview, 118–119
  student-centered learning, 122–124
  time management, 120–122
  trimming the fat, 119–120
NoDerivatives license (Creative Commons), 65
non-accredited courses, 144, 145
NonCommercial license (Creative Commons), 66
NonCommercial-NoDeriveratives license (Creative Commons), 67
NonCommercial-ShareAlike license (Creative Commons), 66–67
nonlinear (dynamic) learning, 122–123

user experience (UX) *(continued)*
  exercise in, 36
  overview, 32
  Universal Design for Learning and, 33–34
  users. *See* design thinking; students; welcoming students

V

validity, assessment, 183, 184
valuing, in affective domain, 149, 150, 152
verification assignments, 118
video
  accessibility of, improving, 56–57
  welcome, 112–114
video descriptions (audio descriptions or descriptive audio), 36, 56–57
Video Text Tracks (VTT) files, 57
virtual meetings, 82, 88
virtual reality (VR), 163–164
vision statement, writing, 10
visual messaging, 32–33
Voluntary Product Accessibility Template (VPAT), 52
Vygotsky, Lev, 126

W

W3C (World Wide Web Consortium), 46, 49
walk-through video, 113, 264
Warning icon, explained, 3
Web Accessibility Initiative (WAI), 46, 49
Web Accessibility Versatile Evaluator (WAVE), 50
Web Content Accessibility Guidelines (WCAG), 14, 46, 49, 50
WebAIM Contrast Checker, 58
webinars, 237
website tools, 74

websites, banner ads on, 246
weekly schedule, 43, 103
welcome letter, 114, 266
welcome modules, 129
welcome video, 112–114, 266
welcoming students
  checklist for, 266–267
  community building and environment decorating, 116–118
  meet and greet, 114
  out-of-the-box approaches, 114–116
  overview, 112
  verification assignments, 118
  welcome letter, 114
  welcome video, 112–114
what is on your plate metaphors, 168
where in the world icebreaker, 117
why behind eCourse, identifying, 19–20
wildcard searches, 13
Word documents, adding Alt Text to images in, 53–55
WordPress, 191
work-life balance, 20, 26–28
worksheets, 160–161
World Wide Web Consortium (W3C), 46, 49
writing effective learning outcomes, 95–97

Y

YouTube, marketing eCourses on, 238
YouTube Ads, 246
YouTube EDU, 254

Z

Zone of Proximal Development (ZPD), 126

About the Author

Amanda Rosenzweig, PhD, is the Assistant Dean of the School of STEM and Canvas Learning Management System Administrator at Delgado Community College. Amanda has spent 20 years teaching biology, human anatomy and physiology courses, and online course design and delivery. In addition, Amanda is teaching in the accessibility studies program at Central Washington University. Amanda is part of numerous initiatives and grants supporting online course design, biotechnology career growth, equity for hiring community college graduates, accessible laboratory design space, and K-12 STEM outreach for teachers and students throughout the region.

Born and raised in Monroe, Louisiana, Amanda ventured off for college, earning her bachelor's degree from William Woods University. She then returned to Monroe for her master's degree at the University of Louisiana at Monroe. The day after Amanda graduated, she moved to New Orleans, where she started her teaching career. After a few years of teaching and the semester of Hurricane Katrina, Amanda decided that she could profoundly impact students and their trajectory, so she completed her doctorate in Curriculum and Instruction at the University of New Orleans. Due to the regional impacts, educational technology, online teaching, and instructor influence became the focus of her dissertation. Fast-forward five years, and she encountered a student who needed digital accommodation that she was not prepared to give. Through that lived experience, Amanda's involvement in accessibility and disability support became a driving force to improve all modalities of education and their digital components. In 2022, Amanda completed a master's certificate in accessibility studies from Central Washington University, earned numerous certifications, and completed many training courses focused on digital accessibility.

Amanda is an animal lover and has a special place in her heart for dogs, horses, turtles, snakes, and sloths.

Dedication

Thank you to my family: Sue, my mom; Ethan and Seth, my older brothers; Julie, my sister-in-law; and my nieces and nephews.

To my best friends that believed in me and allowed the Amanda-isms to flourish.

To my dad, my bubby, my niece Emerite Belle, and my best friend Jason Hatfield, I wish you were here to read this.

Author's Acknowledgments

Thank you to Dayna Leaman for walking into my office 20 years ago as a publisher representative and becoming one of my beloved and most supportive friends. Your love of life, dogs, and reality makes my heart happy. Thanks also to Jennifer Yee for taking a chance on a person with a passion looking for their purpose.

Publisher's Acknowledgments

Acquisitions Editor: Jennifer Yee

Development Editor: Tim Gallan

Copy Editor: Christine Pingleton

Technical Reviewer: Thomas Egan

Senior Managing Editor: Kristie Pyles

Production Editor: Pradesh Kumar

Cover Image: © Morsa Images/Getty Images

Take dummies with you everywhere you go!

Whether you are excited about e-books, want more from the web, must have your mobile apps, or are swept up in social media, dummies makes everything easier.

Find us online!

dummies.com

A Wiley Brand

PERSONAL ENRICHMENT

9781119187790
USA $26.00
CAN $31.99
UK £19.99

9781119179030
USA $21.99
CAN $25.99
UK £16.99

9781119293354
USA $24.99
CAN $29.99
UK £17.99

9781119293347
USA $22.99
CAN $27.99
UK £16.99

9781119310068
USA $22.99
CAN $27.99
UK £16.99

9781119235606
USA $24.99
CAN $29.99
UK £17.99

9781119251163
USA $24.99
CAN $29.99
UK £17.99

9781119235491
USA $26.99
CAN $31.99
UK £19.99

9781119279952
USA $24.99
CAN $29.99
UK £17.99

9781119283133
USA $24.99
CAN $29.99
UK £17.99

9781119287117
USA $24.99
CAN $29.99
UK £16.99

9781119130246
USA $22.99
CAN $27.99
UK £16.99

PROFESSIONAL DEVELOPMENT

9781119311041
USA $24.99
CAN $29.99
UK £17.99

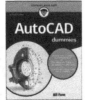

9781119255796
USA $39.99
CAN $47.99
UK £27.99

9781119293439
USA $26.99
CAN $31.99
UK £19.99

9781119281467
USA $26.99
CAN $31.99
UK £19.99

9781119280651
USA $29.99
CAN $35.99
UK £21.99

9781119251132
USA $24.99
CAN $29.99
UK £17.99

9781119310563
USA $34.00
CAN $41.99
UK £24.99

9781119181705
USA $29.99
CAN $35.99
UK £21.99

9781119263593
USA $26.99
CAN $31.99
UK £19.99

9781119257769
USA $29.99
CAN $35.99
UK £21.99

9781119293477
USA $26.99
CAN $31.99
UK £19.99

9781119265313
USA $24.99
CAN $29.99
UK £17.99

9781119239314
USA $29.99
CAN $35.99
UK £21.99

9781119293323
USA $29.99
CAN $35.99
UK £21.99

dummies.com

dummies
A Wiley Brand